George Thomas Stokes

**Ireland and the Celtic Church**

A History of Ireland from St. Patrick to the English Conquest in 1172

George Thomas Stokes

**Ireland and the Celtic Church**
*A History of Ireland from St. Patrick to the English Conquest in 1172*

ISBN/EAN: 9783337162399

Printed in Europe, USA, Canada, Australia, Japan

Cover: Foto ©ninafisch / pixelio.de

More available books at **www.hansebooks.com**

# IRELAND AND THE CELTIC CHURCH.

## A HISTORY OF IRELAND FROM ST. PATRICK TO THE ENGLISH CONQUEST IN 1172.

BY

### GEORGE T. STOKES, D.D.,

*Vicar of All Saints', Blackrock ;*
*Professor of Ecclesiastical History, Trinity College, Dublin.*

SECOND EDITION.

London:
HODDER AND STOUGHTON,
27, PATERNOSTER ROW.

MDCCCLXXXVIII.

[*All rights reserved.*]

# PREFACE.

I HAVE often been asked to recommend a history of Ireland, embodying the result of the latest investigations, and telling a very chequered story in an interesting way. I have been unable to name any work fulfilling these conditions. Mr. Skene's learned volumes embody the result of modern investigations, but they deal as much with Scotland as with Ireland; while the older historians, such as Lanigan, King, and Todd, though very learned and accurate, are largely controversial and most certainly not light reading. I have endeavoured in the following pages to avoid controversy as far as possible, and have necessarily been obliged to make the story as interesting as I could. The form of the book explains the reason why. The lectures contained therein were originally delivered as public prelections in the Divinity-school of Trinity College. As Professor of Ecclesiastical History in the University of Dublin I am bound to lecture twice a week during two terms of the academic year, but no one is obliged to attend my classes. If I wish, therefore, to have an audience, I must attract one. I have had no cause for complaint on this head so far as the following lectures were concerned, and, therefore, I presume they were found interesting by those who attended. I can only hope they may not be found dull and uninteresting by the wider audience to which they are now submitted. I have done my best to improve them by the addition of notes, which will direct the student to the sources whence I have drawn my material, much of which has hitherto lain buried in *Proceedings* and *Transactions*, specially those of the Royal Irish Academy. I am conscious of many omissions in this work. Chapters on St. Brigid of Kildare, and the Ministry of Women in the Early Irish Church, on the Celtic Liturgies and Ritual, and on Celtic Art, should have found a place in a history of the "Making of Ireland." But, then, I have several excuses for these defects.

Publishers do not want ideal histories, complete in form, exhaustive in matter, but histories which will interest the public. Exhaustive histories are sometimes very exhausting to their readers. Again, I wished to give a picture of ascertained facts, and therefore made it a rule to deal with subjects which have been thoroughly discussed by specialists or illuminated by the publication of great works like Bishop Reeves' *Adamnan's Columba*, and Dr. Todd's *Wars of the Gaedhil*.

The question of Celtic liturgies is still in debate. Mr. Warren, in his learned work, has done much towards its solution. The Rev. Dr. MacCarthy read, last year, a very learned paper on the Stowe Missal, which will see the light in the next part of the *Transactions of the Royal Irish Academy*. The whole question, however, forms a part of a much larger subject, viz., the local liturgical uses which prevailed throughout Europe and the East in mediæval times. We are, as yet, only beginning this study, and must await the publication of documents which now lie hidden in many a dusty receptacle before it can be completely and finally settled. I am myself convinced that the Irish and Gallican uses of the fifth century were identical, and have pointed out below, in a note on page 318, a proof of this in the matter of chrism in baptism. The Irish Church of the seventh century had, however, its own liturgical peculiarities, as is evident from the *Antiphonary of Bangor*,[1] a seventh-century Irish prayer-book, now existing at Milan. In that work we find a creed used at Bangor differing in form from every other creed hitherto known.

In conclusion I have only to acknowledge in general what I have acknowledged in detail in the notes,—the great help I have received from the works of those who have, in days gone by, and especially during the last half century, devoted themselves to the study of Irish history, literature, and antiquities. I have omitted none, so far as I knew of them, from

---

[1] The *Antiphonarium Benchorense* was first published by Muratori in his *Anecdota Bibliothecæ Ambrosianæ*, t. iv., pp. 119-59. See also Warren's *Celtic Liturgy;* Migne s *Pat. Lat.*, t. lxxii., 582; *Ulster Jour. of Archæology*, 1853, pp. 168 79; and O'Laverty's *Diocese of Down and Connor*, Appendix.

Ussher, the glory and pride of my own University, to the present Bishop of Down (Dr. Reeves), the Bollandist Mr. Hogan, S.J., and Archbishop Moran, among English writers; and to Zeuss, Zimmer, and Wasserschleben, among the Germans. I have, however, especially to acknowledge the generous assistance afforded by Mr. W. M. Hennessy, M.R.I.A., of Her Majesty's Irish Record Office, who has always most generously placed at my disposal his boundless knowledge of the Celtic language, literature, and antiquities, on which subjects he is now the highest living authority.

I must, in the last place, express the hope that no words of mine may help to deepen the wounds of Ireland, or cause pain to any generous heart, no matter what his religion or politics.

GEORGE T. STOKES.

28, Trinity College, Dublin,
  *October 2nd*, 1886.

# CONTENTS.

## LECTURE I.

### THE ANCIENT CELTIC CHURCH.

Origin of Celtic Christianity—In Galatia—Gaul—England—St. Joseph and Glastonbury—The Holy Grail—Missionary influence of the Roman military system—And of Roman commerce—British Celtic Christianity in the fourth century—Ireland and the Roman empire—Use of the terms Scotia and Scoti—Tacitus and Ireland—Alexandrian geographers on Hibernia—Wars between Irish kings and the Romans—Cormac MacArt; Niall of the Nine Hostages—Claudian—Altus, an Irish soldier, at Calvary—Pelagius and Cœlestius—A typical Irishman of the olden time—Palladius and the first attempt to convert Ireland . . . . . . . 1—24

## LECTURE II.

### ST. PATRICK.

His works: *Confession* and *Epistle to Coroticus*—*Book of Armagh*, contents of—Tirechan's *Annotations*—Life by Maccumacthenius—Test for mediæval biographies—Hymns of SS. Fiacc and Sechnall—Colgan's *Lives*—The *Tripartite Life*—Birthplace of St. Patrick—Dumbarton—His father—A decurion—And a deacon—Clerical marriage and secular occupations in fifth century—Correspondence of Exuperius and Pope Innocent I.—Theodotus of Ancyra—Captivity of St. Patrick in Antrim—The hill of Slemish—His pious life and escape . . 25—45

## LECTURE III.

### ST. PATRICK'S MISSION.

PAGE

Mission of St. Patrick, a controverted question—Dr. Todd's view—Tirechan's statement—Germanus and the Pelagian heresy—The Hallelujah victory—Date and place of St. Patrick's arrival—Work at Wicklow, Strangford Lough, and Antrim—Conversion of Dichu—Description of Dalaradia—The valley of the Braid near Broughshane—Identification of Milchu's farm, where Patrick was a slave—Value of local knowledge—Suicide of Milchu—St. Patrick's prophecy . . 46—61

## LECTURE IV.

### TARA AND THE CONVERSION OF IRELAND.

Celtic nations and tribal organisation—Central national assemblies in Galatia—Gaul and Ireland—Description of Tara—Cormac MacArt—Convention of Tara—Brugh-na-Boinne and burial of Cormac—St. Patrick and Slane—King Laoghaire—Conflict of St. Patrick and the Druids—Easter at Tara—St. Patrick's mission to Connaught—Conversion of King Laoghaire's daughters—St. Patrick at Croagh-Patrick—Legend concerning the expulsion of snakes from Ireland—Mission in Ulster—Foundation of Armagh—Visit to Munster—Death and burial of the saint . . . . . . . . . 62—96

## LECTURE V.

### ST. COLUMBA.

His history written by Adamnan—Life and works of Adamnan—Birth and baptism of St. Columba—Education at Clonard—St. Finnian—School of Clonard—Columba's ordination—Monastic bishops—Visit to Glasnevin—Literary zeal of Columba—Quarrel with Finnian of Moville about the Cathach—Battles between the Irish monasteries—Battle of Cooldrevny—St. Molassius and Columba . . . . . 97—110

## LECTURE VI.

### COLUMBA IN IONA.

PAGE

Causes assigned for Columba's exile, religious and political—Two districts called Dalriada—Scotch Dalriada an Irish colony—Brude, King of the Picts—Columba's voyage to Iona Description of the island—Cashels in Iona, Ireland, and Egypt —Columba's plan of evangelisation—Success among the Picts —Calls SS. Comgall and Canice to his help—Conversion of King Brude—Contest with the Druids—Synod of Drumceatt —Descent of the Royal family from Niall of the Nine Hostages—Connection with St. Columba—Columba's love of nature—His death . . . . . . . 111—130

## LECTURE VII.

### COLUMBANUS.

Missionary activity of Celtic Church—Marianus Scotus in eleventh century—Columbanus and Columba confounded—Distinction in origin—Age—Work—Authorities for life of Columbanus—Writings—*Life* by Abbat Jonas—Education at Bangor—Studies in Celtic monasteries—Mission to Gaul—France in the sixth century—Fredegund and Brunehault—Columbanus in Switzerland—St. Gall—Foundation of Bobbio—Its library and MSS.—Death of Columbanus—His attitude towards the pope . . . . . . . . . 131—148

## LECTURE VIII.

### THE PASCHAL CONTROVERSY.

Origin of controversy concerning Easter—Easter cycles—Quartodeciman view and Jewish controversy—Changes during first five centuries—Irish used old Roman cycle—Reformation of calendar by Victorius and Dionysius Exiguus—Mission of St. Augustine and Easter question—Resistance of Celts to Rome—Bishop Dagan and Columbanus—Munster accepts

Roman view—SS. Fintan and Laserian in controversy—Novel plan of settling a disputed question—Cummian's epistle—Resistance of the Columban order in North England—Conference at Whitby—Colman and the monastery of Mayo—Antagonism of Celtic and Saxon monks—Submission of Iona. . . . . . . . . . 149—165

## LECTURE IX.

### IRELAND AND THE EAST.

Celtic monasticism, origin of—Monasticism in primitive Church—Nitria—Joannes Cassianus and his writings—Letters and influence of St. Jerome—Syria and France in fourth, fifth, and sixth centuries—St. Abraham—Simeon Stylites and enclosed anchorites—Anchorites in the East and in Ireland—St. Doulough's Church—Use of term Disert or Desert in Irish names and in Cassian—Hermit life in Ireland—Marianus Scotus—Anchorite rule—Enclosed anchorite on the Mount of Olives—Description of a Celtic monastery—Inismurray—Iniscleraun and Mount Thabor, monasteries of . 166—188

## LECTURE X

### THE SOCIAL LIFE OF THE EIGHTH CENTURY.

Twofold division (1) The political life, (2) The ecclesiastical life—Authorities—Reciprocal influence of Church and State—Division of Ireland into five kingdoms—Kingdom of Meath represented by present diocese of Meath—*Book of Rights*—Tribal distribution—Perpetual wars—Career of Phelim, King of Munster and bishop—Story of Bishop Corprius and the prince's spirit—Brehon law—Icelandic code—Sitting Dharna of Hindoos—Artistic effort among the Celts—The *Book of Kells* and the *Codex Rossauensis*—Professor Hartley's analysis of colours in *Book of Kells*—College of Slane—And Dagobert II., King of France—Correspondence between Colcu of Clonmacnois and Alcuin . . . . 189—210

## LECTURE XI.

### GREEK AND HEBREW LEARNING IN IRISH MONASTERIES.

PAGE

Influence of Iconoclastic controversy on the West—Communication between East and West in middle ages—A. J. Letronne, and *Liber de Mensurâ Orbis*—Dicuil and Irish travellers in the East in the eighth century—Irish monks on the Sweetwater Canal—*Chronicle* of John Malalas—The *Saltair Na Rann*—Discovery of Iceland by Irish monks—Joh. Scotus Erigena—The *Book of Armagh*, and study of Greek in Ireland—Greek church at Trim—Celtic expositors—Commentaries of Aileran, Augustine, and Sedulius—Virgil, the geometer, and scientific studies in Ireland—Organisation of the Celtic schools . . 211—230

## LECTURE XII.

### THE ROUND TOWERS OF IRELAND.

Modern conception of historical science—Definition of a round tower—Various theories about their origin—Dr. Petrie's views—Modified as to date by Lord Dunraven—Church towers, origin of—Early churches towerless like ancient Irish churches—Origin of church towers in Syria—Count de Voguë and Central Syria—Emperor Justinian and architecture—Byzantine art and its influence—On France—And Ireland—Round towers at St. Gall and Aix-la-Chapelle—Foreign ecclesiastics in Ireland—Litany of Œngus the Culdee 231—250

## LECTURE XIII.

### THE DANISH INVASION OF IRELAND AND THE PAGAN CRUSADE.

Danish invasion a great national movement—Origin—Divisible into three great parts—Date—Turgesius, the first great Danish conqueror of Ireland—His career and death—Foundation of Dublin—Primate Forannan—Social life and civilisation of the Danes—Dasent's *Burnt Njal*—Icelandic literature . 251—266

## LECTURE XIV.

### THE DANISH KINGDOM OF DUBLIN.

Brian Boru and Cormac of Cashel—Battle of Ballymoon—Cormac's schorlaship and writings—Dr. Whitley Stokes' estimate of Cormac's *Glossary*—The Rock of Cashel—King Sitric, and the battle of Kilmashogue—Mercantile prosperity of Dublin under the Danes—Cloth trade with Bristol—Earl Haco's "broadcloth cruise"—Diocese and Danish kingdom of Dublin—Haliday's *Scandinavian Kingdom of Dublin*—The Thingmount and Althing of Dublin—And of Iceland—College Green—The Stayne . . . . . . . 267—282

## LECTURE XV.

### BRIAN BORU AND THE TRIUMPH OF CHRISTIANITY.

Authorities for his history—Descent—Early struggle with the Danes—Mahon and the battle of Sulcoit—Murder of Mahon—Accession of Brian to throne of Munster—Conquest of Connaught—Meath and Ulster—Of the Danes—Internal organisations of Brian—Church-building—Crannoges—Battle of Glenmama—Of Clontarf—Circumstances which led up to it—Queen Gormflaith—Danish allies at Clontarf—Earl Sigurd—Brodar, the apostate—Morrogh O'Brian—Description of the battle—Death of Brian—Authorities for the battle of Clontarf—Rev. Dr. Haughton upon its date . . . . 283—306

## LECTURE XVI.

### THE SEE OF DUBLIN AND UNION WITH ENGLAND.

Conversion of Danes during the tenth and eleventh centuries led to foundation of See of Dublin—At first hostile to Armagh and the Celtic Church—Dependent on Canterbury—All its early bishops consecrated there—Ussher's *Sylloge*—Donatus, first bishop of Dublin—Foundation of Christ Church Cathedral—Patrick of Dublin and Lanfranc of Canterbury—C orrespondence of Lanfranc in the *Sylloge*—Attempt to reform the Celtic Church—Dr. Lanigan on Patrick's submission to Lanfranc—A plundering bishop—Gregory, first archbishop—A valiant soldier, then a prelate—Primate of Armagh seizes Dublin by force—Gilbert of Limerick, and his treatise *De Statu Ecclesiæ*—Synod of Kells—St. Laurence O'Toole—The Priory of All Saints and Trinity College—Dermot MacMurrogh and the Anglo-Norman invasion—Death of St. Laurence   307—329

## LECTURE XVII.

### ST. MALACHY AND THE SEE OF ARMAGH.

Distinction between sees of Armagh and of Dublin—Origin of Armagh—Succession of primates—*Book of Armagh*—Brian Boru and Armagh—Married primates—Gilbert of Limerick—Primate Celsus—Synods of Usnach and Rathbresail—St. Bernard and St. Malachy—Life of St. Malachy—Bishop, first at Connor—Then at Armagh, and lastly at Down—Malachy's visit to York—Clairvaux and Rome—An Irish episcopal journey in the twelfth century—Synods of Holmpatrick and Kells—Cardinal Papiro—Gelasius first archbishop of Armagh who held the pall—Synod of Clane—The primate submits to Henry II.   .   .   .   .   .   .   .   .   .   330—349

# LECTURE I.

## *THE ANCIENT CELTIC CHURCH.*

I HAVE chosen as the subject of my present course the history of the ancient Celtic Church, from its origin down to the conquest of Ireland by the Anglo-Normans. It is an obscure and difficult, but at the same time a most interesting subject. I shall endeavour to treat it truthfully, fearlessly, and impartially. Let me now define clearly what I propose to do in this lecture. I propose to treat of the history of the ancient Celtic Church, not merely of the history of the Irish Church. I certainly intend to devote special attention to the Irish branch of that Church. But Celtic Christianity was both older and more extensive than Irish Christianity, and an exhaustive discussion of our subject will demand an investigation of its sources.

Again, let me warn you at the outset, that in taking up this subject I do not present myself as an original investigator. I am no profound Irish or Celtic scholar, qualified to deal with the recondite mysteries of ancient dialects or well-nigh illegible manuscripts. I am simply a diligent student of the results skilled inquirers have attained, which I, in turn, will endeavour to weave into a connected and interesting narrative. Indeed, I may remark, in vindication of my own attempt, that the most diligent student of Celtic annals or Celtic philology would not necessarily be the most competent historian of the Celtic Church, simply because his intellectual field of vision had been too limited. A man might be very highly skilled in the mysteries of the Cornish, Manx, or Pictish dialects, and yet be wholly wanting in that broad knowledge of ecclesiastical and general history which sheds light on many a perplexing passage.

I have said that Celtic Christianity was older and wider than its Irish form, and I have said so because British and Gallic Christianity were both of them Celtic, and both of them prior in point of time to its Irish form. The subject of this day's lecture will then be Celtic Christianity prior to St. Patrick.

Addressing a University audience, I need scarcely remind them that a Celtic Christianity, with its peculiar national faults and characteristics, finds place even in the New Testament. The Galatians, whose apostasy from pure Christianity has endowed the Church with St. Paul's masterly defence of Christian freedom, were Celts; and let me say at the same time that, though they may have given the apostle trouble, yet nowhere did the Church of Christ find a more loving and a more passionate devotion in those earlier ages than among the Celts of Asia Minor. Yet I must pass over Celtic Christianity in its Galatian form, simply referring you to Bishop Lightfoot's Commentary on the Galatian Epistle, where the subject is exhausted.

Gallic Christianity again was Celtic, and was very ancient. The Gauls were undoubtedly Celts, and Celts, too, very closely allied with the Celtic tribes of Britain and of Ireland. The language, for instance, of ancient Gaul was akin to the Irish tongue. Of that ancient Gallic language we have not many extant monuments.

One of them was brought before the Royal Irish Academy some twenty years ago by the late Professor Lottner of this University. It consisted of a Druidical charm, half in Latin and half in Gallic, which had sorely puzzled French antiquarians, but revealed its secrets to our own professor, because he perceived at a glance that the Gallic words were identical with expressions still used in Irish.[1] I need scarcely delay over Celtic Christianity as it developed itself in Gaul at this early stage. Every tiro in ecclesiastical history knows that Celtic Gaul received the Gospel from the earliest times, while the celebrated story of the martyrs of Vienne and Lyons, as told by Eusebius in the fifth book of his History, proves that the Celtic Christians of the second century were just as ready in Gaul as in Galatia to lay down their lives for Christ. It is important, too, as bearing on our future investigations, to remember that Gallic was intimately connected with Oriental Christianity. The Christians of Lyons and Vienne, under Marcus Aurelius, sent an account of their sufferings to the Church of Asia as to the mother Church. Irenæus, second Bishop of Lyons, was a Greek, and a native of Asia Minor. The whole of southern Gaul was, in fact, Greek and Oriental as much as Roman, and remained so till the Middle Ages;[2] a fact which we shall do well carefully to note for future reference.

---

[1] See "The Gaulish Inscription of Poitiers, containing a Charm against the Demon Dontaurios," by R. T. Siegfried and C. F. Lottner, a paper read before the Royal Irish Academy, April 13th, 1863. See its *Proceedings*, t. viii., p. 308, and a *facsimile* on plate xxiii. in the Appendix.

[2] Ed. Le Blant, *Chrét. Inscrip. de la Gaule*, t. i., pref., p. cxv., and Diss. Nos. 38, 211, 225, 248; t. ii., Diss. Nos. 521, 557, 613. The most interesting of all these dissertations is that on the life of St. Abraham, an Eastern monk of the fifth century, who passed

The ancient Celtic Church of Britain comes nearer home to ourselves. English Christianity is commonly supposed to date from the time of Pope Gregory the Great, and the mission of St. Augustine. You all know the story how Pope Gregory, passing through the slave market of Rome, saw the children exposed for sale, and demanded the name of their nation. Being informed they were Angles, he replied, "Not Angles, but angels if Christians;" whereupon Augustine was sent to found English Christianity. English Christianity, I say, not British. Mark the difference. Take up the last volume published by the lamented historian Mr. Green, *The Making of England*, and you will understand the vast importance of the distinction I have made. English Christianity, the Christianity of the Angles and of the Saxons, dates from Augustine, and was derived from Rome. British Christianity was the Christianity of the Britons; it existed here for ages before Augustine, and must have been derived immediately from Gaul. This, if I am not mistaken, is far from being the ordinary view; people usually think that Pagan darkness covered England and Ireland alike till St. Patrick came in the fifth century and converted Ireland, which enjoyed the light of the Gospel for a century and a half before England, where it did not penetrate till the beginning of the seventh century. Such, I say, is the popular view, due simply to ignorance of such an

---

from the banks of the Euphrates, where he was born, to end his days in Central Gaul. He died about A.D. 476 (Till., *Mém.*, xvi., 258; Ceill., x., 393, xi., 380). *Cf.* Hieron., Liber Secundus, In Epistolam ad Galat., in Migne, *Pat. Lat.*, t. xxvi., 354; Salvian. *De Guber. Dei*, iv., 14; Mabillon, *AA. SS. Ord. Bened.*, i., 662. See also Lenthéric's *La Grèce et l'Orient en Provence* (Paris 1878), and *Les Villes Mortes du Golfe de Lyon* (Paris: 1876—78) —two very interesting works which illustrate this topic.

ordinary authority as Bede's *History of the English Nation*. Let me, then, endeavour briefly to sketch the fortunes of Christianity among the British people during the earliest ages of the Church.

The notices of Christianity in England during the first three centuries of our era are few and far between. Of Christian monuments, tombs, inscriptions, churches, belonging to that period, there are simply none extant. During the first two centuries we have no certain records of any Christian effort in England. Mediæval tradition speaks of Joseph of Arimathea as coming to Glastonbury. But the mere statement of the tradition is a sufficient refutation thereof. The Jews hated, we are told, Lazarus and Joseph so much for their active support of Christ's cause, that at last they arrested them, put them on board a ship without sails or oars, which was miraculously guided first to Marseilles, where Lazarus became the first bishop,[1] and then to Britain, where Joseph founded the Church at Glastonbury.[2] More attention is due to the alleged conversion of some noble Britons at Rome about the time of St. Paul's first visit. Tacitus tells us, in his *Annals* (xiii., 32), that Pomponia Græcina was the wife of Aulus Plautius, the first real

---

[1] The traditions concerning Lazarus and his mission in southern Gaul are still prevalent in that locality. *Cf. Notes sur les Livres Liturgiques des Diocèses d'Autun, Chalon, et Macon*, par M. Pellechet (Paris: 1883), p. 227, and the *Revue Critique*, January 26th, 1885, p. 67.

[2] Ussher, *Brit. Eccles. Antiqq.*, cap. ii. (Works, ed. Elrington, vol. v., p. 25-47), gives the whole of this legend, including the story of the Holy Grail, celebrated in the *Acts of King Arthur*, and by Lord Tennyson in his poems. The story is told at length in Baring-Gould's *Curious Myths of the Middle Ages*, second series, p. 339. The grail itself was the vessel out of which our Lord partook of the Last Supper, and in which Joseph of Arimathea collected His blood, when Christ's side was transfixed by the spear. It was then carried by him to Britain. According to another

conqueror of Britain, about the years 43—47 A.D. She was accused, about the year 57, of holding a foreign superstition, and delivered over to the judgment of her husband, who very naturally acquitted her. The foreign superstition has been identified with Christianity,—and with good reason, as the excavations and investigations of De Rossi at Rome have proved. This simple historical fact has, however, become the basis on which a vast superstructure has been made to rest. Pomponia Græcina has been made a sister of Caractacus, the British prince. Caractacus was, as Tacitus tells us, led captive to Rome, where his daring speech and bearing so impressed the emperor that he gave him life and comparative liberty. At Rome Caractacus and Bran, his father, a Druidical bard, and Gladys, his daughter, were all converted to Christianity. Gladys became the wife of Rufus, from his modesty called Pudens, who is identified with the Pudens of St. Paul's Epistle to the Romans, and with the Rufus and Pudens mentioned by the poet Martial.[1] I need scarcely say, however, that all these suppositions are utterly devoid of

---

version, the grail is preserved in heaven till a race of heroes appear on earth worthy to become its guardians. This gave occasion to the stories about King Arthur's Court, the Knights Galahad, Launcelot, and others, celebrated by Tennyson. See also *Das Evangelium Nicodemi in der Abendländischen Literatur*, by Dr. R. P. Wülcker (Paderborn : 1872); at p. 72 there is an excursus concerning the legend of Joseph of Arimathea and his mission to England. Ireland's freedom from snakes is attributed to St. Joseph as well as to St. Patrick (Ussher's Works, vi., 552). The two articles on Joseph of Arimathea in the *Dict. Christ. Biog.*, t. iii., p. 439, give other authorities about these traditions.

[1] All these stories about Pudens, Rufus, Aristobulus of Rom. xvi., said by the Greek Menæa to have been ordained by St. Paul bishop over the Britons, and also about the baptism of the British King Lucius, will be found in Ussher's *Brit. Eccles. Antiquit.*, cap. iii., in Elrington's edition of his works, t. 5; *cf.* Martial's *Epig.*, iv., 13, xi., 53.

historical evidence, and owe all their currency to mediæval Welsh legends, which represent the Druid bard as returning to Britain and preaching the Gospel to his pagan countrymen. During the second century again we have no historical evidence for the existence of Christianity in Britain. Tertullian, at the close of it, boasting in a rhetorical passage of the wide spread of the Gospel, declares that Christ was worshipped among the Moors, the Spaniards, the Germans, the various nations of the Gauls; while even the parts of Britain impervious to the Roman legions acknowledged the sway of Christ.[1] But on such rhetorical expressions we can lay no stress. It is indeed most probable that Christianity did find an entrance into Britain during those early years, but we have no evidence of this fact. There were numerous channels through which it could percolate. We scarcely ever realise the full meaning of St. Paul's words, that it was in the fulness of time God sent forth His Son, till we grasp the vast, the magnificent, the far-reaching organisation of the Roman Empire, which carried law and order and a thorough system of communication from the borders of the Indian Ocean to the shores of the North Atlantic, so that a traveller could leave Ctesiphon, or Babylon, in Mesopotamia, or the city of Nicomedia in Asia Minor, as Constantine the Great once did, and never draw rein till the public conveyance set him down at Boulogne, on the shores of the English Channel. That system of public roads[2] easily lent itself to the extension of

---

[1] Tertull., *Adv. Jud.*, c. vii.
[2] On the public road system of the Romans, and the construction thereof, see Le Bas and Waddington, *Voy. Archéol.*, t. iii., p. 206; for vast constructions under Domitian, see *Rev. Arch.*, 1873, t. xxvi., 65; *cf. Jour. Hell. Stud.*, 1883, t. iv., p. 30; and *Mittheil. Inst. Ath.*, 1882, p. 130, about road-making under Severus. On British roads see Coote's *Romans of Britain*, p. 55.

the Gospel. But there were two other influences at work which must have introduced Christianity to Britain from the earliest date. One was the army, the other was commerce. The Roman military system is well worth the careful study which modern German scholars, led by the venerable and indefatigable Mommsen, have long devoted to it.[1] That system located the legions permanently in various countries. Some legions were stationed for even three or four centuries in the same province, where the legions settled more like military colonists than soldiers on ordinary foreign service. But while the Romans stationed the legions permanently in the same places, they always recruited them in foreign lands, so that a legion in garrison at York would be recruited in Spain or Asia Minor, while a legion in Asia Minor would draw its recruits from Britain or Germany.[2] I need scarcely remind you that the New Testament itself offers various examples—notably that of Cornelius, the centurion of the Italian band—of this method of military organisation, as also of the influence exercised by it in spreading the Gospel into foreign lands. We can observe the same phenomenon in our own time. The British army is still an active agent in disseminating the various tides of home opinion throughout our worldwide empire.

---

[1] See *Geschichte der Römischen Kaiserlegionen*, von Dr. W. Pfitzner, p. 201, and a series of articles in *Hermes*, t. xix., by Mommsen, on the constitution, location, and recruitment of the Roman legions.

[2] The intercourse between Britain and the most distant East is shown by the inscription in the language of Palmyra, discovered a few years ago at South Shields, and published by Dr. Wright, in the *Transactions* of the Society of Biblical Archæology, vi., 436; *cf.* Clermont-Ganneau, in the *Revue Critique*, February 2nd, 1885, p. 89. Le Bas and Waddington, *Voy. Arch.*, iii., 332, Ins. 1364, notice the presence of British troops in Pamphylia; *cf. Ephem. Epigraph.*, 1884, vol. v., p. 28, no. 41.

The evangelical, the tractarian, the rationalistic movements, have all found devoted and powerful missionaries in the British army. Perhaps the most notable example in modern Church history that occurs to me is the foundation of Methodism in the United States. One hundred and twenty years ago communication between England and America was much slower and more dangerous than between Rome and London in the reign of the Antonines. Yet within thirty years of the foundation of the Methodist Society by John Wesley, a few soldiers in a marching regiment founded a Methodist Society at New York about the year 1765, which has grown so rapidly as to have now become the most powerful and numerous religious community in America.[1] Can we imagine that the religious zeal of the Christians of the second century glowed with a less fervent flame than that of Wesley's disciples in the eighteenth?

Commerce, again, was another influence which must have powerfully assisted the progress of the Cross in these Western Islands. The possession of Britain was not coveted by Rome simply from a lust of power. It was desired because of its commercial value. Its vast herds of cattle served to supply the needs of Gaul. The Romans showed their good taste, too, and valued highly even the delicacies of Britain. The oysters, for instance, the "natives" of Kent, were dearly loved by the epicures of Rome, who imported them from the great Roman station of Richborough, near Thanet.[2] But it was the mines of England which then as now constituted its commercial importance. Lead, tin, copper, iron were extracted by the Roman Government.

---
[1] Stevens, *Hist. of Methodism*, t. i., p. 329 (London: 1860).
[2] Juvenal, *Sat.*, iv., 141; Plin., *Nat. Hist.*, ix., 79, xxxii., 21.

The various museums of England possess about fifty blocks or pigs of lead, marked with the Imperial stamp, —proving that in England, as in Spain, Africa, and the East, the Roman Government retained the mines in their own hands. An active export trade was at the same time carried on by private individuals, who purchased the minerals from the imperial officials. A vigorous trade in tin was, indeed, carried on between England and the Mediterranean long before the Romans conquered the island; not only through the Carthaginian traders, but also by direct export to the opposite coast of Gaul, whence the metal was carried on horseback to Marseilles and Narbonne; and, when we come to Roman times, commerce must have followed much the same track. A block of copper has been found near Conway, addressed by a Roman merchant to his partner in Rome, and destined for exportation probably from the port of Chester. To those interested in the social life of this period I may commend a paper on mining operations in Britain under the Romans, in the *Proceedings* of the Somerset Archæological Society for 1858.[1] This active commercial intercourse must inevitably have brought Christianity in its train.

British Christianity does not, however, appear in history till the fourth century. The British Church is seen fully organised at the Synod of Arles, in A.D. 314, when three Metropolitan bishops signed the acts of the Council,—Eborius, of York; Restitutus, of London; and Adelfius, of Cærleon-on-Usk,[2] representing the

---

[1] Som. Arch. Soc. *Proceedings* for 1858, paper by J. Yates, M.A. On the missionary influence of commerce, see J. Réville, *Religion Sous les Sévères*, p. 49 (Paris: 1886).

[2] So called from Legio ii. Augusta, there stationed; see Hübner's British Inscriptions in *Corp. Ins. Lat.*, t. vii., p. 36.

three great centres of Roman life in Britain.[1] The fourth century showed not merely the organisation, it also proved the life and vigour of the British Church. Its opening decade was marked by the longest, the fiercest, and the most skilfully organised persecution the Church ever encountered. Britain did not experience its fury, which fell upon Italy, Africa, and the East, on Asia Minor, Palestine, Egypt, where thousands sealed their faith with their blood, as the pages of Eusebius and the touching stories of the genuine martyrologies so abundantly record. Britain was under the rule of Constantius, father of Constantine the Great. He was favourably disposed to Christianity, and mitigated, therefore, the severity of the imperial edicts. Yet the desire for martyrdom which at that time seized upon the Church like an epidemic displayed itself in Britain.[2] St. Alban, the protomartyr of Britain, suffered at St. Albans, Aaron and Julius at Chester, and many of both sexes suffered elsewhere throughout the island.[3] But the period of persecution passed away, and then British Christianity rapidly developed itself. British bishops were probably present at Nice in 325, and at Sardica in 347. They were certainly present at the Arian Council of Ariminum in 359, where the British and Gallic bishops displayed their independence of Imperial influence by refusing the public allowance for their maintenance. The British Churches of the

---

[1] Mansi, *Concilia*, ii., 463-468; Hefele's *History of Councils*, i., 180, Clark's trans.; Haddan and Stubbs, *Councils of Great Britain*, i., 1-40, where references will be found for all the stories about early British Christianity.

[2] See, for instance, the stories of the SS. Eulalia of Merida and Barcelona, in the *Dict. Christ. Biog.*, t. ii., p. 276.

[3] *Cf.* Cellier, *Hist. des Aut. Ecclesiast.*, xi., 526, for a notice of St. Sixtus, an early British martyr, reverenced when St. Augustine landed.

fourth century took the keenest interest in Church controversies. They opposed Arianism, but hesitated, like many others, about the use of the word ὁμοούσιος. The British Church, indeed, of this period proved its interest in theological questions by the most vigorous and satisfactory of proofs. It produced a heretic. Pelagius, the founder of the Pelagian heresy, and the antagonist of Augustine, is said to have been a Welshman, whose British name was Morgan.[1] By the close of the fourth century, Christianity must have prevailed universally among the British Celts. This is evident from the simple fact that the Celtic population which retired in the fifth and following centuries before the conquering Saxons were all of them Christians. A quotation proves this. Bede, who hated the Celts with a true Saxon hatred, depicts these original British Christians as guilty of most heinous crimes, disgraceful to their Christian profession. But in lib. i., cap. xxii. he singles out one for which the Divine judgment fell on them,—" They never preached the faith to the Saxons or English who dwelt among them." With a refinement and intensity of national hate, they left them to perish in their sins, determined that if the Saxons were superior to the Celts in this world, the position should be reversed in the next. So much for British Christianity in Celtic times.

Let us turn to Ireland and its history. The his-

---

[1] Ussher, *Eccles. Britan. Antiqq.*, Works, v., 252, ed. Elrington; see also the notes in Migne's *Pat. Lat.*, Hieron., Opp., t. iv., col. 682, where references will be found to Marius Mercator, *Commonit.;* Orosius, *Apologet.;* Prosper, *Carm. de Ingrat.;* August., *Epist.,* 186. St. Jerome expressly asserts in his *Comment. in Jerem.*, Præf., lib. iii., that Pelagius was an Irishman. His words are, "Habet progeniem Scoticæ gentis, de Britannorum vicinia." On the signification of the name Morgan, and its identity with Pelagius, see Dr. Reeves' paper on St. Marinus in *Proceedings* Roy. Irish Acad., viii., 299.

tory of our country is a perplexing maze. It has suffered much at the hands of partisans, on this side and on that. It has suffered still more at the hands of injudicious and uncritical friends, who not distinguishing between the rhapsodies of bards and the solid facts of history, have disgusted common-sense inquirers with the whole subject. I will not bring you back, with the *Four Masters*, or Keating, or Guest, to the flood and the confusion of tongues,[1] but will soberly inquire whether we have any ground for believing that Christianity existed among the Irish, or, as we should rather call them, among the Scots, prior to St. Patrick's mission.

It is very important for you to remember this fact, which bears upon our whole inquiry,—whenever in the first eleven centuries the term Scot occurs, it always means Irishman. During the first seven centuries the Picts were the inhabitants of modern Scotland. It was not till the eleventh or twelfth century that the term Scotland or Scotia was applied in its modern sense.[2] Now, the answer to the question, Was Christianity known in Ireland during the first four centuries? depends upon the answer to a further question, Was Ireland known to the Romans? This admits of a very simple reply. Ireland was known to the Romans, as is evident from two lines of proof,—one direct, the other indirect. In the *Agricola* of Tacitus we have a

---

[1] Thus Keating, in his *History of Ireland*, O'Mahony's edition (New York: 1881), p. 106, tells us how some chroniclers relate that Cain's three daughters were the first who dwelt in Ireland, while another account has it that Cassir, daughter of Bith, Noah's son, arrived in Ireland before the flood, landing near Bantry in the co. Cork.

[2] See Ussher's *Antiqq.*, cap. xvi., Works, vol. vi., p. 276—281; Keating, p. 375; Skene's *Celtic Scotland*, i., 137, 398; Dr. Reeves on Stephen White in *Proceedings* Roy. Irish Acad., viii., 29; Colgan's *Trias Thaumat.*, p. 109.

very full and minute account of the campaigns carried on by the great Roman general Agricola under Vespasian, Titus, and Domitian between the years 78 and 86. These campaigns embraced Wales, Anglesea, and North Britain south of the Firths of Forth and Clyde, or say generally a line drawn from Glasgow to Edinburgh. This campaign must have brought him within sight of Ireland. In fact, Ireland and Scotland are in places so close that, standing on the cliffs of the Antrim coast, I have often seen the houses in Scotland, while I have sailed from land to land in an open boat in three hours. Agricola's curiosity was aroused by the sight of Ireland, and hence in chapter twenty-four we are informed that in his fifth campaign he garrisoned the part of Britain which looks towards Ireland, not so much from fear of invasion as from hope of conquest. He gives us an interesting description of this country. "Hibernia," he says, "is situated between Britain and Spain, and is very accessible from the shores of Gaul. In size it is smaller than Britain, but larger than the islands of the Mediterranean. The soil, climate, manners, and habits of the people are similar to those of Britain. Its ports are well known to merchants." The historian then gives us the first glimpse of actual contact between Rome and Ireland. "Agricola had received one of their chiefs expelled in a domestic feud, and retained him in alliance for future use. I have often heard from him that Ireland could be conquered and held by one legion ; and that it would be profitable for Rome as against the Britons, that their arms should be dominant everywhere, and that freedom should be everywhere abolished out of their sight."[1]

This is the earliest notice of Ireland in real history.

---

[1] Tacit., *Agricola*, c. xxiv.

The earlier Greek historians and geographers mention vaguely Ierne. Strabo and Diodorus Siculus, in the time of Augustus, tell of its existence on the strength of the voyages of Pytheas about the time of Alexander the Great and of the Carthaginian merchants. But Agricola was the first historical personage who came into contact with Ireland, and his notice of it is instructive. It is evident from it that the description left us by Cæsar and Tacitus of the state of Gaul and Britain may be applied to Ireland. Just note two points of similarity. Firstly, in Agricola's time—that is, the first century—its inhabitants were divided, like the Britons, into clans or tribes. Secondly, these clans were torn, as our annals relate, by intestine feuds. Whilst we see that an Irish prince, when beaten by his opponents, was just as ready in the first century to betray his country to the Romans as an Irish prince in the twelfth century to betray it to the Normans. The geography of Ptolemy in the second century shows that a very extended intercourse with Ireland must have prevailed by the time of the Antonines, as the Alexandrian geographer gives a very minute and accurate account of our country. But then we must remember that the second century was an age of great activity on the part of the Roman power in Britain. Voyages of discovery must frequently have been undertaken. Agricola, a little earlier, was not content with conquering Britain as far as the Clyde. He sent his fleet on a voyage round the north coast of Scotland; and surely, if the Roman fleet hesitated not to encounter the dangers of such northern seas, they would not have been deterred by the calmer and bluer waters which surround our coasts.[1] We are not left, however, without evidence that

---

[1] Tacit., *Agricola.*, capp. x., xxxviii.

the naval officers stationed at ports like Chester and the Clyde did extend their voyages to the opposite island. Some thirty or forty years ago Mr. Putland, of Bray, was digging the foundation of a gateway on the side of Bray head, when he came upon a number of bodies interred side by side, each with a copper coin of Trajan and Hadrian lying on their breasts, the obolus, doubtless, to pay Charon, the ferryman. Roman coins, too, extending from the age of Nero to the time of Honorius in the fifth century, have been found in abundance all along the eastern coast, as, for instance, on the Three Rock Mountain, at Rathfarnham, at Downpatrick, the Giant's Causeway, Coleraine, and many other places. At the Causeway, in the year 1831, there were two hundred Roman coins found, extending from Vespasian, A.D. 70, to the Antonines, A.D. 160; while in 1854 two thousand Roman coins and two hundred ounces of silver were discovered at Coleraine.[1]

Between the second and the fourth centuries we hear practically nothing of any contact between Rome and Ireland. In the middle of the third century the Irish annals tell of an expedition against Britain fitted out by

---

[1] On the Roman coins found in Ireland see *Proceedings* of Royal Irish Academy, t. ii., 184—190; t. v., 199; t. vi., 442, 525; and several other references *s. v.* Coins, in the general Index to vol. vii. On the Coleraine find see John Scott Porter in *Ulster Journ. Arch.*, 1854, p. 182—191, and Hübner, Brit. Ins., in *Corp. Ins. Lat.*, t. vii., p. 221, Ins. 1198. The coins found in 1854 were all of the fourth and fifth centuries, ending with Honorius, under whom Britain was finally abandoned by the Romans. Porter mentions several other similar finds in the same locality during this century. Those found in 1854 contained specimens of the name Patricius, which is rare among the British inscriptions. The coins mentioned in *Proc.* R. I. A., t. vi., p. 442 are specially worthy of notice, for they all belonged to the time of the Roman Republic.

Cormac MacArt, King of Ireland and founder of Tara, and they add a long list of booty which he gained on this occasion. It was, however, only in the fourth century, when the warlike energies of the Roman Empire had become relaxed, and vigorous life was fast fading at its extremities, that the Hibernian Scots became the implacable and perpetual foes of the empire. Among the sources of Roman history in the fourth century the works of Ammianus Marcellinus stand pre-eminent. He was the friend of the poet Claudian, whose poems shed many an interesting sidelight on the narrative of the historian. From a comparison of these sources we see how deadly and how continuous were the attacks of the Irish upon Britain. In 343 they seem to have begun the conflict. In A.D. 360 they broke a treaty of peace, and in combination with the Picts, Saxons, and Attacotti kept possession of Britain for ten years under an Irish king, called Crimthann,[1] till Theodosius, landing in Kent in 369, thoroughly subjugated the whole country, and reorganised the public service, appointing two new officials, one to command the Channel fleet and watch the Saxon pirates; the other, the Comes Britanniarum, to guard the western coast against the Irish attacks.[2] The victory of Theodosius was for a time complete, and

---

[1] For Crimthann see Keating, p. 369, and *Four Masters*, A.D. 366. Upon these invasions of Britain by Scots and Attacots, see Amm. Marcell., xx., 1, xxvi., 4, xxvii., 8; Claudian, *De IV. Cons. Honor. Paneg.*, viii., 30-33; xxii. in i. *Cons. Stilich.*, lib. ii., 251; *De Bello Getico Lib.*, 416-418; *Four Masters*, ed. O'Donovan, A.D. 405; Ussher, Works, vi., 116, where the references to Claudian will be found at full length. This is one of the earliest and most interesting allusions in Irish annals that can be verified by external authorities. Niall of the Nine Hostages renewed the war with Rome a few years later (Ussher, vi., 115, 559; Keating, p. 373).

[2] See *Notitia Dignitatum*, ed. Böcking (Bonn: 1839-53).

Claudian exultingly sings of "Icy Ierne" weeping for her heaps of slain, of Thule red with the blood of the Picts, of the Orkneys dripping with Saxon gore, of the general himself conquering the Hyperborean waves with audacious prow.

This defeat seems to have been the means of making the Irish people more closely acquainted with Rome than ever before. Theodosius must have been struck with the vigour and energy displayed by these barbarians in his campaign. So instead of murdering his prisoners, he organised the Attacots into imperial cohorts, which he stationed at Treves, in Gaul, where they were seen by St. Jerome, after the victory of Theodosius, performing the duties of a Roman garrison, but feeding themselves, according to the Saint, on human flesh. St. Jerome had evidently not quite shaken himself free from the influence of those earlier legends which represented Ireland as the abode of perpetual snow, and its inhabitants as cannibals.[1]

You can easily see how this extended commercial intercourse, these continuous wars, these plundering expeditions, must all have helped to convey a knowledge of Christianity to some at least of the Hibernian Scots. The annals of Ireland speak of one Altus, an Irish warrior in the service of Rome, who was

---

[1] The Attacots were a people scattered over the south-western parts of Scotland and the northern parts of Ireland (Petrie's *Tara*, p. 46, and Skene's *Celt. Scotl.*, i., 101 ; O'Donovan's Notes to *Four Masters*, A.D. 405). They were embodied in the Roman army, and make a distinguished figure in the *Notitia Dignitatum* (see Böcking's note, t. i., p. 227). St. Jerome (*Adv. Jovin.*, lib. ii., cap. 7, in Migne's *Pat. Lat.*, t. xxiii., col. 296) says they eat human flesh, and charges the Irish of that day with practising community of wives. Mr. Hennessy considers that the Attacots were the same as the Scots, and that Attacotti is only a Latinised form of the Celtic word Aitechtuatha, signifying peasants.

present at our Lord's crucifixion, and was so impressed with the miracles he beheld that he returned to preach the faith to his countrymen,—a tradition embodied in verse by Sir S. Ferguson in his *Lays of the Western Gael* :—

"And they say, Centurion Altus, when he to Emania came,
And to Rome's subjection called us, urging Cæsar's tribute claim ;
Told that half the world barbarian thrills already with the faith,
Taught them by the god-like Syrian Cæsar lately put to death."

The story is not impossible, though very improbable, because we have of late years learned from extant inscriptions that British troops were sent to garrison Asia Minor, and some of them may have found their way to Jerusalem in the course of military changes.[1] Again, the great invasions of Britain during the latter half of the fourth century must have brought many a Christian captive into Ireland, some of whom may, like the captive maid in Naaman's household, have used their influence for the promotion of the true faith. Indeed, we are not left without instances showing how such border raids upon the empire tended during the fourth century to the spread of the truth. The conversion of Georgia dates from the year 320. That country has ever since retained its faith, notwithstanding the assaults of Parsee Dualism and of Mahometanism. Yet that conversion was originally due to a female captive named Nina.[2] Com-

---

[1] British troops in Pamphylia, Le Bas and Wadd., *Voy. Arch.*, iii., p. 332, Ins. No. 1364. Cf. *Eph. Epig.*, 1884, t. v., p. 28, no. 41.
[2] See arts. "Iberian Church" and "Nina" in the *Dict. Christ. Biography*.

merce, too, constant and extended as it was between Gaul and Ireland, must have introduced Christianity during the fourth century. It was the age of an Athanasius and a Jerome, equally well known on the banks of the Rhine, the Nile, and the Jordan; it was the age of a Hilary of Poitiers, of a Martin of Tours; and can we imagine that none of their converts penetrated to an island so well known to them, especially when we learn from other sources that in this same fourth century the Gospel was spread by Christian merchants far beyond the bounds of the Roman Empire,—to Aden, for instance, where they founded a Church; to Ceylon and to Abyssinia?[1]

The strong presumptions thus created we shall find fully borne out by history. Christian captives must have been carried off from Britain in those raids of the Hibernian Scots about the time of the Emperor Julian. The best chronology fixes the date of St. Patrick's captivity in Ireland some time towards the close of the fourth century. While again we have the clearest historical proofs that Christian Irishmen existed before the close of the fourth century. I have already mentioned Pelagius, the founder of the Pelagian heresy. He was regarded by all his contemporaries as a Briton, as I have already mentioned. Let me call your special attention to him for a moment. His life reveals the intellectual activity of the British Church; it reveals, too, the extended travel and intercourse which found place between the greatest extremes of the Roman Empire. He was born in Britain, spent his earlier manhood in Rome, whence about the year 410 he passed to Sicily, Africa, Syria, and Asia Minor, vigorously maintaining

---

[1] See article on Ethiopian Church in Smith's *Dict. Christ. Biog.*, Cosmas Indicopl., iii., 179; Neander, *H. E.*, iii., 171.

and diffusing his peculiar opinions in all these regions. His bosom friend, the chosen companion of all his journeys and labours, was Cœlestius, an Irishman. Cœlestius, during the first thirty years of the fifth century, was one of the most prominent figures in the religious and in the political world too of that day. His activity was immense. He had developed even in that early age a true Irish faculty for agitation, and realised fully that successful agitation can only be carried on by intense personal exertion. His early training eminently qualified him for his future life. He was a lawyer by education, and practised in the Roman Courts about the year A.D. 400. There he became acquainted with Pelagius and his system. Pelagius was a quiet contemplative soul, who loved to follow out his speculations on the mysteries of grace and providence in the retirement of the closet, but hated, like all such souls, the bustle and din of the controversial world. Now, however, he came in contact with one qualified to do the rough work of life. Cœlestius, the lawyer, was converted from law to theology, and embraced the system of Pelagius with the greatest enthusiasm. In no age, however, have lawyers succeeded in theology. Their training does not fit them for it. Their own peculiar subject develops a hard, sharp, legal tone of mind, which tolerates no mystery, no half-lights, no halting compromises; and in all true theology the mysterious element ever enters in, to disconcert that tone and to demand such compromises. Cœlestius seized on the system of Pelagius, demanded and obtained clear views on the subject, and then set them forth in the most uncompromising and offensive manner. At Carthage against St. Augustine, at Rome before the Pope, at Constantinople before the Patriarch, he sustained and expounded his views. His travels would be regarded as immense even amongst moderns. He penetrated the most distant East, and took counsel with the celebrated Theodore of Mopsuestia. Again and again was he expelled from Rome and from Constantinople by imperial and ecclesiastical rule alike. He brought down upon himself the wrath and the abusive tongue of St. Jerome, who describes him in his usual style as "an Alpine cur reared up on Scotch porridge."[1] He was irrepressible too. In 416 he gained the Pope Zosimus over to his side. The wily Italian, well-skilled in affairs, was no match for the persuasive tongue of the Irishman dealing with the subtleties of theology. Overawed, however, by the authority of an Augustine and of a Jerome, whose dicta were then decisive in the theological world, the pope changed his mind and condemned Cœlestius. Cœlestius, however, was nothing daunted. If the pope agreed with him, so much the better; but if the pope disagreed, why, Cœlestius did not care, but would seek redress in other quarters. The last glimpse we get of this typical Irishman is from Constantinople. The year 431 was marked by the Council of Ephesus and the opening of the great Nestorian controversy, which completely dwarfed the Pelagian in duration and results. Cœlestius, true to his instinct, was there too, bearding the pope from Constantinople, supporting the Patriarch Nestorius against his Roman rival, and finally meeting at

---

[1] See Ussher's Works, ed. Elrington, v., 253, 254; Hieron. in Comment. in Jeremiam Prophetam, Primi Libri Prolog., and Præf. in lib. iii., Migne, *Pat. Lat.*, t. xxiv., col. 682, 758. The *Commonitorium* of Marius Mercator gives us a good deal of curious information about Cœlestius and Pelagius. Jerome clearly describes one of his Pelagian opponents as an Irishman in his Præf. lib. iii. in Jer., saying that he was descended from the Scots, "de vicinia Britannorum." *Cf.* Garnier, Dissert., i., in Migne's *Pat. Lat.*, t. xlviii., col. 266; Noris, *Hist. Pelag.*, i., 3.

the hands of the Ephesian Council that excommunication which was the usual fate of the unsuccessful party.

This brief sketch of Cœlestius proves several things. It shows us that the national character and national tendencies were much the same in the fourth and fifth as in the nineteenth centuries. It also proves the point upon which I have been insisting, that Christianity was not unknown to some Irishmen prior to the time of St. Patrick and the national conversion of Ireland. The exploits, indeed, of this Irishman, and the troubles of the Pelagian controversy, seem to have turned the pope's attention to this out-of-the-way corner of the West. And so we learn from the Chronicle of Prosper of Aquitaine, a contemporary author, that in the year 431, under the consulship of Bassus and Antiochus, "Palladius was consecrated by Pope Cœlestine, and sent to the Scots (or Irish) believing in Christ as their first bishop;"[1] while in another work the same writer, referring to Cœlestine's efforts against heresy, praises him for driving the Irishman Cœlestius from Italy, the British heretic Agricola from Gaul and Britain, and ends by telling us that "by ordaining a bishop for the Scots, whilst he laboured to keep the Roman island Catholic, he made also the barbarous island Christian."[2]

These words are in complete conformity with the conclusions we have otherwise gained. Palladius was from Gaul, a disciple of Germanus of Auxerre, and was doubtless well acquainted with Irish needs.[3]

---

[1] "Ad Scotos in Christum credentes ordinatur a Papa Cœlestino Palladius, et primus episcopus mittitur."—St. Prosper., *Chron.* in Migne, *Pat. Lat.*, t. li., col. 595.

[2] St. Prosper., *Lib. cont. Collatorem*, cap. xxi., in Migne, *Pat. Lat.*, t. li., col. 271.

[3] Palladius was probably Archdeacon of Germanus. He was despatched by him on a mission to the pope in 429; *cf.* Prosper.

He was ordained, therefore, as the first bishop over the scattered Christians in this island. Palladius, however, did not succeed. He sailed from Gaul, landed at Wicklow, preached in the neighbourhood, was expelled by the natives, driven northwards by a storm, and shortly afterwards died in Britain. Thus ended the first attempt to found a Church in Ireland.[1]

*Chron.*, *l.c.*, col. 594; *Bk. Arm.*, fol. 2aa, in *Anal. Bolland.*, t. i., p. 553, makes him Archdeacon of Rome; *Dict. of Christ. Biog.*; and Herzog's *Encyclop.*, *s.v.*

[1] The reader may consult about St. Palladius Rev. J. F. Shearman's work *Loca Patriciana* for the facts and legends connected with his history. He makes an elaborate attempt to identify even the Churches he founded in Ireland.

## LECTURE II.

### *ST. PATRICK.*

ST. PATRICK, his mission, and his work come next in order. In dealing with this subject I know that I shall pass over ground scorched and hot with the fires of manifold controversies. With some controversial matters I must of course deal, but I shall make it my principal object to give a connected view of St. Patrick's life and work, as revealed to us by the latest and best investigators. St. Patrick is by some regarded as a myth, and I can scarcely wonder at such an idea. Some have held that there were one, two, three Patricks, while Dr. Petrie tells us that, from the various histories, there seem to him to have been seven different Patricks. In Smith's *Dict. Christ. Biog.* there are five hundred and ninety-five Johns commemorated in the first eight centuries. Surely then there may have been easily three St. Patricks at work in Ireland during the fifth and sixth centuries, when Patrick (Patricius) was rather a title of honour than a personal name in the strict sense of the word. But I do not think any sound historical instinct will doubt that the tradition of a whole nation, embodied in documents some as old as the seventh century,[1] and

---

[1] The earliest notice of St. Patrick by an extant Irish writer dates from A.D. 634; *cf.* Cummiani *Epist.* in Ussher's *Sylloge*, as will be shown in a later note on p. 29.

reproducing itself in the most permanent of all records, the topography of the country, must have had a solid foundation in fact, and that tradition ascribes our national conversion to one definite person, St. Patrick. Accepting then the tradition of the country, let us first ascertain what materials we have for our historical inquiry.

One great source of information about any historical personage is found in his own works. Now, we have two acknowledged works of our Saint still extant: his *Confession* and his *Epistle* to a Welsh prince called Coroticus. These two works form the basis of all the histories or lives of the Saint which have ever been published.[1]

The history of the *Confession* and the evidence for its authenticity is rather curious. The *Book of Armagh* is one of the great treasures of our own library; it is a very composite volume. It contains the only complete copy of the New Testament transmitted to us by the ancient Irish Church; the manuscript of which fixes its own date, as it expressly tells us that the Gospel of St. Matthew was finished September 21st, A.D. 807.[2] This book is a regular repertory. It contains a charter

---

[1] The writings ascribed to St. Patrick will be found in a collected shape in Migne's *Patrologia Latina*, t. liii., col. 790. Sir J. Ware was the first to print his *Confession* and his *Epistle to Coroticus*, in his *St. Patricio ascripta Opuscula* (Lond.: 1656). Ussher still earlier meditated the publication of St. Patrick's works, but never carried out his purpose, opp. t. xv., 79. Dr. Todd, *St. Patrick*, pp. 311, 346, 425, gives the bibliography of his works. The genuine writings of St. Patrick, with notes critical and historical, have just been published in a cheap form by G. T. Stokes and C. H. H. Wright (Dublin: Hodges & Figgis, 1887).

[2] *Cf.* a paper by the Bishop of Limerick (Dr. Graves) in the *Proceedings* of the Royal Irish Academy (1846), t. iii., pp. 316, 356, on the date and script of the *Book of Armagh;* a Memoir on the *Book of Armagh* by the Bishop of Down (Dr. Reeves); and Mr. Hogan's preface in the *Analect. Bolland.*, t. i., 531-544.

from Brian Boru to the Church of Armagh, written in his name by his chaplain or confessor, when Brian visited that city in the early part of the eleventh century; it contains, too, the most ancient life of St. Patrick, written towards the close of the seventh century, and a copy of his *Confession*, which the scribe professes to have taken from St. Patrick's own autograph. "Thus far," says the scribe, "the volume which Patrick wrote with his own hand." The MS. which the scribe copied must have been very ancient. He frequently complains of its obscurity and illegible state, at which we cannot wonder. The manuscripts written by Irish scribes of the Middle Ages are all noted for their extreme beauty and clearness, as you can at once verify by inspecting those exhibited in our library. But, then, St. Patrick was not a professional scribe, as they were. He expressly describes himself as rude and unlettered; his training, too, had not been the best to perfect him in handwriting. If the Fellows and Professors of this University had spent their youth from sixteen to twenty-two herding swine, as St. Patrick did, their handwriting would not have been improved. And so we cannot wonder that the Armagh scribe grumbles over the difficulty of elucidating St. Patrick's writing. When we take up the *Confession* itself, the internal evidence is all in favour of its authenticity. "It contains," remarks Dr. Todd, "none of the ridiculous miracles which the later biographers of St. Patrick delight to record. It is just such an account of himself as a missionary of that age, circumstanced like St. Patrick, might be expected to compose. Its Latinity is rude and archaic.[1] It quotes the ante-Hieronymian

---

[1] A splendid edition of the works of St. Gregory of Tours was lately (1883-1885) published in two volumes, in the *Monumenta*

Vulgate, and contains nothing inconsistent with the century in which it professes to have been written." So far concerning the *Confession* of St. Patrick.[1]

We possess also an *Epistle* directed to Coroticus, a Welsh prince. It is simply a letter protesting against the unchristian conduct of Coroticus, or Caredig, a distinguished Welsh hero of the first half of the fifth century. The Irish invaded the principality and conquered it. Coroticus organised his countrymen, defeated the invaders, and pursuing them across the Irish Sea committed great outrages in Ireland. Though nominally a Christian, as all the Welsh were in the fifth century, he made no distinction between the Pagan Irish and St. Patrick's converts, slaying or carrying captive to slavery even neophytes with the baptismal waters fresh upon them. The *Epistle* to Coroticus does not occur in the *Book of Armagh*.[2] Its Latinity is apparently of the same age and from the same pen as the *Confession*. It quotes the old Latin version of the Bible, and is, therefore, generally accepted by critics as genuine.[3]

Another source whence we may derive information

---

*Germaniæ Historica*, under the editorship of W. Arndt and Br. Krusch. For the first time we have there presented the text as Gregory wrote it. The Latin style is very similar to St. Patrick's, rude and semi-barbarous in grammar and spelling; see a learned notice of this edition by M. Max-Bonnet, in the *Revue Critique* for March 2nd, 1885, p. 161.

[1] Todd's *St. Patrick*, p. 347.

[2] It is referred to in the MS. of the tenth century, supplementing the last part of *Book of Armagh*, found at Brussels. *Cf. Analect. Boll.*, t. i., p. 577. The Epistle to Coroticus was first published by Sir James Ware from the Cotton MS., and then by the Bollandists from a manuscript found at Treves. See Coroticus in *Dict. Christ. Biog.*

[3] An interesting confirmation of this *Epistle* was brought to light some twenty years ago, when a stone pillar was discovered in Wales with this prince's name inscribed in Latin and in

about the past is found in histories or annals written soon after the events narrated.

The earliest history of St. Patrick which we now possess is contained in Tirechan's Annotations on St. Patrick's life. These you will find in the *Book of Armagh*.[1] This Tirechan was a disciple of St. Ultan, of Ardbraccan, in Meath, who also seems to have written a life of St. Patrick. St. Ultan died in A.D. 656. The earliest extant history of St. Patrick represents, or embodies, therefore, a history composed at the least considerably more than one hundred years after St. Patrick's time.[2]

The next earliest document is a life of St. Patrick, comprised in that same *Book of Armagh*.[3] It was written about the end of the seventh century, by one Muirchu Maccumactheni, son of Cogitosus, who died A.D. 670.[4]

---

Ogham characters; which were duly interpreted by Dr. Graves, then a Senior Fellow of our own College. I am bound to say that some good critics do not agree in the interpretation of Dr. Graves.

[1] Printed by Rev. E. Hogan in the *Analecta Bollandiana*, t. ii., pp. 35-68 and 213-238.

[2] The earliest mention of St. Patrick in any historical document is contained in Cummian's letter, concerning Easter, addressed to Segienus, Abbot of Iona, in 634. His peculiar cycle is there recognised, and he is described as "Sanctus Patricius, Papa noster." In presence of this notice, the silence of Bede about St. Patrick is of no account. He was intensely Roman, and despised the Celtic and Patrician party in England and Ireland alike. Cummian was a very learned man, and had evidently ample historical materials at hand. He could not have been mistaken about events which may only have been separated from himself by one long life. See Ussher's Works, t. iv., pp. 432-443. St. Patrick is celebrated also in the *Bangor Antiphonary*, dating from the seventh century at least, if not earlier. See O'Laverty's *Down and Connor*, ii., 120, App. xx.

[3] Printed by Rev. E. Hogan in the *Analecta Bollandiana*, t. i., pp. 531-585. Dr. Reeves assigns Tirechan's *Annotations* to the close of the ninth century (*Antiqq.*, p. 224).

[4] *Proceedings* of the Royal Irish Academy (1864), t. viii., p. 269, where Dr. Graves very acutely determined the date of Cogitosus. See *Dict. Christ. Biog.*, s.v. "Cogitosus."

These are the only documents upon which we can rely as historical materials for the life of St. Patrick; and they probably embody documents and traditions reaching back to St. Patrick's day. Time, indeed, had even then surrounded the memory of St. Patrick with a thick, almost impenetrable haze. Listen to the opening words of this life of St. Patrick, written by the son of Cogitosus. It was evidently modelled upon the preface to St. Luke's Gospel, and plainly enough confesses the difficulties of his subject. "Forasmuch as many, my lord Aidus (of Sleaty), have taken in hand to set forth in order a narration, according to what their fathers and they who from the beginning were ministers of the word have delivered unto them; but by reason of the very great difficulty of the narrative, and the diverse opinions and numerous doubts of many persons, have never arrived at any one certain track of history. But lest I should seem to make a small matter great, I will now attempt with little skill, from uncertain authors, with frail memory, with obliterated meaning and barbarous language, but with a most pious intention, obeying the commands of thy belovedness and sanctity and authority, out of the many acts of Saint Patrick, to explain these gathered here and there with great difficulty."[1]

The writings of St. Patrick himself, and the collection in the *Book of Armagh*, are, I repeat, the only documents on which a historical critic can rely.[2] There is one

---

[1] *Analect. Bolland.*, t. i., 545; Aidus, or Aedh, anchorite of Sleaty, in Queen's county, died in 698, according to the *Four Masters* (see O'Donovan's note); in 699 according to the *Annals of Ulster;* cf. *Anal. Boll.*, i., 542.

[2] There are plenty of other documents professing to be lives of St. Patrick, but they are mere mediæval compilations, none of which can stand the tests of real criticism. Colgan, in his

test for such documents which admits of easy application in this case. In studying acts of martyrs and saints one universal canon of criticism is this,—the more genuine and primitive the document, the more simple and natural, and, above all, the less miraculous; the later the document, the more of legend and miracle is introduced. Turning our minds for an instant from Ireland to the wider field of universal Church history, we shall see how this rule works. Take up, for instance, the genuine acts of the martyrs recorded by Eusebius, the acts of the Martyrs of Vienne and Lyons under Marcus Aurelius. There you will find no miracle at all. The acts of Polycarp are genuine. There again is no real miracle. The acts of Perpetua and Felicitas are genuine; they are marked by visions, indeed, yet nothing miraculous is recorded. But take up the acts of the martyrs as set forth in the fifth and following centuries, and no miracle is too absurd or too incredible for the writer. In fact, the monks were very sincere believers, they believed thoroughly in their heroes. They had a very narrow knowledge of the world, and of God's ways and laws of action therein. They above all things desired edification and comfort for their own spirits from the example of the saints, and so they gave loose rein to their imaginations in the panegyrics they composed for the days of their commemorations. For, as we must ever bear in mind, a great number of these exaggerated and falsified narratives are due to the sermons composed for the saints'

---

*Trias Thaumaturga*, has collected the greater portion of them. The *Tripartite Life* is the most celebrated of them. An English translation of it will be found in Cusack's *St. Patrick*, made by that eminent Celtic scholar Mr. Hennessy. Another, that by Joceline, abounds with well-known legends. It was translated and published by E. Swift, Dublin, 1809.

natal days, and intended, like many a modern biography, to conduce to the greater glory of their heroes.[1]

Now let us apply this test, which is used as boldly by the Roman Catholic Bollandists as by Protestant critics, and we shall find that the writings of St. Patrick himself contain no miraculous stories; they are simple and natural histories. Two centuries elapse, and miracles begin to cluster round the memory of the saint. Yet the historical details of the earliest life in the *Book of Armagh* can be easily separated from them. But now advance a step. We have two ancient hymns in honour of the saint, purporting to have been written by a contemporary of St. Patrick. One is the hymn of St. Fiacc, of Sleaty, near Carlow. The other is the hymn of St. Secundinus, one of the companions of St. Patrick.[2] Examine them in conjunction with the *Tripartite Life*. They simply teem with miracle, some of them not very creditable to the temper or the courtesy, nay even to the common humanity of the saint.[3] In

---

[1] If the stories retailed in some modern sermons were printed verbatim, the monks would be proved not to have had a monopoly of miracles and legends.

[2] The hymns of SS. Fiacc and Sechnall (Secundinus) were first published by Colgan in his *Trias Thaumat.*, p. 210. The hymn of St. Sechnall will be found in the *Book of Hymns of the Ancient Church of Ireland*, published by the late Dr. Todd, part i.; while a critical dissertation on St. Fiacc's hymn finds a place in part ii., p. 287. The hymn of St. Sechnall was also published in the *Catholic Layman*, t. ii., No. 24, December 1853, and in Cusack's *St. Patrick*, p. 562, where also, on p. 558, is St. Fiacc's hymn. St. Fiacc's hymn has lately been thoroughly discussed from a philological point of view by Zimmer in his *Keltische Studien*, Hft. ii. (Berlin: 1884). For the life of St. Fiacc see Boll. *AA. SS.*, Oct. vi., 96-106, and sup. tom. 119-121; *Dict. Christ. Biog.*, t. ii., p. 508.

[3] Thus St. Patrick's sister, Lupait, was a nun. She broke her vows, however, and became the mother of a son, afterwards eminent for sanctity. Repenting of her sin, she cast herself prostrate before St. Patrick's chariot on the public road, beseech-

St. Fiacc's hymn we hear of the permanent impression of angels' feet on a rock, of the apparition of angels summoning St. Patrick back to Ireland, of the voices of the children from Mayo calling him back from France to Connaught, of his healing the blind and lepers, of his raising the dead, of a burning bush in which an angel appeared to him and foretold the future greatness of the Church of Armagh.

These hymns are, however, far surpassed by later biographies. Colgan, in the seventeenth century, was a Franciscan, gifted with varied and profound knowledge of Irish antiquities. To him and to the Bollandists associated at Louvain we owe the preservation of much valuable material for the past history of Ireland. This distinguished writer produced in 1645 two volumes in the Latin language; two copies of which at least will be found in our own library. One volume describes the lives of those Irish saints whose festivals occur between the 1st of January and the 31st of March. The other, called *Trias Thaumaturga*, is devoted exclusively to the lives of St. Patrick, St. Bridget, and St. Columba. In this work Colgan embodies seven distinct lives of St. Patrick, the most celebrated of which is called the *Tripartite Life*, because divided into three great divisions or books. That Life was originally composed partly in Irish and partly in Latin.[1] It was

---

ing him for pardon. The saint drove his chariot over her. She rose up bruised and injured, and cast herself again before the chariot. Again he drove over her. This was repeated a third time, and the penitent having sustained this ordeal was at length restored to favour. This story is also told of St. Patrick and St. Secundinus. St. Patrick drove over his friend when celebrating mass. See Cusack's *St. Patrick*, p. 382, and the *Tripartite Life* in Cusack, p. 519, and Colgan's *Trias Thaumat.*

[1] The substance of the *Tripartite Life* is in Mr. Hennessy's opinion older than A.D. 800. See O'Curry's *Lectt.*, xvi.

based upon the life of St. Patrick contained in the *Book of Armagh*, but is an enlarged if not a very improved edition of the same. The writer of it simply revels in the region of the miraculous. Some of you may have glanced at those interesting documents of early Christian antiquity, the Apocryphal Gospels, such as the Gospels of the Infancy and of Nicodemus. Our Blessed Lord is there represented as working miracles from His earliest infancy, some of them, too, very mischievous and foolish miracles indeed. His schoolmaster boxes His ear, and the offending arm is at once paralysed. A playmate strikes Him, and dies at once; He forms birds of clay, and then breathes life into them for His own amusement. But the Apocryphal Gospels are far surpassed by the *Tripartite Life*, which some would gravely represent as the most ancient and most authentic biography of St. Patrick. His baptism was marked by miracles. He was brought to a blind priest, who was so ignorant that he could not even read the service. Another difficulty, too, interposed itself. There was no water for the sacrament. So the sign of the cross was made over a rock with the infant's hand, water at once burst forth from it, the priest's eyes were at once opened, and, strangest of all, the priest at once gained the power of reading the service without any previous study. While yet a child, his nurse required a fire to cook his food; the wondrous boy took five drops of water and flung them on the ground, which straightway were transformed into five flames of fire. In the middle of winter the nurse wanted fuel for her fire. St. Patrick went out, collected a bundle of icicles, and heaped them round the fire. The saint breathed on them, when they at once burned like faggots. Some later lives still tell us how a leper desired to sail with St. Patrick from Gaul to Ireland. The saint desired his company, while the crew very naturally refused it. St. Patrick flung his stone altar overboard, seated on which the leper safely followed the ship, and landed with him in Wicklow harbour. These few specimens will, I am sure, satisfy you that, valuable as these lives may be for folk-lore, and the study of the social life of the Middle Ages, they have no claim whatsoever to the position of real historical records. Let us, however, take the writings of St. Patrick himself, the Patrician documents in the *Book of Armagh*, together with the hymns of SS. Fiacc and Secundinus, and with these as our guides let us investigate the personal history of our national saint.

Where, then, was St. Patrick born? To this query there have been very many conflicting replies. Ireland itself has claimed the honour. Scotland and France have each their vigorous champions. The claim of Ireland we may at once dismiss. It is founded on a passage in St. Patrick's Epistle to the British prince Coroticus, where he speaks of the contemptuous feeling cherished in the hearts of the Britons towards Irishmen,—a feeling which fourteen centuries have not sufficed quite to destroy. Listen to this early protest against a sentiment which has wrought untold mischief. "The Church," he says, 'weeps and wails over her sons and over her daughters, whom the sword has not yet slain, but who are exiled and carried away to far-off lands, where sin openly prevails and shamelessly abounds. There Christian freemen are reduced to slavery, and that by the most unworthy, most infamous, and apostate Picts. . . . The unrighteousness of the unrighteous hath prevailed over us. We are become as aliens. Perchance they do not believe that we have received one baptism, that we have one God our Father. With them it is a crime that we have been born in Hibernia; but it is said, have ye not one God? Why do ye wrong one to another?"

These words—"with them it is a crime that we have been born in Hibernia"—constitute the whole foundation of Ireland's claim to have been the birthplace of St. Patrick. It is evident, however, that he is thereby merely identifying himself with his converts; while in other parts of his works he asserts in the clearest and most positive manner that he was not an Irishman by birth.

Some, again, have maintained the claim of Boulogne, others that of Dumbarton on the Clyde.

St. Patrick himself gives us but little information on this point, save that in general he speaks of Britain as his place of birth and the residence of his parents.

The opinion of critics seems now inclined to assign the honour to Dumbarton, which in ancient times was called Alcluith, and formed the western termination of the great Roman wall, extending from the Forth to the Clyde, constructed by Agricola about the year 80, and renewed under Antoninus Pius, to protect Northern Britain from the attacks of the savage Highlanders.[1] To this view, as I have hinted above, the greater number of modern critics seem inclined, though, like all such questions, there is much to be said on the other side, and if one be inclined to argue, it will be impossible to demonstrate the erroneous character of his views. All the circumstances, however, tend to confirm the claim

---

[1] Concerning the construction, etc., of this wall, see Hübner's remarks in *Corpus Lat. Ins.*, t. vii., p. 3; and the dissertation on "Graham's Dyke," p. 191. Dumbarton, with its great rock, so prominent a feature as one sails up the Clyde, would form a natural stronghold and post of observation against the Dalaradian freebooters, from the opposite Antrim coast.

of Dumbarton. Its local position is in its favour. The
"finds" of Roman coins upon the opposite Antrim
coast, dating in such quantities from St. Patrick's
day, sustain it, while again another circumstance cor-
roborates it. Mark how this was. St. Patrick tells us,
in the Epistle to Coroticus, that he was of noble birth ;
that his father was a decurion, a member of the local
town council,—an institution which prevailed as a useful
species of local government in all colonies and munici-
palities throughout the wide domains of Rome, from
the farthest East to the shores of the North Atlantic
Ocean. Let me dwell upon this point, which is rather
obscure ; for, indeed, with all our classical studies, there
is no subject over which a thicker darkness prevails
among English students than the methods of government and administration used by the Roman Empire.
Of late years there have come to light in Spain some
very curious documents which illustrate these methods.
In pursuing the course of some ancient Roman mines,
the explorers came across tablets containing laws made
to regulate the imperial mining colonies during the first
and second centuries of our era. These laws descend
to the minutest particulars, proving the comprehen-
siveness and perfection of Roman legislation and of
the Roman civil service. Among other regulations we
find that town councils or local senates, composed of
decurions, were appointed as soon as a few hundred
persons were assembled together in a town or village.
Decurions, therefore, must certainly have existed at
Dumbarton at the close of the fourth century.[1] Again,
St. Patrick tells us he was carried captive with some

---

[1] About the office of decurion in the colonies, see Marquardt
and Mommsen, *Handbuch der Römischen Alterthümer*, t. iv.
p. 501-516; *Nouveaux Bronzes d'Osuna* in *Jour. des Sav.*, 1877

thousands of his countrymen, whom God visited for their sins. Now, at the end of the fourth century Northern Britain was ravaged by Picts and Scots, and thousands were led captives, till the most famous generals of the empire, Theodosius and Stilicho, were sent to restore tranquillity to the desolated island.[1]

St. Patrick, in his writings, always speaks of Britain in the plural, denominating it Britanniæ, which was strictly accurate.[2] Theodosius, after expelling the Irish

---

p. 132, by M. Ch. Giraud. *Cf. Ephem. Epig.*, t. ii., p. 137, and t. iii., p. 103, where Hübner and Mommsen discuss this topic with vast learning. The two latter references show that the institution of decurions prevailed in all the towns established by the Romans wherever they found mines. They must have existed, therefore, all along the west coast of Britain about the year 370. The title decurio occurs twice among the British inscriptions, edited by Hübner, *Corp. Ins. Lat.*, t. vii., Nos. 54 and 189.

[1] The following quotations from the *Four Masters*, under date 405, show that the Irish sovereign who reigned during St. Patrick's youth extended his ravages much farther than the western coast of Britain. "After Niall of the nine hostages had been twenty-seven years in the sovereignty of Ireland, he was slain by Eochaidh, at Muir n-Icht, *i.e.*, the sea between France and England,"—a spot which O'Donovan in his notes on the year 405 identifies with Boulogne. Keating had access in the seventeenth century to Munster documents which are now lost. He gives a long account of these Irish invasions of England and France, exactly corresponding to the statements of the Roman historian Ammianus Marcellinus and of the *Four Masters*. See his *History of Ireland* (Mahony's edition), p. 369-390. Sidonius Apollinaris commemorates the fame of the Picts and Scots, as well as of the Saxon pirates. He calls, indeed, the invaders of the Gallic coast Saxons; but the Scots may easily have been confounded with them; see his *Epp.*, viii., 6, 9, and *Carm.*, vii. in Migne's *Pat. Lat.*, t. lviii., col. 597, 601, 680, 688, 689.

[2] Three points seem to me conclusive as to the age of St. Patrick's Confession: 1. The Version of Holy Scripture used, which was the old Latin; 2. State organisation of decurions, divisions of, and name used for Britain; 3. Ecclesiastical organisation and discipline, specially the notice of a married clergy, engaged in secular occupations. We cannot conceive an ignorant monk of the Middle Ages, or even a monk of two cen-

and Pictish foe, organised Northern Britain into a separate province, called Valentia, the names of the other provinces being Britannia Prima, Britannia Secunda, Maxima Cæsariensis, and Flavia Cæsariensis.[1] His original name, too, was Succath, a Celtic name, such as naturally would find place in a population living in the midst of Celts, even if his family was not originally Celtic, as probably was the case, though at the same time conforming themselves, as the Britons largely did, to the institutions, language, religion, and civilisation of Rome.[2]

So much as to the place of his birth. The father of St. Patrick was called Calpurnius, a deacon. His grandfather was Potitus, a priest.[3] His father then was a clergyman, a town councillor, and a married man. Observe this, he was the son of a deacon and the grandson of a priest. In the beginning of the fifth century the law of celibacy had not yet been effectually enforced on the clergy of Gaul or Britain. In fact, the marriage of the clergy successfully resisted the denunciations of popes and councils during the next six

---

turies later, imagining such a state of affairs, or composing such a work. The organisation among Gallic and Roman Christians for the redemption of captives from the Franks is another piece of evidence, which I have discussed at some length in the article on St. Patrick in the *Dictionary of Christian Biography.*

[1] *Cf.* Hübner's British Inscriptions in the *Corpus Ins. Lat.*, t. vii., p. 4; and Böcking's *Notitia Dignitatum.*

[2] See a learned paper on St. Patrick's names by Dr. Todd, read, January 14th, 1856, before the Royal Irish Acad. *Proceedings,* vi., 292. *Analect. Bolland.,* ii., 35, where Tirechan mentions four names, e.g., Patricius, Succetus, Magonus, and Cothraige.

[3] The name Patricius occurs in Hübner's volume *C. I. L.,* t. vii., nos. 1198 and 1336. The other names Calpurnius and Potitus do not occur among the British inscriptions, but the cognate ones, Potitianus and Kalpurnianus, are found there. Patricius was found among the Coleraine coins discovered in 1854, already referred to.

hundred years.[1] But let us take the case of Southern Gaul during St. Patrick's youth. There was a celebrated bishop of Toulouse, named Exuperius, who lived during the end of the fourth and the beginning of the fifth centuries. He was the intimate friend and correspondent of St. Jerome, and famous for his holy life and conversation. This bishop addressed a letter to Pope Innocent I., about the beginning of the year 405. In it he asked the pope a number of questions, some of which throw interesting light on the social and religious life of Southern France at that time. He wished for information upon a burning question in the nineteenth as in the fifth century. He asked whether a man might marry his deceased wife's sister; whether retired soldiers might be ordained; whether divorced persons might remarry; what books are contained in the Canon of Scripture; and how he should treat married priests and their children. The pope, in his reply, gives us a glimpse into the inner life of the times. Those who have held judicial posts may not be ordained without doing penance, on account of the sin necessarily connected with their office. Retired soldiers may not be ordained at all, because of the loose morals of the army. While as to the clergy, while disapproving in general of their marriage, he tolerates it under certain circumstances, proving conclusively that the law of celibacy, which had been first promulgated at Rome less than twenty years before, had made as yet but little way in Southern Gaul. If so, it must have been practically unknown in Britain.

---

[1] See Wilkins' *Concilia*, t. i., p. 367, where the Council of Winchester, A.D. 1076, decreed that "married priests living in castles or villages should not be compelled to abandon their wives."

Here now arises a very natural question. St. Patrick's father was a decurion or town councillor. How, then, was he ordained? The reply is simple enough. In his capacity of decurion he did not act as a magistrate at all. In colonies like Dumbarton the only magistrates were ædiles and duumvirs. The decurions, however, in council assembled, controlled the whole social and municipal life of the place; instituted and regulated the games, managed the water supply, the public buildings, local taxes and education. In addition to his public employments his father Calpurnius was also a farmer, and possessed a country house from which St. Patrick was carried captive. This union of spiritual and of secular offices,—decurion, cleric, farmer,—was by no means uncommon during the earlier ages of the Church. It was, in fact, only about the opening of the third century that the clerical office became a profession separate from secular cares or employments. Cyprian, in Africa, bent all his energies in this direction about the year 250, but the old system still maintained itself.[1] Here and there, in remote out-of-the-way corners of ecclesiastical history, we get glimpses of the earlier order and its long-continued existence. Let me give you an instance or two. Among the genuine acts of the martyrs which have survived the wreck of time, those of Theodotus, the innkeeper of Ancyra, hold a high position.[2] They are valuable for many reasons. They give us interesting glimpses into the social condition of the empire just before its conversion to Christianity; they present us with pictures of paganism drawn from life, and they

---

[1] See Cyprian., *Epp.*, i.
[2] *Cf.* Ruinart., *Acta Sincera*, p. 354: Mason's *Diocletian Persecution*, Appendix; Theodotus, in *Dict. Christian Biography*

show us the organisation and discipline which enabled the Church to triumph over the power and determination of a Diocletian himself.

Theodotus was an innkeeper in the Celtic town of Ancyra, at the beginning of the fourth century. He was celebrated for his devotion and love to the martyrs who were suffering under Diocletian's edict. Ancyra became at last too hot for him, when he fled and took refuge with a priest in a country village. This priest ministered every day at stated hours in a village church, but at the same time worked a farm, and regularly visited the great market of Ancyra, driving his own cart and selling his wares. On one of these journeys which he thus undertook in the course of his regular business, he was enabled to perform a kindly office for the earthly remains of the devout innkeeper. Theodotus, having long escaped the persecutor, was at last arrested, tortured, and slain. The prefect determined that his body should lie unburied, exposed to the beasts and birds, which the Christians counted a disgrace to be avoided at all risks. So the magistrate appointed a strong guard to watch the body, some of whom he had just flogged for neglect on a similar occasion. And now the narrative becomes strikingly lifelike. The body lay where Theodotus had been beheaded in the place of common execution, just outside the city. The evening was cold and late, and the guard had lit a fire, and made a booth of branches, when the priest drove up with his cart laden with barrels of wine, the produce of his vineyard. They invited him to remain all night with them, as the gates were already shut. He learned whose body they were guarding, treated them plenteously to his best wine, made them all drunk, and triumphantly drove off with the body of his devout innkeeper.

In the fourth century, then, a priest could be a farmer and a wine-merchant, without any reproach on that account; while as a sufficient evidence that the union of the clerical and secular office continued to much later than St. Patrick's time, I shall simply quote an inscription [1] on the walls of Assos, in Asia Minor, telling us how the walls were restored, about the time of Justinian, by Helladius, a presbyter and chief magistrate of the city, corresponding to the union among ourselves of such diverse offices as Dean of St. Patrick's and Lord Mayor of Dublin.

Having thus illustrated and explained the position of his family, I must hurry on to other portions of my story. At sixteen years of age St. Patrick was carried captive into Antrim by the Irish pirates, who also wounded his father, and carried off his sister, whom they sold into slavery in Connaught. His boyhood, if we are to believe his own account, far from being specially saintly, as his more credulous biographers describe, was marked by spiritual darkness, and even by gross immorality. But then we can never take devout men at the estimate they form of themselves in moments of deep contrition. The holier they grow, the more of the vision of God they enjoy in this life, the more intense their abhorrence of themselves and of their wasted opportunities in the past. Augustine's *Confessions* tell us of boyish scrapes and tricks as if they were sins of deepest dye. Bunyan speaks of his youthful frolics, his May-day dances and Sunday bell-chiming, as if they were the vilest immoralities. And St. Patrick attributes the misfortunes of himself and of his fellow-captives to their gross wickedness. Thus he

---

[1] Boeckh, *Corp. Ins. Græc.*, No. 8838; *cf. Contemporary Review*, June 1880, p. 983.

tells us in his *Confession*, "I was taken captive when I was nearly sixteen years of age. I knew not the true God, and I was brought captive to Ireland with many thousand men as we deserved, for we had forsaken God and had not kept His commandments, and were disobedient to our priests, who admonished us for our salvation." He was carried to the opposite coast of Antrim, and retained as a slave in the family of a chieftain of Dalaradia. We are able to identify the very place of his captivity. It was close to the village of Broughshane, five miles from Ballymena. The name of his master was Milchu.[1] He lived in a valley near the hill of Slemish, now called the valley of the Braid, from the river which flows through it. There St. Patrick spent six years tending cattle. St. Patrick's solitude and misfortunes were blessed to his soul. He was recalled from the world to a higher life. "He was every day frequent in prayer." He tells us that the love of God increased in him so much, that he would often in a single day say a hundred prayers, and in the night almost as many, so that he frequently arose to prayer in the woods and mountains before daylight, in snow and frost and rain, and "I felt no evil," he adds, "nor was there any laziness in me, because as I now see the Spirit was burning within me."

The time of his escape, however, drew nigh. He had been enslaved at sixteen. When he arrived at three-and-twenty the highly-strung imagination of the young Christian received an intimation that his deliverance was nigh. One night, as he tells us, he heard in a dream a voice saying unto him, "Thy fasting is well; thou shalt soon return to thy own country."

---

[1] Milchu, A.D. 388, was son of Hua Buain, King of North Dalaradia.—Reeves, *Antiquities*, p. 339.

He waited a little, and again had a dream in which the same voice told him the ship was ready, but was distant two hundred miles. Whereupon he fled from his master, reached the ship, and safely made his escape, apparently to France, whither his family seems to have meanwhile removed. St. Patrick's preparatory work was now done. He had learned the language, manners, and customs of the Irish. His affections were engaged. Like many another, he had become Hibernior Hibernis. His direct missionary work will next engage our attention.

## LECTURE III.

### ST. PATRICK'S MISSION.

ST. PATRICK had spent his youth in Ireland. There God had revealed Himself to his soul, and Patrick ever longed to return to the same country with the tidings of salvation. He felt, like Livingstone or our own Bishop Patteson, the martyrs, one of Africa, the other of the Southern Ocean, as if the voices of the perishing multitudes whose needs he well knew were continually sounding in his ear, "Come over and help us." His manner was restless. His life was unsatisfied, because missing its great end and object. His own words in the *Confession* prove this : " Again, after a few years, I was with my relations in Britain, who received me as a son, and earnestly besought me that then at least, after I had gone through so many tribulations, I would go nowhere from them. And then I saw in the midst of the night a man, who appeared to come from Ireland, named Victor(icus), and he had innumerable letters with him, one of which he gave to me. I read the commencement of the epistle containing 'The Voice of the Irish,' and as I read aloud the beginning of the letter, I thought I heard in my mind the voice of those who were near the wood of Fochlut, which is near the Western Sea; and they cried out, 'We entreat the holy youth to come and walk still amongst us.' And my heart was greatly touched, so that I could not read any more.  So I awoke.  Thanks to God that after very many years the Lord hath granted them their desire." St. Patrick, in fact, had been seized by an enthusiasm which must find an outlet.  Like Francis Xavier and Howard and Wilberforce ; like George Fox the Quaker, who tells us that the burden of the Lord brought him nigh to the gates of death till he yielded to the inner call ; like a greater than all of them, like St. Paul, so too St. Patrick felt " necessity is laid upon me, yea, woe is unto me if I preach not the Gospel."

The mission of St. Patrick to Ireland—using the word mission in its technical sense—has been the subject of bitter controversy.  Some maintain that St. Patrick was sent straight from Rome to Ireland by Pope Cœlestine in 432.  Others deny with equal vigour that he had any commission from that pope.  "The *Confession* of St. Patrick" (says Dr. Todd, p. 310, who strenuously upheld the latter view) "contains not a word of a mission from Pope Cœlestine.  One object of the writer was to defend himself from the charge of presumption in having undertaken such a work as the conversion of the Irish, rude and unlearned as he was. Had he received a regular commission from the see of Rome, that fact alone would have been an unanswerable reply.  But he makes no mention of Pope Cœlestine or of Rome, and rests his defence altogether on the Divine Call which he believed himself to have received for the work."  The evidence on this question is, I am bound to tell you, very conflicting.  The writings of St. Patrick himself undoubtedly contain not even the remotest hint of such a mission.  Nay, they even use language, such as I have just recited, *apparently*, though not *necessarily*, at variance with such an idea.  On the other hand the documents and traditions which date from the seventh century appear more or less to favour such a view. The facts of St. Patrick's life in the interval between his captivity and his return to Ireland are subjects of much debate. Miss Cusack, in her *Life of St. Patrick*, gives as intimate and minute an account of his history as the special correspondent of the *New York Herald* or of the *Daily Telegraph* could have done. But then she is a lady, and, therefore, gifted with an imagination. According to the Brussels document found a few years ago by Smedt, and which supplements the *Book of Armagh*, St. Patrick set out to visit Rome, but, meeting with Germanus, went no further, receiving clerical education at his hands. He is said to have visited the famous monastery of Lerins, which was founded upon the model of the Egyptian monasteries. If this were so, it would help to explain certain Oriental customs and ideas in ritual and in architecture prevalent in the Irish Church. Thus the annotations of Tirechan, which date from the seventh century, tell us that "in the thirteenth year of the Emperor Theodosius the Bishop Patrick was sent by Cœlestine, Bishop and Pope of Rome, to instruct the Irish. Bishop Palladius was first sent, who was also called Patrick by a second name, and he was martyred among the Scots, as the old saints have said. Then the second Patrick was sent by the Angel of God Victor and by Pope Cœlestine. All Ireland believed, and nearly all were baptized by him."[1]

Though I have no fancy to take part in this controversy, I must still say a few words concerning it. I do not, indeed, believe in the Roman mission of our national apostle, not only because his own

---

[1] Hogan, in *Analecta Bollandiana*, ii., p. 67.

language appears inconsistent with it, but also upon broader grounds. People who read Church history through the spectacles of the nineteenth century are very apt to fancy that the pope occupied then for the whole Western Church the same position as he does now in the Roman Communion. The Congregation De propaganda Fide now controls the whole missionary activity of that Church. No faithful son thereof would dream of starting any important missionary work without the sanction and support of that body, and through it of the pope; and that sanction is not easily given. About forty-five years ago an enthusiastic Alsatian, named Liebermann, a converted Jew, was anxious to establish a brotherhood devoted to the conversion of the negroes. He made a journey to Rome on foot in December 1839, and spent twelve months there before he could obtain the papal sanction for the Society of the Holy Ghost, which has now become one of the most important missionary as well as educational organisations connected with the Church of Rome. But at the beginning of the fifth century it was not so. The pope then neither exercised the control nor received the reverence afterwards yielded to him. The bishops of the province of North Africa flouted the claim of the same Pope Cœlestine who is said to have sent St. Patrick, when he attempted to exercise supremacy over the province of Africa. Columba never sought papal sanction for the conversion of the Picts, St. Columbanus for the conversion of the Germans and Swiss. Metropolitan and provincial jurisdiction and rights were then respected. Each province claimed, as Africa did, the right to manage its own affairs, and to convert the heathen in its own neighbourhood. Athanasius and Egypt sent Frumentius to Abyssinia;

Ambrosius and the province of North Italy sent Vigilius and his companions to convert the pagans of the Alps; and the bishops of the British province, or more probably still Germanus of Auxerre, whose connection with Celtic Christianity was very close indeed, consecrated Patrick for the conversion of the Irish. Let me just briefly state the reasons which lead me to this conclusion. Germanus was a distinguished bishop of Gaul, and noted for his opposition to Pelagianism.[1] About the year 425 a Briton, named Agricola, introduced that heresy to Britain. The British bishops, living in perpetual anxiety, and deprived, through the incursions of the Scots and Saxons, of that peace and tranquillity without which study or learning cannot flourish, summoned Germanus to their aid from the happier and more tranquil Church of Gaul.[2] The pope, too, tormented in Asia, Africa, Constantinople, and Italy by the obstinate and persistent attacks of the Pelagian heretics, supported the proposal of the British bishops. The career of Germanus in Britain was a triumphant one. He defeated and expelled the heretics, and not only so, but falling back upon his old experiences as a soldier (for he had been a general before he became a bishop), he organised the Britons and routed the combined forces of the Saxons and Picts. This

---

[1] *Cf.* the article on Germanus in Smith and Wace's *Dictionary of Christian Biography*.
[2] The Church of Gaul, especially on the northern and eastern frontiers, was in a disturbed state enough during the second half of the fifth century. The writings of Salvianus of Marseilles, Sidonius Apollinaris, and Zosimus, lib. vi., prove this. Zosimus, *l.c.*, shows how a ring fence of semi-barbarian powers grew up, separating the rest of the empire from Britain, and explaining the want of intercourse between it and the rest of Christendom, which led Gregory the Great to consider it utterly pagan. See Coote's *Romans of Britain*, p. 137, and *Girala. Cambr. Opp.*, t. iii., p. 77 (Rolls Series), where he expressly asserts this separation.

battle is celebrated in history (Bede, i., 20) as the Hallelujah Victory, and was fought near Mold, in Flintshire. These events occurred when Patrick's heart was drawn towards Ireland. Palladius had just been sent by Pope Cœlestine to Ireland, and had received the crown of martyrdom at the hands of the Picts. He had been the friend and probably the archdeacon of Germanus, who recognised in Patrick an instrument suited to carry on the work thus inaugurated by Palladius and sanctioned by the pope. But, after all, why should there be bitter contention about the mission of St. Patrick? Suppose that he was consecrated and sent to Ireland by Cœlestine himself, what does it matter? Every one confesses that Augustine of Canterbury was sent to England direct from the pope; does that fact affect in any degree the independent claims of the English Church? A parallel instance is a sufficient reply. Every one admits that the first bishop who ministered in the United States derived his orders from the Episcopal Church of Scotland; does that fact imply the supremacy of the Scotch bishops over the American Church? Let us return to St. Patrick's work and mission.

About the year 432, according to the usually received chronology, St. Patrick, with a few companions, sailed for the shores of Ireland. He landed at the mouth of the river Vartry, on the spot where the town of Wicklow now stands. This place seems in those ages to have been a favourite harbour of resort. Palladius landed there a year or two earlier. Three or four centuries later the Danes founded a settlement there, and very naturally. Wicklow Head is the most prominent object to persons coming up the Channel, and running far out into the sea forms a convenient place of refuge for ships sailing before a southern breeze. The nature of the ground, too, made it especially suitable for the ships of that age, as it renders it specially unsuitable for the ships of our age. The ships of ancient times were many of them large and commodious, but they were shallow and almost flat-bottomed. We may derive a sufficient notion of them from a specimen of a war galley discovered some years ago in a Sleswick peat bog.[1] The boat was flat-bottomed, seventy feet long and eight or nine feet wide. Its sides were of oak-boards, fastened with bark ropes and iron bolts, while fifty oars propelled it over the waves. It is evident to any one who knows the ground that the Murrow and great strand of Wicklow presented to such shallow but commodious barks the most fitting shelter, as they were never anchored if it was at all possible to draw them up on shore. In fact, the ancient life of St. Patrick in the *Book of Armagh* expressly calls the harbour "opportunum et clarum," commodious and famous, terms which no one would now dream of applying to it. The neighbourhood of Wicklow, and all the coast lands as far as the Three Rock Mountain, were then occupied by a tribe named Cualann, or Cualanni, who were expelled by the O'Byrnes and O'Tooles in the thirteenth century, but have left their name imprinted upon the wild, lovely valley of Glencullen, within seven miles of this spot. Palladius, the predecessor of Patrick, a few years before, was received with hostile demonstrations at this place. Palladius, however, knew nothing of Ireland. He was a Gaul indeed, and acquainted probably with a kindred tongue, but he had not that command over the language which St. Patrick had, and which enabled him at once

---

[1] *Cf.* Lubbock's *Prehistoric Times*, pp. 8, 9; Green's *Making of England*, p. 16; and Glasgow Archæol. Soc. (1886), N. S., t. i., pt. ii., No. IX.

to gain the hearts and ears of the natives. Patrick did not tarry long at Wicklow. His heart was set upon Dalaradia and the scenes and personages of his youthful captivity. He sailed, therefore, along the coast, touching here and there at convenient points. He landed at a spot still called, after him, Inis Patrick, a small island off Skerries. The parish to which it belongs is still called Holmpatrick. He then proceeded northwards, coasting along a shore which then, as now, affords only at long intervals any shelter from the storm. He stopped at the Boyne, passed Carlingford Bay, and came to land at the next natural harbour, Strangford Lough, where he found his farther progress barred by the terrific race which prevails at this point. There St. Patrick landed, and proceeded, with his companions, to explore the country. They had not gone far when they met a swineherd. Supposing them to be pirates or robbers,—a very natural supposition under the circumstances,—the swineherd ran away and called his master, whose name was Dichu. He was a chieftain of high birth, descended from Fiatach Finn, King of Ireland in A.D. 116. Hearing that pirates had landed in his territory, Dichu came out, sword in hand, to oppose the invaders; but, struck with the venerable appearance of St. Patrick, he received him with kindness, took him to his house, listened to his preaching, and finally became a believer in Christ—"the first of the Scots," say more than one of the lives, "who confessed the faith under Patrick's ministry." Dichu, having been baptized, became a convert, not only in word, but in deed. Tradition tells, that he at once presented to St. Patrick the ground on which they were standing, upon which the saint erected a church, since called Sabhall Padhrig, in Latin Horreum Patricii, or in English, Patrick's Barn. Dr. Lanigan, t. i., p. 213, the celebrated Irish historian, well suggests that this church was called a barn because it was built according to the form and position of Dichu's barn, or perhaps it was nothing else than a real barn which Dichu presented for the preaching of the Gospel, just as many an edifying service has since been held in such a building. This barn, Sabhall, or Saul, as now it is called, was the earliest church founded by St. Patrick, and continued to be a favourite haunt of his till death overtook him, for it was in the monastery of Saul, the site of his earliest missionary success, that he entered into his rest. Saul has ever since continued to be a Christian church, and still exists a parish of our own Church, the most ancient and most venerable of Christian parishes and Christian churches in Ireland. St. Patrick did not tarry too long at Saul. He committed his boats, or coracles, to Dichu's charge, and thence made his way to Dalaradia, the scene of his captivity. No place connected with the ancient history of Ireland has been more clearly identified than Dalaradia, and few places retain more vivid traditions concerning the sojourn and actions of our saint. Let me now describe it, though the description would most fitly have occurred in my last lecture. It is a beautiful district, and must have been more beautiful, because clad with woods of oak, in St. Patrick's time.[1] Dr. Reeves, in his *Antiquities of Down and Connor*, has devoted much space and much learning to the elucidation of its ancient history.[2]

---

[1] See Reeves, *Antiquities*, pp. 86, 300, 345; concerning Saul, see pp. 220, 223.
[2] Reeves, *Antiquities of Down and Connor*, Dissertations on Dalriada and Dalaradia, pp. 318-348.

Let me state the substance of his remarks in a few words. There are two districts in the county Antrim which in ancient times had names closely akin. One was called Dalriada, a name which continues in use in the corrupted form of the Route, by which the district is still known. It extended from Coleraine to Larne, embracing all the coast district of the Giant's Causeway and the glens of Antrim. Dalaradia was a distinct division, forming the centre of the county bounded roughly on one side by Lough Neagh and on the other by the glens. These districts have made their mark on more than Irish history. They formed during the occupation of Britain by the Romans the land whence issued some of the most deadly and persistent of their foes. In the second century Marcus Antoninus sent to Britain one Lollius Urbicus, afterwards famous in Christian history as the prefect whom Justin Martyr has pilloried in his second *Apology* for his unjust persecution of the Christians.[1] Urbicus erected another fortification besides that of Agricola between the Forth and the Clyde. He showed his fear of the Scots of Antrim by placing his loftiest and strongest fort at Barhill, near West Kilpatrick, on the Clyde. Later, too, the district became famous. In the beginning of the sixth century, about the year 502, the Antrim men invaded the opposite coast of Scotland, and successfully established a kingdom which perpetuates itself in the modern name of Argyleshire. This event is thus recorded by the Irish annalist Tigernach under the year 502: "Fergus the Great, son of Erc, accompanied by the race of Dalriada, occupied a part of Britain and died there." Some people,

---

[1] See Lightfoot's *Ignatius*, t. i., p. 493, and the article on Lol. Urbicus in the *Dictionary of Christian Biography*.

many of them too calling themselves Irishmen, are ever inclined to treat the Irish Annals with scorn. Such persons may perhaps regard this notice with more respect when I mention that the Venerable Bede in the first chapter of his first book gives exactly the same account, telling us that the Scots, who then invaded Britain, established themselves, "vel amicitia vel ferro," as he tersely puts it, and were thence called Dalreudini, "nam lingua eorum daal partem significat."

This, as Dr. Reeves says (*Antiquities*, p. 337), "is a very condensed account, but of the highest value as an external testimony to the correctness of our domestic records."[1] We can even form some conception of what the inhabitants were like in St. Patrick's time, thanks to the researches of archæology, which is every day proving more and more the truest handmaid of history.

All along the Antrim coast, from Carrickfergus to Glenarm, there runs a series of chalk cliffs, where the chalk is abundantly mixed with flint. These cliffs in ancient times formed a perfect magazine for the inhabitants of the county Antrim, whence they drew implements for domestic service and weapons for the chase and for war. The strand, indeed, of Larne is to this day the greatest source of flint-finds in Ireland, or perhaps in the British Islands. Some twenty years ago a large number of these flint weapons, and even a complete arrow with a flint head, were discovered in the very neighbourhood of St. Patrick's captivity, scattered all over the hills which had been uncultivated since his time, proving that the companions of his

---

[1] See Keating's *History of Ireland*, ed. O'Mahony, p. 422; and *Four Masters*, ed. O'Donovan, A.D. 498, for the Irish account.

youth and the converts of his later years belonged to that rude race which had not abandoned the use of flint weapons, at least for the purposes of the chase, though acquainted with the use of iron and the nobler metals.[1]

It was to this district that St. Patrick was now making his way to visit his old master Milchu, bearing with him the tidings of salvation. The earliest life of St. Patrick—that by Maccumacthenius—now indulges in legend. Patrick wished to revisit Dalaradia and the hill of Slemish, not only to preach the Gospel there, but also to see the place where his guardian angel Victor or Victoricus had ascended into heaven before his eyes. The perpetuity of Irish tradition is strikingly illustrated by this notice. Indeed, the more you investigate the more will you be struck with the firm, tenacious grasp tradition, traditional scenes, traditional history, traditional games and celebrations take of the popular mind. And no country is richer in these unexplored mines of traditional history than our own. Its backwardness in other respects has been advantageous from this point of view. Nothing destroys tradition so utterly and so rapidly as education. Give a peasant a penny newspaper and teach him to use it, get him to take an interest in the politics of Europe, and the great political questions which may be exciting his own country, and you deprive him of the keen interest he once took in the stories handed down from generation to generation and told round the fireside on the winter evenings as the rain and storm raged without. In the course of my investigations for these lectures, I have been greatly struck by the perpetuity and accuracy of Irish traditions. There was, for instance,

---
[1] See *Journal* of the Kilkenny Arch. Society, N.S., t. iii., p. 218.

a tradition in the neighbourhood of Kilkenny that the Danes of Waterford, in the ninth century, had pursued a band of native Irish to a large natural cave in the neighbourhood of that city, had shut them in, and smothered or starved them to death. In the beginning of the last century Dr. Thomas Molyneux, a distinguished scholar of that time, visited Kilkenny, and explored that cave, when human bones in immense quantities were found in the exact spot which the tradition designated.[1] The traditions about St. Patrick correspond with facts in much the same way. The ancient life in the *Book of Armagh*, speaking of Slemish, says, " From which mountain a long time before when he served as a slave he saw the angel Victor ascend into heaven, his footstep being marked in stone on another hill." Now let us come to facts. Take up Dr. Reeves' *Antiquities of Down and Connor*, pp. 83, 84, and you must be struck with the topographical accuracy of this ancient life.

The valley where St. Patrick lived as a slave is divided into two parts by the river Braid. One side of the river is the parish of Skerry, the other side is the parish of Rathcavan. In the parish of Rathcavan, on one side of the valley, is the mountain of Slemish whence Victor ascended into heaven. On the other side, in the parish of Skerry, is the basaltic hill of Skerry, on which you can still see the ruins of a church said to have been founded by St. Patrick; while at a few yards' distance from the north-west angle of the church is a patch of rock, on the edge of which is a depression having a faint resemblance to the print of a shoe, which the Ordnance Survey, agreeably to the tradition

---

[1] See *Journal* of the Kilkenny Archæological Society, N.S., iii., 299.

as old as the seventh century, notices as "St. Patrick's footmark." Nay, it is possible that we may identify even the very spot, the very farm where St. Patrick resided. In the townland of Killycarn, parish of Skerry, just across the river Braid (Ordn. Maps, Antrim, Nos. 28 and 29), is a large rath under which are some beehive constructions, usual in such places. This is said to have been one of the residences of Milchu. But I am inclined to think that we have a surer indication of its locality. In the valley of the Braid, and lying in a straight line between Slemish and Skerry, is the townland of Ballyligpatrick. This word means the place or town of Patrick's Hollow (Bally = town, lig = hollow, Patrick). In this hollow are still some remains of a fort or rath. Now, remembering that St. Patrick says he got up in the night and resorted to the woods and mountains for prayer, what is more natural and more probable than that this townland preserves in its name the memory of the residence of St. Patrick in the days of his slavery? Slemish is on the southern side of it, while stepping-stones over the Braid and a short walk lead to Skerry Hill on the northern side, either of them forming such a resort for spiritual exercises as a youth of St. Patrick's temperament would have eagerly desired at that time.

I have dwelt at some length on this point, because every day's experience is teaching that a careful personal survey, an intimate knowledge of the ground where events happened, is absolutely necessary for their true comprehension. Oftentimes, too, a name preserved perhaps by local tradition or in some local landmark, will shed a flood of light upon some doubtful point. Mr. Freeman's present position as a historian of England is due very largely to such careful studies made by him of all the scenes which he depicts. Lord Macaulay personally visited every part of the battle-field of the Boyne, and, therefore, his narrative reads like an eye-witness's.

To this region which I have thus described, and which still bears various evidences of his residence therein, St. Patrick now approached. But as legend clusters round his slavery there, so legend again clusters round his first visit as a Christian missionary. Milchu,[1] his former master, heard of the approach of his fugitive slave and of the triumphs which accompanied his march. Milchu feared that he should be unable to withstand the magical powers by which, as he believed, Patrick was attended, and should, therefore, become a slave himself in turn. So, by the direct instigation of the devil, the chief gathered all his substance into his house, and standing on it as a funeral pile burned himself to death. St. Patrick meanwhile had arrived at the northern side of Slemish, whence a view is gained over the Braid valley; and longing to impart to his former master the tidings of salvation, saw Milchu's house on fire. There the saint stood astounded for several hours at the sight of the burning homestead. Maccumacthenius, who wrote the account, had evidently visited the locality, for he tells us all the local details with great exactness, and mentions that the precise spot where Patrick thus stopped was then marked by a wayside cross.[2] St. Patrick gave vent to his feelings in sighs,

---

[1] Milchu was a historical character. He is thus mentioned in the *Annals of the Four Masters*, A.D. 388: "Milchuo, son of Hua Bain, King of North Dalaradia." *Cf.* Reeves' *Antiqq. of Down and Connor*, pp. 78, 83, 339.

[2] The exact words of the narrative in the *Book of Armagh* are: "Ubi primum illam regionem, in qua servivit, cum tali gratia adveniens, vidit, ubi nunc-usque crux habetur in signum." *Analecta Bollandiana*, i., 559.

groans, and prayers, and then prophesied that none of Milchu's seed should sit upon his throne for ever, but that they should ever be subjects, not rulers. His family, however, received the faith at St. Patrick's hands. His son Guasacht was a bishop in the Church of Granard, and is commemorated in the *Martyrology of Donegal* on January 24th, while two of his daughters became consecrated virgins. St. Patrick straightway returned to his convert Dichu, on the shores of Strangford Lough, to prepare for his next great step, his assault on Tara, the very centre of Irish paganism.

# LECTURE IV.

## TARA AND THE CONVERSION OF IRELAND.

GREAT missionaries would be great generals. They require the peculiar talents demanded in great conquerors. They must be able to form comprehensive plans of warfare, they must be able to grasp details, and they must have an eagle eye to detect that central point round which the really important battle should be fought. Such men were St. Paul, Francis Xavier, Ignatius Loyola, John Wesley, Bishop Selwyn, and such an one was St. Patrick. He recognised at once that triumphs for Christ won beside Strangford Lough, or amid the picturesque but distant mountains of Antrim, might be very important in themselves, but were as nothing compared with the impression which would be made by a victory gained at the capital and centre of national life. For you will observe there was a centre of national life in Celtic Ireland. Ireland was just the same as all the other branches of the Celtic family. That family has retained longer than any other section of the Aryan race the tribal formation. In Galatia, for instance, the Celts were three centuries settled there before our era; they had passed, too, under the mill of Roman provincial despotism; yet they retained the tribal organisation down to the first century. In the great *Corpus of Greek Inscriptions*, edited by Boeckh, you will find an inscription from Ancyra, number 4039 describing games celebrated in that city every fifth year. This inscription glorifies the officials in the celebrations. It mentions the spectacles, the gymnastic contests, the gladiatorial shows, the wild beast fights, the frequent sacrifices, for the Celts in Asia were evidently as fond of uniting religion and amusements as the modern Irishman. And they had another point of contact. No modern race-course or fair would be complete without a house of refreshment and entertainment. And in like manner we are told of the ancient Galatians that in addition to the games they did not forget the refreshments, for the inscription celebrates the hospitality of the officials who gave banquets to two whole cities, and entertained three entire tribes, the Tectosagæ, the Tolistobogii, and the Trocmi.[1] Now, you must bear in mind why I have adduced this example. The tribal organisation pervaded Galatia, but still the tribes found a central point of meeting and of union in Ancyra, and in the games connected with their national assembly which the Romans permitted them to hold in that city. The case was the same with ancient Gaul. The tribal organisation was not only tolerated, but even utilised by the Romans. Certain things the Romans did not tolerate. They put down the Druids and Druidical practices. The Roman state could find better use for her subjects than ruthlessly sacrificing them in hecatombs

---

[1] See Lightfoot's *Galatians*, p. 243, and *Macmillan's Mag.*, Oct. 1882, "Home Rule under the Roman Empire." The Romans utilized for the purposes of local government the tribal and communal organisation which they found existing throughout the empire. See on this topic a series of articles by Pallu de Lessert in the *Bulletin des Antiquités Africaines*, 1884, on "Les assemblées Provinciales de l'Afrique Romaine," and a monograph by him styled *Études sur le droit public et l'organisation sociale de l'Afrique Romaine* (Paris: 1884).

(*cf. Rev. Celtique*, t. v., p. 44). But the tribal organisation was legalised by them. Yet the tribes were not independent of one another. The bond of union may have been a loose one, but yet it was a reality. They met every year for common consultation at the city of Lyons, celebrated games, held literary contests, passed votes of thanks to former governors, instituted prosecutions against unjust ones. In Lyons, however, as at Ancyra, we find the same union of business, pleasure, and refreshment. Britain again was split up into tribal organisations when conquered by the Romans, but they could unite at times under a common head ; and the Celtic coinage of Britain proves that, while the several chieftains ruled their separate clans with all independence, yet there was an overking, a supreme governor, to whom they all paid allegiance. As it was in other Celtic countries, so was it in the Ireland of St. Patrick's time. The population was organised on a tribal basis. Each tribe was ruled by its own chief. But there was a supreme king who governed the district or kingdom of Meath, and held a great convention of his subordinate chiefs every three or seven years (it is not quite settled which) at Tara, where the same happy combination of business and festivity found place, which I have noticed in very different localities. To Tara therefore St. Patrick now directed his course. Setting sail from Strangford Lough he sailed back to the mouth of the Boyne, landed at Colp in the barony of Lower Duleek, where he laid up his boats, and made his way towards Tara.

Let me now pause in the course of our narrative to set before you some facts concerning Tara, for Tara as well as St. Patrick is the subject of my lecture. The popular notion about Tara is gained from Moore's melody of worldwide fame—

" The harp that once through Tara's halls the soul of music shed,
Now hangs as mute on Tara's walls as if that soul were fled.
So sleeps the pride of former days, so glory's thrill is o er,
And hearts that once beat high for praise, now feel that pulse no more."

The usual idea is that Tara was a splendid city and a magnificent palace, like Windsor, where the kings of Ireland held high festival until the Anglo-Norman conquest in the twelfth century, when the glories of Tara were finally destroyed. Now, this notion is without a shadow of historical foundation. Tara, as a royal residence, ceased to exist hundreds of years before Strongbow. The last assembly of the tribes was held there in the sixth century. Its desolation too, A.D. 563, was due not to the cruel invader, but to the action of an indignant priest. A criminal had fled for sanctuary to the Abbey of St. Ruan, now Lorha near Roscrea, was dragged thence, and executed at Tara. The enraged abbat went in procession to the royal palace and cursed it. And no king sat in Tara from that day forth. The malediction was commemorated by the name afterwards bestowed on the monastery, " The Monastery of the Curses of Ireland."[1] Let me explain to you the origin of Tara, so far as it can be historically ascertained. The Hill of Tara is about twenty-five miles from this spot. Petrie, its great historian, describes it thus : "'The Hill of Tara, though undistinguished either for altitude or picturesqueness of form, is not less remarkable for the pleasing and extensive prospects which it com-

---

[1] See about St. Ruan, or Ruadan, Ussher's Works, t. vi., pp. 472, 529, 590, 597 ; O'Curry's *Lectt.*, i., 337, 343.

mands, than for the associations connected with it, as the site of the residence of the Irish monarchs from the earliest times. In both these circumstances it bears a striking similitude to the hill of Aileach, near Derry, the residence of the kings of Ulster; and to the hill of Emania, near Armagh, another residence of the Ulster kings of a different race. All these localities have shared a similar fate in the destruction of their monuments at distant periods, and all equally present striking vestiges of their ancient importance." Now as to the history of Tara. The Irish bards tell us that the Hill of Tara became the chief residence of the Irish kings on the first arrival of the Firbolgs or Belgæ in Ireland. But as they tell us that 136 kings reigned tl ere in succession before St. Patrick's arrival, we must decline to follow them into times so near the antediluvian period. Petrie declares that all the monuments now remaining at Tara are due to Cormac MacArt. His period is the earliest date to which we can trace the genuine history of Ireland. He lived in the third century. He was grandson of Conn of the hundred battles. He reigned from A.D. 218—260. He was a vigorous ruler and an active warrior. He never neglected what then (if not in later years) was regarded as a sacred duty, the spoiling of Great Britain. Under date of the year 222 the *Annals* tell us that " the large fleet of Cormac MacArt went over the sea for the space of three years;" which simply means that he was ravaging the English and Scotch shores with fire and sword. This statement receives a striking confirmation from Roman history. The Emperor Severus waged a series of campaigns against the Celtic insurgents from 208—211, with but very small success. He was, in fact, practically defeated, which seems to have encouraged the foes of Roman rule, and amply accounts for the raids of Cormac MacArt.[1] But our hero gained more from the Romans than mere spoil. He carried back notions of a higher civilisation and of a purer faith. He brought back a beautiful captive with whom he fell in love. She apparently did not like the coarse food of the Irish, the bread was not fine enough. So to please her, he sent to England for a millwright, and thus introduced water-mills into Ireland, instead of the kerns, or hand mills, alone previously used.[2] From the same source, too, he may have imbibed those monotheistic, if not Christian ideas, which gained for him the bitter hostility of the Druids, which Sir Samuel Ferguson has celebrated in his poem on the burial of Cormac MacArt.

Cormac was not only a warrior, he was also a legislator and a ruler. He organised the Brehon laws, the army with the aid of his son-in-law, Finn MacCumhaill,[3] the literary classes, the poets, bards, and chroniclers of Ireland, and settled the national convention on a regular basis, appointing a meeting every third year for the administration of public affairs. Perhaps it

---

[1] See article on L. Sep. Severus in Smith's *Dictionary of Greek and Roman Biography*.

[2] "It is an interesting circumstance that the historical fact thus recorded respecting this mill is still vividly preserved; and a mill, now called Lismullen Mill, still exists on the reputed site of the ancient one. It may also be worthy of remark, that the present miller considers himself, and is considered by the people of the district, as the lineal descendant of the Pictish millwright brought over by King Cormac, though the original name of the family, MacLamha, or Hand, has through the failure of the main line in his grandfather become extinct."—Petrie's *Tara*, p. 162; *cf.* Keating's *History of Ireland*, ed. O'Mahony, p. 350.

[3] Finn MacCumhaill, commonly called Finn MacCoul, was a historical character (see O'Curry's *Lectures on MS. Materials of Irish History*, vol. i., pp. 301-306. He was the Fingal of Ossian's poems).

may interest you to hear a bardic description of this national convention from a poet of the year 984 :[1]—

> "The feis of Temur each third year,
> To preserve laws and rules,
> Was then convened firmly
> By the illustrious kings of Erin.
> Cathaoir of sons-in-law convened
> The beautiful feis of regal Temur,
> There came with him (the better for it)
> The men of Erin to one place,
> Three days before Laman always,
> Three days after it, it was a goodly custom.
> The host of very high fashion spent
> Constantly drinking during the week.
> Without theft, without wounding a man
> Among them during all this time,
> Without feats of arms, without deceit,
> Without exercising horses,
> Whoever did any of these things
> Was a wretched enemy with heavy venom;
> Gold was not received as a retribution from him,
> But his soul in one hour."

Such was the general convention or general assembly of the tribes at Tara, as organised on a fixed basis by Cormac MacArt.

But now, what was the appearance of Tara? The bards tell us of the halls and buildings erected at Tara by Ollamh Fodhla, in the year of the world 3922. They are very particular in their details about this man. He ruled Ireland for forty years, and died in his own house at Tara. He was the first king by whom the assembly of Tara was instituted, and he erected the poets' house at Tara. He also appointed a chief over every barony, and a farmer over every townland, and he was called Ollamh, or chief poet, because he was first

---

[1] O'Donovan's *Book of Rights*, p. 10.

a learned bard, and then king of Ireland. But though we may feel a natural interest in one who rose to be king of Ireland through literature, and not through the more popular course of arms, yet we must be excused from going back beyond Cormac, to whom Petrie attributes the erection of all the buildings which have left any trace upon the present Hill of Tara. I cannot, indeed, attempt to enter upon a description of these ruins. That has been exhaustively done for all time by Mr. Petrie, in his memoir contained in vol. xviii. of the *Transactions* of the Royal Irish Academy. There you will find the fullest description of them as they appear at present, and the most careful, learned, and critical account of them as they are described by poets and historians who must have seen Tara in its highest glory. There you will find a description of the feasts of Tara, the order of precedence observed therein, and the character of the viands served up for the entertainment of the guests. But Mr. Petrie does not leave us under any false impression. He tells us that exactly the same customs and the same rude magnificence were to be found in the household of every chief, not only in Ireland, but also in the Highlands of Scotland, so late as the sixteenth century. Indeed, he might have come down still later, for any of you that have ever read the *Legend of Montrose* or *Waverley* or *Rob Roy* will remember how Sir W. Scott depicts customs and feasts, which find their aptest illustrations in the banquets of Tara as described by the bards whom Petrie has translated for us.

And now for the buildings which Moore has celebrated, and about which so many false impressions prevail. Buildings there were certainly, and some of them very extensive. The Hall of Assembly, or the banqueting hall, is situated on the northern slope of the hill. It measures 759 feet in length, was originally 90 feet in breadth, and retains marks of fourteen distinct entrances. This is the hall where the great national assembly or convention of Tara was held. But now we may fairly ask, What was the character of the buildings? They were simply composed of wood and clay. "Though stone houses," says Petrie, "as well as stone fortresses are commonly found along the northern, western, and southern coasts of Ireland, nothing of the kind, with one exception, ever existed at Tara. But though the houses were unquestionably of wood and clay, it must not be inferred that they were altogether of a barbarous structure, or inferior in point of comfort to the contemporaneous structures of other nations, equally remote from examples of Greek and Roman civilisation. It is probable they were not unlike or inferior to those of the ancient Germans, of which Tacitus speaks (*De Germania*, c. 16) in terms of praise, and which he describes as being overlaid with an earth so pure and splendid, that it resembled painting" (Petrie, p. 231). In corroboration of Mr. Petrie's statement, that, though the buildings were only of wood and clay, yet this does not imply a state of barbarism, I may just note that all of you can any day see a convincing proof that a certain degree of civilisation must have existed among the princes which assembled at Tara. In the year 1810 two magnificent golden torques were found at Tara, and are now preserved in the Museum of the Royal Irish Academy. They are of a spiral or screw fashion. One is five feet seven inches from one extremity to the other, and weighs 27 oz. 9 dwts. The other is of equal diameter, but of more delicate construction and greater lightness, weighing only 12 oz. 6 dwts. Seeing, then, that history and legend alike tell us of Tara, that the remains of Tara are still to be seen exactly corresponding to ancient descriptions, and that the evidences of ancient art have been there discovered, we have certainly as good ground to accept the convention of Tara as a historical fact, as classical archæologists have for accepting the statements and conclusions of Schliemann about ancient Troy.

Tara then and its barbaric glory may be accepted as a historical fact. Let me now describe for you another feature which marks the neighbourhood, and proves the rude magnificence of the ancient kings of Ireland. The burial-places of the kings of Tara have astonished the minds and roused the curiosity of scholars and inquirers of every land. They form, in fact, collections of prehistoric remains well-nigh unrivalled. There are several royal burial-places in Ireland. The most celebrated, however, is Brugh, or Brugh-na-Boinne, "the fort or town of the Boyne," to which reference is made in almost every ancient Irish manuscript. It is thus described by Sir W. Wilde in his *Beauties of the Boyne and Blackwater*:—" About two miles below Slane the river becomes fordable, and several islands break the stream. Here, upon the left or south-western bank of the river, is the place called Ross-na-ree, or Wood of the Kings, and upon the opposite swelling bank of the river occur a series of raised mounds, raths, forts, caves, circles, and pillar stones, bearing all the evidence of ancient Pagan sepulchral monuments." The raised mounds amount to twenty in number; some of them are of world-wide fame, as Knowth, New Grange, and Dowth. Knowth occupies an acre in extent, and rises to the height of eighty feet. New Grange covers two acres, and is perhaps the most remarkable Celtic monument now existing. Sir W. Wilde's description of it is too long for quotation. He justly remarks, however, upon our neglect, that while visited by antiquarians from every land, it is practically unknown to Irishmen, though within a two hours' drive from Dublin.

As Schliemann and Mycenæ and Greece are now all the rage, I may mention that the interior chamber of the New Grange Moat has often been compared to the great cavern variously called the tomb of Agamemnon and the treasury of Atreus. Both are constructed on exactly the same principle, the roof being dome-shaped, but built without any knowledge of the principle of the arch. The central chamber is nineteen feet six inches high, twenty-two feet long, and eighteen broad, while the passage which leads to it is sixty-three feet long, and in general six feet high. Again, a mile from New Grange the third great Rath of Dowth presents very similar features. This vast cemetery was existing in the same state as now in St. Patrick's time. One thousand years ago, in the year 862, it was plundered by the Danes of Dublin, and the raths were rifled of their treasures. Earlier still we have a notice of it. Cormac MacArt, King of Tara, in the third century, became a Christian, or at least imbibed Christian ideas and rejected Druidism. He died from the bone of a Boyne salmon sticking in his throat. His burial is thus described in the Irish Annals: " He " (Cormac) "told his people not to bury him at Brugh, because it was a cemetery of idolaters; for he did not worship the same God as any of those interred at Brugh; but to bury him at Ross-na-Righ, with his face to the east. He afterwards died, and his servants held a council, and came to the resolution of burying him at Brugh, the place where the kings of Tara, his predecessors, were always buried. The body of the king was thrice raised to be carried to Brugh, but the Boyne swelled up thrice, so that they could not cross. They afterwards dug his grave at Ross-na-Righ, as he had ordered."[1]

I have bestowed considerable time upon these details, because they strikingly illustrate and confirm the history of St. Patrick at this great crisis in his missionary career. St. Patrick arrived at the mouth of the Boyne. There, as Maccumacthenius tells us, he abandoned his boats, and proceeded a day's journey up the river's bank, till he came to the graves of the sons of Feic, this very pagan cemetery of Slane which I have described. There St. Patrick determined to tarry, that he might

---

[1] This incident has been vigorously painted by a poet of our own, Sir S. Ferguson, in his *Lays of the Western Gael.* Let me just quote you one or two stanzas ; the whole poem is well worth careful study. King Cormac is represented as thus speaking on his death-bed :—

> "Crom Cruach and his sub-gods twelve,
> Said Cormac, are but lawen treene ;
> The axe that made them haft or helve
> Had worthier of our worship been ;
> But He Who made the tree to grow,
> And hid in earth the iron stone,
> And made the man with mind to know
> The axe's use, is God alone."

He then orders his burial at Ross-na-ree, not among the pagans of Brugh-na-Boine. The attempt of the pagans to bury him there, and their defeat by the Boyne itself, are depicted, and then the poem ends:—

> " Round Cormac Spring renews her buds
> In March perpetual by his side ;
> Down come the earth-fresh April floods
> And up the sea-fresh salmon glide ;
> And life and time rejoicing run
> From age to age their wonted way,
> But still he waits the risen sun ;
> For still 'tis only dawning day."

keep the great feast of Easter, pitching his tent on the hill of Slane. At the same time the king of Ireland and his priests were observing a great pagan feast at Tara, whence Slane is easily visible. Maccumacthenius was well versed in Scripture, and his narrative now becomes steeped in Scripture phraseology. Let me give the substance thereof. King Laoghaire, like another Nebuchadnezzar, had assembled to his feast his kings, satraps, dukes, princes, and counsellors, together with his magicians and priests. It was their custom, proclaimed by royal edict, that no fire should be lit on that night over all the plain within sight of Tara, before the beacon light shone out from the royal palace; and that, if anyone did light a fire, that soul should be cut off from his people. The holy Patrick, however, was ignorant of the edict, and even if he knew of it, would have treated it with contempt. He, therefore, commenced the celebration of the Paschal feast by lighting a sacred and blessed fire, according to custom, which was seen with amazement by the inhabitants of Tara.[1] The king speedily summoned a council of his great men, that he might be ascertained as to the offender; whereupon the Druids declared, "O King, live for ever! This fire which has been lighted before the royal fire will never be extinguished, unless it be extinguished this night. Moreover, it will conquer all the fires of our religion. And he who has lit it will conquer us all, and will seduce all thy subjects, and all kingdoms will fall before him, and he will fill

---

[1] The Easter fire is authentic. Let me say a word about it, as it illustrates the details of ancient Christian life. A great authority on Christian antiquities speaks thus : " One special solemnity indicating the festival character of Easter eve was the lighting of lamps and candles,—a custom which is repeatedly referred to by writers from the fourth century downwards. Eusebius records

all things, and will reign for ever and ever."[1] Upon this the king was greatly enraged. He ordered nine chariots to be prepared, and, taking his two principal magicians, proceeded to visit and punish the bold individuals who had dared to violate the royal edict. And now the *Book of Armagh* relates a series of encounters between St. Patrick and the magicians, very similar to stories of encounters between Christians and heathen priests, told in the acts of the martyrs, and modelled apparently upon the legends current from early times concerning the conflicts of St. Peter with Simon Magus in the city of Rome. Let me tell you the story of the first encounter, which must serve as a sufficient instance of them all. The magicians advised the king, as they drew near Slane, not to enter the

---

that Constantine observed Easter eve with such pomp, that he turned the sacred or mystical vigil into the light of day by means of lamps suspended in every part, and setting up huge waxen tapers as big as columns through the whole city. We find a reference to the same custom in Gregory Nazianzen, who speaks of persons of all ranks, even magistrates and men and ladies of rank, carrying lamps and setting up tapers, both at home and in the churches, thus turning night into day. Gregory Nyssen describes the brilliancy of the illumination as a cloud of fire mingling with the dawning rays of the sun, and making the eve and the festival one continuous day, without any interval of darkness. Prudentius, at the end of the fourth century, has a poem on the lighting of the Paschal torch. In later times, one special wax taper of large size was solemnly lighted from the newly-lighted Easter fire, and was blessed as a type of Christ's rising from the dead, to give light to the world. The institution of this custom was attributed to Pope Zosimus, A.D. 417." See Bingham's *Antiqq.*, bk. xxi., ch. i., sec. 32, and Smith's *Dict. Christ. Antiqq.*, vol. i., p. 595. Tirechan tells us the name of the man who carried the blessed fire St. Patrick used. It was Kannanus, or Ciennanus (in modern times, Keenan), who afterwards presided over the Church of Duleek.

[1] *Cf. Proceed.* Roy. Irish Acad., t. vi., p. 50, for a feast or convention like that of ancient Tara, held in 1351 at Castle Blakeny, in the co. Galway.

circuit of St. Patrick's fires, lest their magical influence might overcome him, but to remain outside the circle and summon the stranger thither. St. Patrick was accordingly summoned to the king's presence, the magi advising that no one should rise when he approached, as whoever did so would believe in him. St. Patrick drew nigh, and, seeing many horses and chariots, he uplifted his voice in the words of the Psalm, "Some trust in chariots, and some in horses, but we will walk in the name of our God." No one rose up at his approach, save Erc, son of Dego, one of the royal pages. He was converted by our saint's preaching, and in after-years appointed the first bishop of Slane, the spot where he was converted, and where his relics were still preserved in the seventh century.[1] Then commenced a vigorous discussion, one Druid, named Lochru, making himself specially prominent in abusing the Catholic faith. His career was but a short one, however, for the saint sternly beholding him, as formerly St. Peter beheld Simon Magus, cried out aloud to God, "O Lord, Who canst do all things, by Whose power all things consist, and Who hast sent me hither, let this wretch who blasphemes Thy name be forthwith raised aloft, and let him speedily perish." Whereupon the unfortunate magician was caught up into the air, dashed head foremost against the earth, and thus miserably perished. Tirechan, indeed, tells us that he himself had seen the very stone on which his brains had been dashed out.

The king, seeing his favourite Druid dead, wished to slay St. Patrick, and ordered his attendants to seize him.

---

[1] A small chapel, called St. Erc's Hermitage, still exists in the Marquis of Conyngham's demesne on the banks of the Boyne. It is beautifully situated, looking up one of the most charming

The saint, perceiving their threatening movements, arose, and intoned in a loud voice the words of the sixty-eighth Psalm, "Let God arise, and let His enemies be scattered. Let them also that hate Him flee before Him." Whereupon a horror of darkness fell upon his foes, and they began to fight one with another. An earthquake also added its terrors, when all the guards took to headlong flight, and never halted till they had reached a plain halfway between Dublin and Drogheda, leaving the king and queen and two attendants in St. Patrick's presence. The queen drew near, and entreated St. Patrick not to slay her husband, and promised he should worship St. Patrick's God; whereupon the king approached, and did obeisance to the saint; but it was only a feigned conversion on his part, for the king immediately afterwards tried to kill the saint and his attendants, when St. Patrick in a moment turned himself and his seven attendants into stags, who skipped away before the astounded monarch. I need scarcely delay you with more of the prodigies which happened at Slane. Let me just sum up the narrative. Next day being Easter day, St. Patrick proceeded to Tara, and there again encountered another arch-Druid. The pagan performed miracles, but Patrick far surpassed them all. This part of the narrative is modelled upon the contest of Moses with the magicians of Pharaoh. This second Druid also perished in the contest. Again the king strove to kill St. Patrick, but finally, at the prayer of his chief men, accepted the faith, was baptized, and gave St. Patrick a safe conduct through Ireland. His conversion was

---

and romantic stretches of the Boyne, resembling portions of the Rhine above Coblentz. It stands close to the bridge of Slane, where the decisive struggle took place between William III. and James II.

only nominal, however. Laoghaire lived to an advanced age, but died a pagan at heart, for he ordered himself to be buried after the manner of his forefathers. They had a feud with the Leinster men and their king, who lived near Naas, and were always buried with their faces looking towards Leinster, and with their arms by their side, to signify the intensity and perpetuity of their hate.

Now you may ask me a very natural and proper question—What about the shamrock all this time? did not St. Patrick preach the faith at Tara and illustrate the doctrine of the Trinity by that national emblem? I am obliged to tell you, however, that, like many another interesting tale, this legend has no foundation in history. The use of the shamrock as an emblem in this country is very ancient, derived probably from the times of paganism, when the trefoil was held sacred. It is possible, then, that the emblem begat the legend. Men used the shamrock when pagans. They continued it, like many other pagan practices, in Christian times, and then Christianised the emblem by developing the legend about St. Patrick's use of it.[1]

St. Patrick's direct success at Tara was not at once very great. He gained, indeed, two or three of the king's courtiers who afterwards became bishops, but the

---

[1] The legend about the shamrock can be traced back to the year 1600. It formed the subject of a prolonged controversy in the pages of *Notes and Queries*, series iii. and iv., 1864-1869, when Mr. F. R. Davies, K.J.J., M.R.I.A., a well-known Dublin antiquarian and student of heraldry, gave the best explanation of it. He referred its origin to the reverence of the Druids for trefoil. See also Moore's *Cybele Hibernica*, p. 73. None of the mediæval lives of St. Patrick mention it. I have consulted several eminent Celtic scholars, including Mr. Hennessy, who possesses an unrivalled knowledge of such legends, and they all profess their ignorance of any historical foundation for it.

memories and associations of Tara were too closely connected with the native worship to yield to a single assault.

Patrick then set out on a series of missionary excursions through Meath. He came to Telltown, where a brother of Laoghaire lived. It was the time of the great feast or fair of Telltown,—a feast, by the way, which is mentioned by Tirechan in the seventh century, and is described by Sir W. Wilde as existing within living memory.[1] It was just like Donnybrook fair. Carbri was the name of this chief. He, like his brother Laoghaire, was an obstinate pagan, and therefore Patrick, after offering him the faith, denounced him, and went on to another brother Conall at Donagh-Patrick, a mile or so lower down the Blackwater. Conall accepted the faith in sincerity, was baptized and blessed by St. Patrick, and promised the reversion of his brother's kingdom. From this Conall St. Columba was descended, and many of the kings of Ireland till the eleventh century.[2]

The assault delivered by St. Patrick on Irish paganism at Tara was typical of his missionary policy. St. Patrick recognised the facts of Celtic nature, and delivered his message accordingly. He knew the devotion of the tribes to their chiefs, and that if the chiefs were secured the conversion of the tribes would naturally follow. He and his followers always aimed, therefore, at the chiefs, and thus made rapid progress. If he delivered his message, however, in accordance with the facts of human nature, he ruled his movements according to the physical formation of the country.

---

[1] Wilde's *Beauties of the Boyne and Blackwater* offers a charming guide to the scenes of St. Patrick's preaching in Meath.
[2] Keating's *History of Ireland* ed. O'Mahony, p. 425.

St. Patrick conquered at Tara, and must have spent a considerable time in that central district of Ireland. But though Meath had received the Gospel, the four other provinces remained in darkness. Tara was then the centre of Ireland towards which all the great roads of the kingdom converged. These roads were five in number. One road ran north-east from Tara through Duleek and Drogheda, in which direction a road still exists. Another, called Slighe (Sligi) Cualann, was the Wicklow road. You remember that I told you the Cualanni inhabited Wicklow at that time. The Wicklow road passed through Ratoath, down through the classic locality of our own city, called Stonybatter, crossed the Liffey at Ath-Cliath, or Dublin, the ford of the hurdles, passed south through Booterstown, which gained its name from it, and so on into Wicklow. Another road led southwards to Ossory and Eastern Munster. It is probably identical with a road which now leads in that direction. A fourth road was called the Slope of the Chariots. It still exists, and though partially disused for a long time, has been well restored within the last few years at the public expense. This road led north-west. A fifth road, called Slighe Mor or the great road, led to Connaught. It is probably identical with the present road to Trim, where it joined the great western road across Ireland.[1]

There is a very curious physical feature which marks the centre of Ireland. About five miles from Dublin, in the neighbourhood of Tallaght, there rises a series of drift gravel undulations, called the Green Hills. This range, varying from one to three or four hundred feet in height, traverses the whole central plain of

---

[1] On the roads leading from Tara see Petrie's *Tara*, in the *Transactions* of the Roy. Irish Acad., t. xviii.

Ireland. Anyone who takes a ticket from Dublin to Galway can trace it side by side with the Midland Railway the whole way, sometimes on one side, sometimes on the other. This ridge has determined the course of the railway. Two thousand years ago it determined the course of the great road from Dublin to Galway Bay, which passed from Dublin to Trim, from Trim to Mullingar, Ballymore, Athlone, thence west by Ballinasloe to Galway, or by Roscommon to Mayo. Now, these great lines of road determined the course followed by St. Patrick, just as the line of the Egnatian road across Macedonia determined St. Paul's course of labour, or the course of the Roman roads connecting Lystra, Derbe, and Iconium determined his field of work in Asia Minor.[1]

St. Patrick went first into Connaught. His mind had ever been drawn towards Connaught. After his escape from captivity, he heard in sleep the voices of the children from the wood of Fochlut, near the Western Sea, calling him to their aid.[2] And now an accidental circumstance determined him to proceed thither. Tirechan, in the *Book of Armagh* (*Anal. Bolland.*, ii., 42), tells the story. St. Patrick had converted, as I have already mentioned, a Brehon lawyer, named Erc, one of King Laoghaire's courtiers. He was baptizing him at the Well Loigles, the situation of which has been ascertained by Dr. Petrie on the slope of the highest part of the Hill of Tara. The well, indeed, has been filled up, but the ground is still marshy just beneath it.

---

[1] The value of such considerations has been clearly shown by the Bishop of Durham in his great work on *Ignatius and Polycarp*, vol. i., p. 348.
[2] On the identification of this locality see *Analect. Bolland.*, ii., 42 ; and O'Donovan's *Hy-Fiachrach*, pp. 463, 464.

While baptizing Erc and many thousands of other converts, he overheard two chiefs talking together behind his back. They were strangers to one another. One of them asked the other whence he came. Whereupon the man who was questioned, one Endeus by name, replied that he was from the western parts, from the plain of Domnon, and from the Wood of Fochlut. Then the holy Patrick rejoiced in spirit, and said to Endeus, "I will go with you if I shall be alive, for God has told me to go." Endeus demurred to this, until St. Patrick told him he never should arrive home alive unless he himself went with him. Endeus then asked baptism for Conall, his young son, but declared that he and his companions could not accept it till they consulted their tribe, "lest they should be laughed at."[1] St. Patrick committed young Conall to a bishop named Cethiacus, whose "relics," says Tirechan, "are now" (seventh century) "in Patrick's great church in the Wood of Fochlut." Now, we can identify by the aid of the Ordnance Survey and the list of townlands compiled by the Census Commissioners of 1861, the places here mentioned. Endeus said he was from the pailn of Domnon; and to this day "Dun-Domnon," or the fort of Domnon, is found in the barony of Erris, co. Mayo. Again, the relics of the Bishop Cethiacus, who educated Conall, are said to have been in the great church of Patrick—magna ecclesia Patricii—in the

---

[1] There is a striking parallel to this in the history of Russia in the tenth century. "When one of the soldiers of the Grand Prince wished to become a convert, he was not prevented, but only laughed at. The efforts of the Empress Olga for the conversion of her son Sviatoslaf were fruitless. He did not like exposing himself to the ridicule of his soldiers by embracing a new faith. 'My men will mock me,' he replied to the prayer of his mother."—Rambaud's *History of Russia*, t. i., p. 61.

Wood of Fochlut. Now the Irish of "magna ecclesia Patricii" is Domnach-Mor, or Donaghmore. And to this day there is a Domnach-Mor and a cross of Patrick near Killala, thus clearly identifying the position of the Wood of Fochlut.[1]

St. Patrick set out from Tara along the great western road of which I have spoken, having purchased a safe conduct at the price of fifteen slaves (Tirechan in *Analect. Bolland.*, t. ii., p. 43). He was accompanied by the chiefs from the west, and also by a number of attendant clergy, whom he placed in various churches along his route. These seventh-century details of this first missionary journey across Ireland are very interesting, as told by Tirechan. Patrick came to the river Inny, a well-known trout stream, draining the Westmeath lakes into Lough Ree and the Shannon. On the one side there is the barony of Granard and the modern county of Longford, on the other side Westmeath, the whole district forming, however, Teabhtha or Teffia, the western section of the kingdom of Meath.[2]

---

[1] See Cusack's *Saint Patrick*, pp. 423, 424. Domnach, which signifies a church and also Sunday, comes from the Latin *dominica*, the Lord's day. According to the *Tripartite Life*, Joceline, Ussher, etc., all the churches which bear the name of Domnach or Donagh were originally founded by St. Patrick, and were so called because he marked out their foundations on Sundays (see Reeves' *Antiqq.*, p. 107; O'Donovan's *Hy-Fiachrach*, p. 463).

[2] See O'Curry's *Lectt.*, i., 286, about Teffia or Westmeath. The *Tripartite Life* tells us that Granard in the north of this district was presented to St. Patrick, who appointed his old master's son, Guasacht, son of Milchu, to preside over the monastery established there. This monastery became very famous from its connection with St. Patrick. The monks in later times used its patrician reputation to absorb for it the ecclesiastical revenues of the best parishes lying along the Shannon, such as Athlone, an arrangement of which we find traces till long after the Reformation. Thus we find the rectorial tithes of these parishes leased to laymen in 1578, and described as lately the possessions

There Patrick appointed St. Mel first bishop of Ardagh, and made Guasacht, son of his old Antrim master, bishop of Rahan, near Tullamore.[1] Thence St. Patrick made his way across the Shannon, somewhere near the site of Clonmacnois, in the King's county. The *Tripartite Life*, of course, makes his crossing miraculous. "Patrick afterwards went into the territory of Connaught across the Shannon, where he found a ford. The bed of the river rose up under Patrick, and the learned will yet find that esker." I am afraid, however, that the Shannon Commissioners must in their improvements have made short work of the esker, as the Shannon is now navigable for large vessels in the spot where our saint crossed. Thence he passed into western Mayo and Galway, or the district answering to the modern Connemara. He spent seven years in Connaught, leaving his mark to this day in the dedications of various churches and in the traditions of the people concerning his teaching. Mr. Petrie and Sir W. Wilde, indeed, thought they had discovered a

---

of the priory of Larro, *alias* Granard. See 13*th Report of the Deputy Keeper of the Public Records in Ireland* (1881), p. 75, No. 3300. Charles I., at the instance of Strafford, restored the rectorial tithes of Athlone, which the monastery of Granard had absorbed. See some papers on the history of Athlone contributed by me to the *Meath Parochial Magazine*, 1886.

[1] The original rude Latin of Tirechan, in the *Book of Armagh*, is very accurate in its local details. It runs thus: "Et venit per flumen Ethne" (now Inny) "in ii. Tethbias et ordinavit Melum Episcopum; et æclesiam Bili fundavit et ordinavit Gosactum, filium Milcou Maccubooin, quem nutrivit in servitute vii. annorum, et mittens Camulacum Commiensium in campum Cuini et digito illi indicavit locum de cacumine Graneret, id est, æcclesiam Raithin." St. Patrick indicated with his finger the site of Rahan Church—still a church and parish as in the eighth century—near Tullamore, from the summit of the moat at Moate Grenogue, in Westmeath; the intervening country being a plain and a part of the Bog of Allen (see *Analecta Bollandiana*, ii., 44).

most interesting memorial of his visit. Let me describe it in the words of Sir W. Wilde, whose book concerning Lough Corrib and its beauties is a most charming guide to the archæology of those western scenes. On p. 134 he says, "Tempull Phaidrig, or St. Patrick's Church, is situated on the island of Inisghoill, in Lough Corrib, in the parish of Cong. It measures thirty-four feet seven inches long. Its walls are nine feet thick, and its doorway is six feet high. That this church is of the age of St. Patrick, as tradition relates and its name would indicate, can scarcely admit of a doubt. A stone is there preserved containing one of the earliest Christian inscriptions in Ireland. It is a single four-sided, unhewn pillar, of hard greyish Silurian stone. On the east face is an inscription in the uncial or old Latin character which Dr. Petrie first published in 1845 as the stone of Lugnædon, son of Limenach, the sister of St. Patrick."[1] However, I am bound to tell you that our later archæologists do not agree in this view. Mr. Whitley Stokes was the first to challenge the opinion sanctioned by Petrie, O'Donovan, Wilde, and Todd, that here we have the veritable tombstone of St. Patrick's nephew, the son probably of that very sister who was carried captive with himself and sold a slave into Connaught. He and Sir S. Ferguson, in the *Proceedings* of the Royal Irish Academy, t. i., "Polite Literature and Antiquities," 2nd series, p. 259, read this inscription as "the Stone of Lugnædon, son

---

[1] Lugnædon was a presbyter, but the presbyters attendant on St. Patrick were not confined to clerical duties alone. They were more like a modern missionary party, where one man may be doctor, another an agriculturist, and another skilled in mechanics. So was it with St. Patrick's attendants. One man was a smith, another man a maker of book-satchels, and Lugnædon's office was that of pilot or navigator.

of Menuch,"—a solution which, of course, leaves it in doubt whether it really is the tombstone of St. Patrick's nephew or not. St. Patrick's success in Connaught was very decided. He is said to have founded churches in every direction, and to have appointed bishops at Killala and Elphin, which have ever since continued to be episcopal sees.

Two or three incidents during this seven years' mission have caused discussion, and been surrounded with abundant legends. After St. Patrick entered Connaught, he came to a great plain between the towns of Roscommon, Elphin, Castlerea, and Strokestown, in which was Cruachan (Croghan), the ancient palace of the kings of Connaught, and the site to this day of very interesting remains of antiquity. Here was a large Druidical establishment as well as a royal residence, and hither had king Laoghaire sent his two daughters, Ethne the fair, and Feidelen the ruddy, to be reared up. These young ladies were early risers, and, like another king's daughter of whom we read in Exodus, they were fond of cold baths in the early morning. There is still a weil at the Rath of Croghan, surrounded by a double fosse, which may be the identical fountain which the young ladies frequented, just as still at Tara we find the same wells which were flowing in St. Patrick's time. Ethne and Feidelen were greatly surprised one morning to discover a synod of grave clerics sitting there clad in white garments, and with their books before them.

Let me now give you the exact words of the ancient historian in the *Book of Armagh*. You will notice that the young ladies overwhelmed the saint with questions. "The virgins said unto them, 'Whence are ye, and whence come ye?' And Patrick said unto them, 'It were better for you to confess to the true God than to inquire concerning our race.' The first virgin said, 'Who is God? And where is God, and of what nature is God? And where is His dwelling-place? Has your God sons and daughters, gold and silver? Is He ever-living? Is He beautiful? Did Mary foster His Son? Are His daughters dear and beauteous to men of the world? Is He in heaven or on earth, in the sea, in rivers, in mountainous places, in valleys? Declare unto us the knowledge of Him? How shall He be seen? How is He to be loved? How is He to be found? Is it in youth? Is it in old age that He is to be found?' But St. Patrick, full of the Holy Ghost, answered and said, 'Our God is the God of all men; the God of heaven and earth, of the sea and rivers. The God of the sun, the moon, and all stars. The God of the high mountains and of the lowly valleys. The God Who is above heaven and in heaven and under heaven. He hath an habitation in the heaven and in the earth and the sea and all that are therein. He inspireth all things. He quickeneth all things. He is over all things. He sustaineth all things. He giveth light to the sun. He hath made springs in a dry ground; and dry islands in the sea. And hath appointed the stars to serve the greater lights. He hath a Son co-equal and co-eternal with Himself. The Son is not younger than the Father, nor is the Father older than the Son. And the Holy Ghost breathes in them. The Father, the Son, and the Holy Ghost are not divided. But I desire to unite you to the heavenly King, inasmuch as you are the daughters of an earthly king. Believe in Him!' And the virgins said as with one mouth and one heart, 'Teach us most diligently how we may believe in the heavenly King. Show us how we may see Him face to face, and whatsoever thou shalt say unto us we will do.' And Patrick said, 'Believe ye that by baptism ye put off the sin of your father and your mother?' They answered, 'We believe.' 'Believe ye in repentance after sin?' 'We believe.' 'Believe ye in life after death? Believe ye the resurrection at the day of judgment?' 'We believe.' 'Believe ye the unity of the Church?' 'We believe.' And they were baptized, and a white garment put upon their heads. And they asked to see the face of Christ. And the saint said unto them, 'Ye cannot see the face of Christ, except ye taste of death, and except ye receive the sacrifice.' And they answered, 'Give us the sacrifice that we may behold the Son, our spouse.' And they received the Eucharist of God, and they slept in death. And they buried them near the well Clebach, and they made a circular ditch like to a ferta. And this ferta or tumulus was granted with the bones of the holy virgins to Patrick and his successors after him for ever. And he made a church of earth in that place."[1]

This story bears the marks of the highest antiquity. The ritual is of the most ancient character. The baptismal queries proposed by St. Patrick are just those specified by writers as old as St. Cyprian and Tertullian, while the white cloth placed on the virgin's head pertains to a very ancient rite. The early Church used a double unction. Catechumens were anointed when they were baptized. They were again anointed by the bishop when they were confirmed. The white cloth or napkin—called in old English Chrisom—was bound round their heads at baptism to prevent the

---

[1] See Tirechan's narrative in *Analecta Bollandiana*, ii., 49.

oil of unction falling off.[1] But the special point of interest about the narrative concerns the death of the neophytes. Some forty years ago a learned writer in the twenty-sixth volume of the *British Magazine*, the Hon. Auberon Herbert, appealed to this transaction to show that the early Irish Church had esoteric as well as exoteric teaching, and that one of its sacred doctrines was the efficacy of human sacrifice and the certainty of salvation to those who submitted to voluntary death, such as the Albigenses prescribed. However, there does not seem any ground for this charge as far as our present narrative is involved. St. Patrick simply tells the virgins they cannot see Christ till they taste of death and partake of the Holy Communion. And then, some time after their Communion, they die in or about the same time, an event by no means impossible, though the simultaneous character of their deaths may be improbable.

Another event famous in legend is St. Patrick's visit to Croagh-Patrick, formerly called Croach-Aigli, or Hill of the Eagle, situated over the bay of Westport. This visit is also mentioned in the *Book of Armagh*. Tirechan (*Anal. Boll.*, ii., 58) describes it briefly, the *Tripartite Life* enters into the most copious details, while as for Joceline, writing somewhat later, he is the source of our most famous popular story. This is a typical instance of the growth of legend. The *Book of Armagh* tells us that on the approach of Lent St. Patrick retired to Croagh-Patrick, to spend forty days in fasting and prayer after the example of

---

[1] *Cf.* Smith's *Dictionary of Christian Antiquities*, t. i., pp. 163 356, and the article on unction in the second volume. In the Gallican and Irish Churches of the fifth century only one unction was used. See decree of the Synod of Orange, A.D. 441; Hefele's *Councils*, iii., 160; Mansi, vi., 444.

Moses and Elijah. To this historical fact Joceline adds a story that the saint brought together on the top of the mountain all the serpents, toads, and other venomous creatures of Ireland, and drove them into the sea with the aid of his miraculous staff (the *baculus* or *baculum Iesu*) which our Lord is fabled to have given our saint in one of the islands of the Mediterranean Sea. There is a deep hollow on the northern face of the mountain looking down on Clew Bay, called to this day Lugnademon (the Lug or Hollow of the Demons), into which they all retreated on their way to final banishment. I need scarcely delay to point out the absurdity of this tale. It is not found in the early authentic lives of St. Patrick. Solinus too, a Roman geographer of the third century, and Bede in the eighth century, mention Ireland's exemption from reptiles. Doubtless, as I have already noticed, the fact of our exemption produced the legend in order to explain the fact.[1] Tirechan, however, does refer to some mysterious spiritual conflict which St. Patrick endured upon Croagh-Patrick, and the *Tripartite Life* enlarges upon it, telling how the demons assaulted St. Patrick in the shape of immense flocks of black birds, who so tormented the saint that he flung his blessed bell at them and smashed it in his impetuosity. Evidently the poor man's digestion was out of order, or he had fasted too much, and was in much the same state as Luther when he flung his ink-bottle at the devil, who was making faces at him across the table.[2]

---

[1] See Bede's *Ecclesiastical History*, bk. i., ch. 1; Reeves' edition of Adamnan's *St. Columba*, pp. 142, 200; above, p. 6.

[2] The origin of this famous legend is as follows. Tirechan states in the *Book of Armagh* (*Anal. Bolland.*, t. ii., p. 58) that Patrick spent forty days and forty nights fasting, after the example of Moses, on Croagh-Patrick. There is evidently here

From Connaught St. Patrick next proceeded to visit Ulster. He preached in Donegal, revisited his old friends in Antrim, and finally founded the great primatial See of Armagh in the year 445, a century and a half prior to the foundation of the See of Canterbury. As this fact more nearly concerns ourselves as Irish Churchmen than any other, I may be pardoned for dwelling a little upon it. There is an old-standing contest between the Churches of Trim and Armagh. The Church of Trim, according to a tradition preserved in the *Book of Armagh*, was built by St. Patrick twenty-two years before the foundation of Armagh. It is still called St. Patrick's Trim, and is the nearest approach to a cathedral which the diocese of Meath possesses. I will not, however, undertake to decide upon the question of its antiquity, for whether older or not it has long since been eclipsed by Armagh.[1] Now

as elsewhere an elaborate attempt to parallel the career of Patrick with that of Moses. During that period he was assaulted by large birds, in such numbers that he could not see either heaven, earth, or sea. Joceline, in the twelfth century, improved this notice into the legend in its present shape. Solinus, as I have already stated, noticed Ireland's freedom from snakes in his *Polyhistor*, cap. 22, where he also gives many other interesting details, showing the accurate knowledge of Ireland possessed by the Romans. He tells us of the mildness of its climate, so that cattle had seldom to be housed in winter, of the stormy character of the Irish Sea, amply verified by modern experience, of the boats or coracles used by the inhabitants, and of the perpetual feuds waged within its shores. See for other notices of the Croagh-Patrick legend Adamnan's *Life of Columba*, ed. Reeves, pp. 142, 200; and also the article on St. Patrick in the *Dictionary of Christian Biography*, t. iv. About Patrick's bell, see O'Curry's *Lectt.*, i., 337.

[1] There evidently was a very close connection between the See of Armagh and various portions of the diocese of Meath. The See of Armagh, in virtue of its primatial position, held property in places which had no ecclesiastical connection with it. Thus I find the following grant among the patents of James I., p. 267, ed. Morrin:—"Licence to Christopher Hampton and John

as to Armagh. The district round Armagh was owned or ruled in St. Patrick's time by a chieftain named Daire. St. Patrick, in the course of his missionary tour in Ulster, came and preached to him, and demanded as usual a site for a church. " The rich man said unto the saint," continues the *Book of Armagh*, " 'What place askest thou ?' 'I ask,' said the saint, 'that thou give me that height of land which is called Dorsum Salicis (Ridge of the Willow Tree), and there I will build a place.' But he would not give the high land to the saint ; he gave him, however, another place in lower land, where now is Fertæ Martyrum, near Ard-Machae. And there St. Patrick dwelt with his followers." St. Patrick was not satisfied with this gift. He wished for the high ground, or ridge, while the chief was unwilling to entrust such a strong military position to any stranger. Miracles, however, came to the aid of St. Patrick. Both Daire and his horse suddenly died and were as suddenly revived by St. Patrick, when the saint at once received the ridge of ground on which to this day stands the metropolitan church of St. Patrick's Armagh.[1]

---

Jeeve to keep taverns or wine cellars in the towns of Armagh, Termonfeckin, Dromiskeene, Eniskeen, Nobber, and Kilmone, in the Manor of Tirlaugh in Mayo, and in all other towns and manors of the Archbishop of Armagh." Tirlaugh in Mayo is in the west of Connaught, while Nobber is in Meath diocese. To the present day the local tradition of Nobber is, that if the fairs are not held on certain fixed days the town becomes forfeited to the Primate. The See of Armagh once possessed property in Limerick. These scattered estates were probably relics of the ancient tribute paid to St. Patrick's See.

[1] See *Analecta Bollandiana*, t. i., p. 572, and Dr. Reeves' *Churches of Armagh*. St. Patrick must have endowed the Church of Armagh with some special privileges, as we find from the earliest dawn of Irish Church History that the heirs of St. Patrick, as his successors at Armagh were called, were always claiming superiority and increasing jurisdiction over other churches throughout Ireland.

After the foundation of Armagh, the *Tripartite Life* and Joceline indulge in some of their usual romance. St. Patrick goes off to Rome. There the Pope invested him with the pallium, made him his legate, and confirmed by the authority of the Holy See whatever he had done in Ireland. They do not even hesitate to impugn the saint's honesty. St. Patrick, says the *Tripartite Life*, was not long at Rome on this occasion when he contrived by a pious fraud, whilst the keepers of the holy places were asleep and unconscious, to carry off a great quantity of relics of apostles and martyrs, a towel stained with our Saviour's blood, and some of the hair of His blessed mother. It is added that this pious theft was committed with the connivance of the Pope himself. And then the writer exclaims in rapture, "O wondrous deed! O rare theft of a vast treasure of holy things, committed without sacrilege, the plunder of the most holy place in the world!"

Disregarding such fables, let us return to the historic documents of the *Book of Armagh*. From them I must very briefly sum up the remaining events of our saint's life. St. Patrick departed from Ulster to the south. He preached at Naas, the palace of the King of Leinster. He preached in the plain of the Liffey, on which occasion he may have penetrated to the site of our present city of Dublin. It is an evidence, however, of the ancient character of the lives in the *Book of Armagh* that they make no reference to this city, which only rose into note, either from an ecclesiastical or civil point of view, after the coming of the Danes to Ireland, who first appeared off these coasts in the year 795. Joceline indeed tells us that St. Patrick came to Dublin, a noble city, but then he wrote only in the twelfth century, and he betrays the anachronism by representing it as inhabited by Danes in St. Patrick's time, and also by telling us that St. Patrick predicted its future eminence in these words, "Pagus iste, nunc exiguus, eximius erit." It is to Joceline and such writers that all the legends are due about St. Patrick's wells in our own College Park, and in Cantrell and Cochrane's Yard, and in St. Patrick's Cathedral, and concerning the multitudes there baptized.

St. Patrick also proceeded into Munster, and legend says that as he spent seven years in Connaught so did he spend seven years in Munster. Dr. Todd, indeed, is inclined wholly to reject our saint's visit to Munster, declaring that the *Book of Armagh* does not give any hint of such a journey. In this, however, Dr. Todd was mistaken. The *Book of Armagh* does mention a visit to Munster, but it tells us nothing of the legends and wonders with which his journey has been embellished by later writers.[1] According to these he went to Cashel, the seat of the kings. As he approached, the idols fell before him, like Dagon before the ark. The king of Munster, Aengus, came out to meet him, and received him with the greatest reverence. However, all this is quite fabulous, the simple fact being that there is no notice of Cashel in the Irish annals as a place of ecclesiastical importance until the middle of the ninth or the beginning of the tenth century.

But now St. Patrick's end drew nigh, and he made his way back to the scene of his earliest labours beside Strangford Lough. Concerning the death of our saint legend has been again busy. An angel in a burning bush predicted his approaching dissolution, a light from heaven indicated the spot where his remains should lie, St. Bridget, moved by Divine inspiration, embroidered

---

[1] See *Analecta Bollandiana*, ii., 66.

his shroud with her own hands. For a whole year the sun stood still over his grave, and the district of Maghinis enjoyed a perpetual day. The historical fact seems to be that St. Patrick was overtaken by death at Saul, near Downpatrick. Round this simple kernel an accretion of abundant legends has grown, bearing manifest proof of their later origin. His first wish, we are told, was to reach Armagh and be there interred, but an angelic voice sent him back to Saul, announcing that the four petitions he had asked of God had been granted: (1) That his jurisdiction should have its seat in Armagh; (2) That whoever repeated at the hour of death St. Sechnall's hymn in his honour should have Patrick as the judge of his repentance;[1] (3) That the descendants of Dichu should receive mercy and not perish; (4) That Patrick, as the Apostle of Ireland, should be the judge of all the Irish in the last day, according to the promise made to the other apostles, "Ye shall sit upon the twelve thrones judging the tribes of Israel."

The burial of St. Patrick was the cause of much contention. The men of Armagh wished to have his bones, the men of Down wished to retain them. However, the matter was settled according to biblical precedent. The monks of Saul yoked two untamed oxen to the cart which bore his body, and left them without guidance. They went forth and stopped on

---

[1] The *Book of Armagh*, in Hogan's opinion, speaks of his own hymn, *i.e.*, the hymn composed by St. Patrick himself. Its words are (*Anal. Boll.*, i., 580), "Secunda petitio, ut quicunque ymnum qui de te compossitus est, indie exitus de corpore cantaverit, tu judicatis pœnitentiam ejus de suis peccatis." St. Patrick's hymn will be found in Petrie's *Tara*, pp. 57-67; Whitley Stokes' *Goidelica*, p. 149; Todd's and Cusack's Lives of St. Patrick; Windisch, *Irische Texte*, p. 52. St. Sechnall's hymn has been already discussed, p. 32 above.

the site of the present cathedral of Downpatrick, where since the year 700, when Maccumacthenius wrote, the body has been believed to lie, for that ancient writer tells us that when they were building a church at Downpatrick, the workmen coming on the relics of St. Patrick were compelled to desist by the flames which issued from the tomb.[1]

---

[1] About the burial-place of St. Patrick see Dr. Reeves' dissertation in *Ecclesiastical Antiquities of Down and Connor*, p. 223.

## LECTURE V.

### ST. COLUMBA.

ST. PATRICK is the most celebrated of the saints connected with Ireland. But he was not an Irishman, though his name has become inextricably bound up with Ireland. Patrick, Patricius, a Roman title of aristocratic dignity, has now become the most popular and most plebeian of names. St. Columba, on the other hand, is the most celebrated of saints purely and thoroughly Irish,—Irish by birth, Irish by education, Irish in their life's work and devotion. To St. Columba, then, and his age, we shall now devote our attention.

St. Columba[1] may be taken as a representative of the Irish Church when it first emerges into the clear light of history. Whatever doubts may be felt about the existence of a historical Patrick, the most incredulous feels none about St. Columba, but most fully admits the existence of our saint. To what is this due? How is it that Columba's history, who was born certainly within fifty years of St. Patrick's death, basks in the light, while St. Patrick's is surrounded with clouds and thick darkness? The difference is

---

[1] Skene's *Celtic Scotland*, vol. ii., and Montalembert's *Life of St. Columba*, published in English by Blackwood & Sons (London: 1868), are the best popular accounts of St. Columba, to which may be added the article on "Columba" in the *Dict. Christ. Biog.* Bishop Reeves' edition of Adamnan is, of course, the one great authority.

due to the labours of one man. Adamnan was abbat of Iona, and ninth in succession from St. Columba himself. He was of St. Columba's own family; was born some twenty-five years after his death; spent a long life in his monastery; enjoyed many opportunities of conversing with his friends and contemporaries; had abundant access to the literary remains of the saint, the records of the community; beheld the relics of Columba, his very clothes, which were there preserved; and as the result has bequeathed to us the life published by Bishop Reeves, which every historical student recognises as one of the most valuable extant specimens of ecclesiastical antiquity. I shall, after my usual custom, first describe that work, which is our great authority and guide on this subject, just as Maccumacthenius and the *Book of Armagh* were our great authorities about Patrick's life. With this important difference, however: St. Patrick's life was written more than two centuries after St. Patrick's death; Adamnan wrote his life of Columba within one hundred years of Columba's death. Let me, then, say a few words about the biographer and his work before I treat of the subject of his biography.

Adamnan was a Donegal man, born about the year 625. He entered the monastery of Iona some time about the middle of the seventh century, where he remained till he became abbat in 679,—a post which he continued to hold till his death in 709. He was a man of very wide culture considering the age in which he lived. He has left us two works: one, the life of Columba; the other, a treatise on the holy places of Palestine. The treatise, *De Locis Sanctis*, is a very interesting narrative of travel in Palestine, Syria, Egypt, and Constantinople, of the state of Jerusalem with its churches and relics, while yet Christianity stood firm, and the authority of Rome prevailed, or had till lately prevailed, in these lands. Adamnan did not, indeed, travel thither himself. Arculf, a French bishop, undertook a voyage to Palestine, accompanied by one Peter, a Burgundian monk, about the year 690. On his return voyage he embarked at Rome for some port on the west coast of France; but, encountering a storm, was driven northward upon the coast of Scotland, where he took refuge with Adamnan, spending a whole winter with him, till he could secure a passage to Gaul in one of the ships which traded to the neighbouring ports. The winter seems to have passed in diligent conversation concerning the wonders he had seen. We can imagine how eagerly this distant and primitive community would have drunk in all his stories during the long dreary nights, lasting eighteen or nineteen hours. Arculf had been a wise as well as a diligent traveller. He had preserved careful and extensive notes on waxen tablets, with plans and measurements of the buildings he had inspected. These sketches Adamnan copied, and worked up into his treatise *De Sanctis Locis*, which he divided into three books. The first, deals with Jerusalem; the second, with the rest of Palestine,—Bethany, Hebron, the Jordan, the Dead Sea, Damascus, Tyre, and Joppa, whence he sailed to Alexandria; the third book tells of Constantinople, where Arculf spent eight or nine months.[1]

The other work of Adamnan was the *Life of St. Columba*, his kinsman and predecessor. It is divided, like the treatise on the holy places, into three books.

---

[1] This treatise on the Holy Places deserves careful study by those interested in the development of art and architecture. Their theories often require the tests which history supplies.

The first describes the prophecies; the second, the miracles; the third, the visions of the saint. In doing so, he relates many marvels, some of which we must regard as legends pure and simple; others we may accept and explain on purely natural principles. This life has been preserved in seven MSS., the oldest of which belonged to the famous Irish convent of Reichenau, on the Lake of Constance. From this work I now propose to offer a sketch of the life of St. Columba.

Columba, or Columcille, was born at Gartan, a wild district in Donegal, on December 7th, A.D. 521. He belonged to the O'Donnells, a clan famous in the annals of Ireland, and not yet extinct in Donegal. He belonged to the royal family of Ireland, being the great-great-grandson of Niall of the Nine Hostages, who reigned towards the close of the fourth century. He was baptized at the church of Temple Douglas, half-way between Gartan and Letterkenny, where he received the twofold and opposed names of Crimthann, a wolf, and Colum, a dove, to which was afterwards added the suffix "cille," as some say, from his close attendance at church, and, as others say, from the numerous churches founded by him. His birth as well as the events of his later life abundantly prove the rapid spread of Christianity in Ireland; since we find that within fifty years of St. Patrick's death the Gospel had penetrated the remotest wilds of the Donegal highlands, had converted the kinsmen of that very Laoghaire who so vigorously resisted St. Patrick at Tara, and had established Christian churches and priests even in such a distant region. Columba was educated principally at the monastic school of Clonard, which St. Finnian, a friend of St. Brigid, founded in the beginning of the sixth century. Clonard was then the most distinguished school which Ireland possessed, and was resorted to from every quarter. " From the school of Clonard," says Ussher, " scholars of old came out in as great numbers as Greeks from the side of the horse of Troy. The usual number of pupils in attendance is set down at three thousand, so that the ancient annalists call St. Finnian himself 'a doctor of wisdom and tutor of the saints of Ireland in his time;' while from the fact that he taught St. Columba, Kieran of Clonmacnois, Brendan of Clonfert, and a number of other celebrated bishops and abbats, he was styled preceptor of the twelve apostles of Ireland."

Let me here interrupt the course of our narrative, and strive to make Finnian and Clonard and its monastery somewhat more real for you;[1] for the mythical character of early Irish history has been so accepted as a matter of course, that we are apt to treat such persons and things as names and nothing more. St. Finnian was the first of the great Irish scholars who made this country famous throughout the earlier Middle Ages.[2] He was, like all the ancient Irish saints, specially devoted to the study and exposition of Holy Scripture. One of the hymns, rhymed in monkish fashion, anciently sung at his festival, brings out this point as his leading characteristic. It begins thus :—

" Regressus in Clonardiam,
Ad cathedram lecturæ,

---

[1] Sir W. Wilde, in his *Boyne and Blackwater*, chap. iii., gives a good account of the ancient and modern state of Clonard.
[2] See for the life of St. Finnian and his disciples, the office and hymns used at his commemoration, and the annals of his monastery till the twelfth century; Colgan's *Acta Sanctorum*, Feb. xxiii., p. 393-407; Ussher, *Antiquitates Ecclesiarum Britannicarum*, cap. xvii. (Opp., ed. Elrington, t. vi., p. 472-477, 580); Smith's *Dictionary of Christian Biography*, ii., 518.

Apponit diligentiam,
Ad studium Scripturæ."[1]

He studied for many years under St. David[2] and Gildas,[3] celebrated doctors at Menevia, in Wales, and then, returning to his own country, founded Clonard. The site of that monastery is well known. Clonard is a village upon the head waters of the River Boyne, where it first takes shape as a definite river, draining the vast morass of the Bog of Allen. It is situated on the Great Western or Connaught road from Dublin, and within a short distance of the Midland Western Railway. Clonard does not now retain many vestiges of its ancient ecclesiastical splendour; but till the thirteenth century it was one of the most famous sees of Ireland. One fact alone shows this,—it was pillaged no less than twelve times; five of them by those persistent robbers, the Danes. The church and adjoining buildings were fourteen times consumed by fire, which doubtless must often have happened, since they were usually constructed of timber. Thus we read that in 1045 the town of Clonard, together with its churches, was wholly consumed, being thrice set on fire within one week. But neither the Danes nor fire were the worst enemies of Clonard. Domestic faction helped to lay it low. Thus in 1136 we read that "the inhabitants of Breffny plundered and sacked Clonard, and behaved in so shameless a manner as to strip O'Daly, then chief poet of Ireland, even to his skin, and leave him in that situation; and amongst other outrages they sacrilegiously took from the vestry of

---

[1] Ware's *Writers of Ireland,* p. 13; cf. Colgan, *Acta Sanct.,* p. 400.
[2] Smith's *Dictionary of Christian Biography,* i., 791.
[3] *Dictionary of Christian Biography,* ii., 670-672.

this abbey a sword which had belonged to St. Finnian, the founder." The library was burned in 1143. The village was again sacked by Dermot MacMurrough and his English allies in 1172 or 1173, and its ecclesiastical ruin was completed in 1206, when Simon Rochford, Bishop of Clonard, removed the episcopal seat from Clonard to Trim, and styled himself Bishop of Meath. Clonard preserved till the beginning of the present century some traces of its ancient glory. Archdall, in his *Monasticon Hibernicum*, describes the remains of the abbey which, within the present century, were completely extirpated, the very site of them having been with some difficulty ascertained by Sir W. Wilde. The monastery and scholastic buildings stood on the western bank of the Boyne; the present church and churchyard occupying a part of the site. The modern church was built out of the materials of the ancient abbey, and contains a splendid font, one of the few remains of Clonard's former grandeur. It is beautifully carved, and is still used, while in the adjoining churchyard the lavatory, a large stone trough for washing the pilgrims' feet, was preserved in Wilde's time, buried in the ground.[1] I may add that any of you who will extend your rambles as far as Tallaght can still find, buried in the graveyard, the ancient lavatory or stone trough of that famous monastery, formerly used for the very same purpose of washing the pilgrims' feet.[2]

---

[1] For the decree concerning the change of Clonard see into Meath, see Wilkins' *Concilia;* Archdall's *Monasticon*, and Cæsar Otway's *Tour in Connaught* in 1832 tell more about Clonard.
[2] Tallaght is an interesting spot from an ecclesiastical point of view, five miles south-west from Dublin. It was a famous monastery and seat of learning in the ancient Celtic Church. After the Norman Conquest it became the country seat of the Archbishops of Dublin, till abandoned by them in the early part of the

It was at Clonard, in the days of its primeval glory, that St. Columba received his education and training for his future work. He came to Clonard a deacon. He assisted St. Finnian in Divine service, and at the same time advanced rapidly in knowledge, especially in the art of copying and illuminating MSS., which, as the *Book of Kells* in our own library proves, attained the highest perfection in the schools and houses of the Columban Order. Columba remained several years at Clonard, and while there received priest's orders. The story of his advancement to that dignity illustrates the constitution and social life of the ancient Irish Church. That Church was, as I have often said, intensely monastic in all its arrangements. Its monasteries were always ruled by abbats who were sometimes bishops, but most usually presbyters. This does not prove that they were Presbyterians in Church government; for, if not themselves bishops, the abbats kept a bishop on the premises for the purpose of conferring holy orders. The abbat was ruler of the monastery by virtue of his monastic or collegiate position, and was so far superior to the bishop; but recognised his own inferiority in ecclesiastical matters, whether in celebrating the Eucharist or in conferring Holy Orders,—a function which appertained to the bishop alone. You will at once understand the distinction by supposing a fellow or professor of this University consecrated a bishop while still retaining his fellowship or professorship. From a collegiate point of view he would be subject to the provost, though merely a presbyter; while

---

present century. The episcopal seat is now in the possession of the Dominicans. The well-known pulpit orator, Father Burke, presided over the monastery till his death. See Handcock's *History and Antiquities of Tallaght* (Dublin: 1877).

in ecclesiastical matters the provost would at once acknowledge his superior rank and power.[1] Attention to this distinction would have saved our Presbyterian friends from the mistakes they have made when claiming the ancient Irish Church as an adherent of their modern ecclesiastical polity.[2]

At Clonard St. Finnian, the abbat, desired to have Columba as a domestic bishop to discharge episcopal functions. With this end in view, he sent him to Etchen, bishop of the monastery of Clonfad, in the neighbouring county of Westmeath.[3] Columba took his

---

[1] Returned colonial bishops have been known to act as curates to presbyters. As curates they were inferior to their rectors and subject to them; as bishops they were superior.

[2] The position of the bishops in connection with the ancient Irish monasteries has been discussed by Bishop Reeves in his *Ecclesiastical Antiquities*, pp. 124-140. Wasserschleben, in his Introduction to the second edition of *Die Irische Kanonensammlung* (Leipzig: 1885), p. xlii., has shown that the custom of monasteries having their own bishop under the government of an abbat, was not peculiar to the Irish Church, but was spread as far as Mount Sinai. He quotes the *Chronicon Ademari* out of Labbe, *Nov. Biblioth. MSS. Libr.*, t. ii., p. 175 (Paris: 1657); *cf.* Pertz, *Mon. Ger. Hist.*, iv., 137, Hannov.: 1841 (which contains the best edition of the Chronicle), as speaking of "monasterium montis Sinai, ubi quingenti et amplius monachi sub imperio abbatis manebant, habentes ibidem proprium episcopum." In the *Epp.* of S. Nilus, ii., 160, Migne, *Pat. Græcæ*, t. lxxix., col. 275), we find a fifth-century instance of the union in the same neighbourhood of the abbatial and episcopal offices in one person. Dr. Reeves notices a similar union at Down and Connor (*Antiqq.*, pp. 95, 175, 261). The connection between the early monastic and diocesan systems is manifest from this one fact alone, that no less than three Irish dioceses were without deans and chapters till the reign of James I., viz., Meath, Connor, and Down; of which number Meath still continues in the same condition. Previously to 1609 the archdeacon and clergy of each diocese, in synod assembled, acted instead of a chapter in succession to the monasteries out of which the sees were developed. See Reeves, *l.c.*, pp. 177, 262.

[3] The history of Etchen, and the authorities for this story, are collected together in the *Dictionary of Christian Biography*, ii., 208.

way thither, and inquired for the bishop. He was told that he was ploughing in the field. Columba went up to him, was heartily welcomed, and by mistake ordained priest instead of bishop,—a circumstance which has been the source of much perplexity for those who imagine that the early Irish Church was an off-shoot from Rome, and governed in all its respects by the cast-iron ritual and laws of that Church. St. Columba soon left Clonard and made a round of the other leading colleges of Ireland, after the fashion of the Schoolmen. Amongst others, he studied at the school and monastery of Glasnevin, near Dublin, situated on the banks of the river Tolka. Columba's life from this period was one of intense activity. He entered upon a course of earnest evangelisation, founding churches and monasteries in every part of Ireland. To him is ascribed the origin of three hundred churches, among which are numbered those of Derry, Kells, Tory Island off the Donegal coast, Drumcliffe in Sligo, Swords in the county Dublin, Raphoe, Lambay near Malahide, and Durrow, which became the largest and most important of all St. Columba's monasteries. Some of these foundations retain to this day traces of their early connection with St. Columba. Thus, at Kells is a small arched and stone-roofed building called St. Columba's House. It contains a kind of garret, an apartment between the stone ceiling of the lower apartment and the slanting roof. This garret is only six feet in height, and yet in it we find St. Columba's penitential bed, a flat stone six feet long and one foot thick; while at Durrow, in the King's county, there exist in the churchyard St. Columba's cross and well.

I have already said that St. Columba was celebrated as a scribe. Like the Venerable Bede, whose final scene is so famous, Columba was found when death overtook him engaged in copying the Scriptures.[1] His monasteries followed in this respect the example of their master, and the *Book of Durrow*, an evangeliarium, which professes to have been written by St. Columba himself, testifies in our own University library to the perfection attained in this direction.[2]

St. Columba's life and history were indeed strangely modified by his literary zeal. The first forty years—the first half, in fact—of his life, were spent in Ireland; the latter half in Scotland, evangelising the pagan Picts. His missionary labours are said to have been thus occasioned. St. Finnian of Clonard was famous as a teacher in Meath and the central parts of Ireland. St. Finnian of Moville, near Newtownards, in the county Down, was equally famous in the north.[3] His tastes were similar to St. Columba's own. He was distinguished as a scribe and as a teacher. St. Columba, in the course of his scholastic wanderings, borrowed a Latin psalter from this latter St. Finnian, which he forthwith proceeded to copy. This act of

---

[1] Cummian, Abbat of Iona, in the seventh century, tells us that on the day preceding his death, A.D. 597, Columba was occupied in copying a psalter which he left to be finished by Baithene, his brother's son, who succeeded (see below, p. 129). Upon the curious law of succession to office prevalent in the ancient Celtic Church the student may consult Maine's *Early History of Institutions*, pp. 235-238; Reeves' *Proceedings* Roy. Irish Acad., January 12th, 1857, t. vi., p. 447.

[2] A now partly obliterated entry in Latin on the back of fol. 12 prays "remembrance of the Scribe Columba, who wrote this Evangel in the space of twelve days." I have not devoted space to the description of the early Irish manuscripts still extant, because this has been amply done by specialists. For a handy statement I may refer to Mr. J. T. Gilbert's work, *Account of Facsimiles of National MSS. of Ireland* (1879).

[3] See on Finnian of Moville *Dictionary of Christian Biography*, ii., 518.

literary piracy the original owner immediately resented, and claimed the copy as well as the original. Columba refused to part with the result of his own labour; whereupon the case was carried before Diarmait, King of Meath, who decided against Columba, according to the principle of brehon law, that, as "to every cow belongs its calf, so to every book belongs its copy."[1]

Thereupon ensued a commotion. Columba was a thorough Celt. Christianity, indeed, had spread itself through Ireland, but it was as yet only a thin veneer over the Celtic nature, rash, hot, passionate, revengeful. It had indeed conquered some of the grosser vices, and made them disgraceful.[2] It had elevated somewhat the tone of morals, but it had scarce touched the fiery, unforgiving spirit which lay deep beneath, and still exhibits itself in the fierce and prolonged faction fights of Limerick and Tipperary. In the sixth century the tribal organisation of the Irish people intensified this spirit. The very women, and monks, and clergy yielded

---

[1] This fateful book is said to be still in existence. It is popularly identified with the Cathach of St. Columba; see Reeves' *Adamnan*, pp. 319-321, Gilbert's *National MSS. of Ireland*, pp. 7-10, where an account of its vicissitudes is given. It is now preserved in the Royal Irish Academy.

[2] Sir H. Maine, in his *Early History of Institutions*, pp. 58-61, points out in the brehon laws ample evidence proving the low state of morals among the Irish in the tenth century. The *Book of Aicill* is the oldest of the ancient law tracts officially translated and published. Maine remarks that it assumes the temporary cohabitation of the sexes to be part of the accustomed order of society. If so, it is no wonder that Pope Adrian should have spoken so severely of Ireland and the Irish in his Bull, handing over the country to Henry II. Sir H. Maine's work, as noted above, will be found most useful for the study of the brehon laws. He points out their numerous points of contact with Hindoo law; specially in the custom of fasting upon a debtor or offender, which, as practised in ancient Ireland, exactly corresponds to the "Sitting Dharna" of the Hindoos. See Maine, *l.c.*, p. 39, and *cf. Ancient Laws of Ireland*, vol. i., p. 113.

themselves up to its fascination. Just as in the days of the Land League and of the tithe agitation, and in the Belfast riots, and at many an election contest in bygone times, the women were the fiercest combatants, so in the sixth century the women went to battle as regularly as the men, and it was only the influence of this very Columba which obtained a decree from the national assembly, held at Drumceatt in 590, exempting women from their liability to military service.[1] But we cannot wonder at the weaker sex going to battle when their spiritual guides showed them the example. The monastic communities were not exempted from military service till the year 804, and even then they do not seem to have very ardently desired the exemption. When left to themselves, the monasteries often diversified the monotony of their existence by a vigorous fight. In the year 673 a battle was fought in King's county between the monasteries of Clonmacnois and Durrow. Each could place no contemptible force in array when all their tenants, and servants, and dependants were summoned to warfare. On this occasion Dermod Duff, son of Donell, the leader of the Durrow faction, and two hundred of his people were slain by the victorious men of Clonmacnois ; while even after they were exempted from attending battle at the call of the king, the monasteries still continued to follow the customs of their fathers; for we learn from the *Annals* that in 816 no less than four hundred men were slain in a battle between rival monasteries. The very synods of the clergy were not

---

[1] A law which seems to have had so little effect that Adamnan, his biographer, had to renew it at the synod of Birr, 697 ; see *Annals of Ulster*, A.D. 696, and Bishop Reeves' article on "Adamnan" in the *Dictionary of Christian Biography;* with which compare his *Adamnan's Columba*, p. 179.

exempt from such un-Christian practices. The MS. *Annals of MacFirbis*, one of the most learned of Irish annalists and historians, tell us that till the time of Adamnan, that is, the year 700, "the clergy of Ireland went to their synods with weapons, and fought pitched battles, and slew many persons therein."[1] Such being the spirit of the age, such being the habits and customs of the time, even in classes most naturally bound to peace, it is no wonder that Columba, a child of the great northern Hy-Neill, took his judicial defeat very badly, and summoned his tribesmen to a contest which, as he represented, touched most keenly their tribal honour. The decision of the king against Columba's claim became, in fact, the occasion of a great conflict between the rival northern and southern branches of the Hy-Neill, which terminated in the battle of Cooldrevny, fought between Sligo and Drumcliffe in the year 561, and won by the Ulster men, the party of St. Columba, when no less than 3,000 of the Meathmen were slain.

The story then runs that St. Columba retired to the monastery of Inismurray, lying off the coast of Sligo, which I shall hereafter describe. The abbat, St. Molassius, was his soul-friend or confessor. Columba consulted him as to his conduct. A synod had already excommunicated him. Molassius advised submission, not resistance, and prescribed as a penance that St. Columba should retire to Pictland, the modern Scotland, and there convert the pagans to Christ, in return for the scandal he had occasioned and the blood he had shed. His celebrated work in Scotland will form the subject of our next lecture.

---

[1] See Dr. Reeves' *Colton's Visitation*, pp. 93—97, where he gives a list of desecrated churches, which proves how warlike the Irish monasteries were.

# LECTURE VI.

## *COLUMBA IN IONA.*

THE early Celtic Church was intensely monastic and intensely missionary. It presented truly Celtic features. Go where you like throughout the world at the present day, and there you will find an Irishman who yet declares there is no place half so sweet or half so charming as Ireland. So was it in Columba's age. The Celtic clergy were wanderers over the face of the earth, and yet they ever carried with them memories of the land whence they came out. The period of missionary activity began with Columba, whom we may designate the first Irish missionary, the apostle of pagan Scotland. I have already alluded to one cause which some allege for his exile to Iona. He had been ordered to abandon Ireland for ever, and gain as many souls for Christ in Scotland as he had destroyed in Ireland, in return for the bloodshed he had caused.

This may indicate one cause of his departure to Iona. His life in Ireland was not up to our conception of the saintly character; and his saintly reputation must be based, not on it, but on his life and work in Iona. Like St. Peter or St. Paul, his life divides itself into two parts,—the unconverted portion and the converted portion. During his Irish life he could not forget either his high birth or tribal and family antipathies, or his hot, vengeful Celtic temper. During his Scottish life, while the old character can be oftentimes traced, he was evidently a very altered man.

Another and a more reputable reason may be, however, offered for his departure. Columba was a very energetic and forcible character. The monastic life had taken a firm and permanent hold upon the temper and imagination of the Celtic people. They flung themselves with all their wild unreasoning enthusiasm into the movement, and the monasteries were teeming with monks, many of whom must necessarily have soon wearied of a life of pure devotion, and have longed for a life of active piety, which should make known the truth whose value they had themselves proved. Such spirits and such aspirations found a willing and a qualified leader in St. Columba.

We can plainly see, too, another occasion for his departure to Scotland. Political and religious events urged him in the same direction. Columba was, as I have told you, of the royal family of Ireland, and very nearly akin to the reigning monarch. He was, in fact, of high social rank, and as such possessed, not merely the imperious disposition, but also the wider, the more extended mental horizon which lofty station confers. St. Columba looked across the narrow channel which separated the coasts of Alba, or Scotland, from those of Scotia proper. He saw the Irish colony which inhabited the Scotch Dalriada, and the Christian Britons of Strathclyde, in imminent danger of utter extinction at the hands of the pagan Picts, who inhabited the highlands; and he determined to bring effective assistance to his brethren, not the might, indeed, of temporal warfare, but of those spiritual weapons which alone can curb and restrain unregenerate nature. Let me explain what I mean, because this fact is the key-note of all St. Columba's later career. If you grasp it, you will easily understand the plan and object of his work in Iona. If you miss it, it will be simple chaos to you. There were two districts called Dalriada. One is in Ireland, on the north coast of Antrim, and is now called the Route. This was an ancient kingdom in St. Patrick's time, and its inhabitants all accepted Christianity during the fifth century. At the beginning of the sixth century, that is, about the time of St. Columba's birth, the Irish Dalriadani, urged on by the restless genius of the Celtic race, crossed the Channel, and founded a second Dalriada in Argyleshire, which in course of time became the dominant power in Scotland, and the germ out of which the mediæval kingdom of Scotland was developed. It will be well for you to remember that the very name, the kingdom, and the royal family of Scotland, and, therefore, of England (through the Stuart line), drew their origin from this Irish colony. Its earliest fortunes in Scotland, however, gave no indication of its brilliant future. Scotland was then groaning beneath the rule of the savage Picts. The Romans had subdued and civilised it as far as Edinburgh and Glasgow. Their departure left it for a century subject to the inroads of the northern pagans, till at last, about the year 500, the tribesmen of Antrim came to the rescue of their brethren, and established this Christian outpost. The Irish settlers maintained their ground successfully for half a century, under three different kings. In the year 560, however, they sustained a crushing defeat at the hands of Brude, King of the Picts, whose royal seat was at Inverness. This battle entailed the loss of a great portion of their territory, and threatened the extinction in Scotland of the Irish colony and of Christianity itself. Columba was closely connected with the kings of the Scottish Dalriada through his grandmother.[1] His imagination was fired by the prospect of such a dangerous work, and the thought may have dawned upon him that the martyr's crown, which so many had longed for, awaited him in the land of the pagan and bloodstained Picts. In the year 563, or thereabouts, "the saint with twelve disciples, his fellow-soldiers, sailed across to Britain," as his earliest biographer puts it, and took up his abode at the Island of Iona, which he has rendered so famous. I shall now divide this lecture into four sections, each of which I will treat as concisely as possible. These four will be: 1. Iona itself; 2. Columba's missionary work there; 3. The Synod of Drumceatt; 4. His death and the results of his work.

Where, you may ask, is Iona, and how did Columba get there? Iona, let me say first of all, rejoices in various names. The oldest form of the name is Hii, Ia, or I; on the tombstones in the local cemetery it is called Y or Hy. Adamnan usually calls it Iova, which by a misprint has given rise to the name Iona. If you wish to visit Iona, the best way is, first, go to Glasgow, then take a ticket to Oban upon one of those magnificent Clyde steamboats which have made sailing on that river synonymous with comfort. At Oban you will arrive late in the afternoon, and next day a sail of three or four hours will bring you to Iona. Iona, in fact, is a little island lying off the larger island of Mull, on the west coast of Scotland. Two stories are current, assigning reasons for Columba's choice of

---

[1] See Reeves' *Adamnan*, p. 94, for Columba's genealogy (*cf.* pp. 32, 40), and his *Ecclesiastical Antiquities*, pp. 318-322; Skene's *Celtic Scotland*, t. ii., p. 84.

it. One, and the more probable, tells that Iona was given him by the king of Dalriada as a fitting station for his missionary labours. Another story is connected with his alleged exile from Ireland. The penance imposed on him for his quarrelsome conduct was, that he should leave Ireland for ever, and never behold it again. The saint in pursuance thereof set sail from Ireland in the coracles of the period, made of skins of beasts and wicker rods; a kind of boat which, frail as it may seem, is still commonly used in Arran, Achill, and the western coast, and is able to live in seas where stouter barks would utterly perish.[1] He sailed doubtless from his favourite monastery of Derry, and landed upon the island of Oronsay, north of Islay. Upon climbing a hill, however, he perceived Ireland in the dim distance; whereupon he again took to his boat, and sailed north to Iona, where no traces of Erin any longer appeared. The memory of this is kept up by the name affixed to a cairn on a hill at the south end of Iona, called the Cairn of Farewell, overhanging the bay where he landed, called Port-na-currach. Iona is a small island, but three miles by two in extent, divided from Mull by a stormy sound just one mile broad, across which the pilgrims and monks were able to call for the ferry-boat to carry them over. I need not spend much time in describing it, as any guide-book to Scotland will give you full particulars, and Dr. Reeves' edition of *Adamnan* contains a map with the Celtic names of the various localities. As it may not, however, be convenient for you all to

---

[1] They can also be seen on the Boyne at Drogheda, where they are used in salmon-fishing. They demand very cautious management; an unskilful step into one has sent me headlong into the Boyne.

make an immediate visit thereto, and as a visit to Iona at this season could probably be made only in a bark not much superior to that used by St. Columba,[1] I may mention that you will find three modern books in our library on the subject. The Duke of Argyle has written one, the late Bishop Ewing of Argyle wrote another, while a third was published in 1850 by Mr. H. D. Graham. This last is miserable as far as the letterpress is concerned. It was written before Dr. Reeves' book was published, which introduced a new epoch in Scottish ecclesiastical history. But its illustrations are very admirable, offering the best substitute for a personal visit to Iona. A journey to the spot cannot introduce you, however, to any buildings St. Columba ever erected. Ruins there are in abundance. You can see the cathedral, and the monastery, and St. Oran's Chapel, and the nunnery, and plenty of carved tombstones; but they are all mediæval. The old Celtic community were expelled, or at least absorbed, by the Benedictine order of monks and nuns introduced in 1203, when the churches were raised of which the ruins still exist.[2] The monastery established by St. Columba was of the usual Irish type. Its buildings were like Brigid's at Kildare, of wattles and clay, or at best of oak planks.[3] The attentive reader of Adamnan's *Life* of Columba will see abundant proofs of this. The monastery was still in the same state, even when more than a century old, for Adamnan tells of the toil he and his brother monks endured bringing home trees to repair their wooden huts. Some traces of the site and surroundings of the Columban monastery are still

---

[1] These lectures were delivered during Michaelmas and Hilary terms.
[2] Skene, *l.c.*, ii., 415.   [3] See Reeves' *Eccles. Antiqq.*, p. 195.

pointed out.[1] The mill and kiln, the hill, the pond, the anchorites' cells, have all been identified. The outline of the cashel, or fortification, of the convent can be traced, just as you can trace to this day the cashel of Rathmichael old church, near Bray, or, better still, the cashel which surrounds the churches in the cemetery at Glendalough.[2] From Adamnan's *Life*, and from a study of other Columban foundations, we can reconstruct the monastery of Iona as Columba built it. There was a vallum, or cashel, of mixed stones and earth surrounding the monastery. There was a stone kiln, of which some remains are still to be seen, a mill, and a barn. The monastery proper contained a refectory of considerable size, in which was a fireplace and a stone vessel full of water, probably used for washing the pilgrims' feet. There was then the hospitium, or guest chamber, of wattles and clay, and the cells or huts of the monks,

---

[1] See Skene, *l.c.*, and Reeves, Adamnan's *Life*, pp. 357—364.
[2] Concerning cashels and their ecclesiastical use see the lecture on "Ireland and the East," where their existence to this day in Egypt is noticed. See also Petrie's *Round Towers*, pp. 440—446; Reeves' *Adamnan*, p. 24, and his *Eccles. Antiqq.*, pp. 182, 196. Bede, *H.E.*, iv., 28, describes the cashel of St. Cuthbert's hermit's cell as so high that he could see nothing but heaven. Prof. Joyce, in his useful and interesting book on *Irish Names*, p. 276, writes thus on the word caiseal: "The word caiseal is very common in Irish, and is always used to signify a circular stone fort. It is a simple word, and either cognate with, or, as Ebel asserts, derived from the Latin castellum. It is found in the most ancient MSS., such as those of Zeuss, Cormac's Glossary, etc. In the modern form, Cashel is the name of about fifty townlands, and begins the names of about fifty others, every one of which was so called from one of those ancient stone forts. The cashels belong to the same class as cahers, raths, etc., and like them are of pagan origin; but the name was very often adopted in Christian times to denote the wall with which the early saints surrounded their establishments." Lord Dunraven, *Notes on Irish Architecture*, i., 46-54, gives beautiful views of the cashel on Inismurray, see further below, pp. 184—188.

made of planks and situated round a central court. The church was built of oak, and possessed an exedra, or vestry, while at some distance and upon the highest ground was placed St. Columba's hut of timber.

Such was the outward appearance of this Christian colony, thus settled to convert the pagans of northern Scotland. It was well and wisely planned, and it was successful with a success never vouchsafed to modern missions, because we have rejected the experience and the wisdom of the ages when nations were born to God in a day. Columba's idea in settling in Iona was not to spend his life in meditation or penitential exercises. His idea was first of all that Iona should be a Christian community, where a number of Christian men should present a picture and model of what Christianity was, what Christian civilisation meant. Doctrine and practice went hand in hand in the Columban venture. Modern missions have almost without exception reversed the process. Doctrinal controversies and prepossessions have dictated a wrong course. The heads of our missionary societies have scorned the notion of calling civilisation to their aid. As for sending out associated bodies of men to work in common, and show an example of civilised life to the heathen, they have regarded such an idea as downright Romanism. They have interpreted the texts which speak of the Gospel of Christ and the cross of Christ as the power of God unto salvation, as excluding all other helps; and they have sent out lone men here and there to preach and to pine, and then either to die or return home, poor miserable failures. I can just now only recall two instances where the Columban idea has been carried out by Protestants. One is the case of the Moravians, and they have been successful.

The other is that of the Universities or Central African mission, and it too has been successful, though working only for a very short time. Columba, however, intended his society to be something more than a model Christian colony. He made it a centre of active evangelistic effort, whence wise and well-planned attacks could be made on the surrounding districts, and whither the wearied evangelists could retreat for rest, for sympathy, and for meditation.

We may now pass to the second division of our subject, and ask what missionary work and missionary successes were achieved by St. Columba. St. Columba landed in Iona, and necessarily took some months to arrange his monastery. His companions numbered at least quite two hundred persons. The wants of such a multitude demanded no small care and foresight. Houses had to be built, provisions stored, fields brought under cultivation, flocks and herds acquired and tended. As soon as this preliminary work was done, Columba vigorously applied himself to his missionary labour. In the first two years of his residence he converted large numbers of the peasants in the adjoining island of Mull and upon the mainland, though he had to struggle with all the difficulties of an unknown tongue. Two years after landing in Iona he determined to assail Pictish Paganism at its centre and stronghold. Columba's plan of attack was similar to St. Patrick's, as I have already described it. Let me briefly recall it. Patrick first settled in Down and Antrim, and made good his footing therein, founding churches and securing a place of retreat in case of need. Then he advanced to Tara. So did St. Columba act. He first established himself at Iona, studied the language of the Picts, converted his neighbours, and then, following the windings of that long line of loughs and lakes which now form the Caledonian canal, he penetrated to the fort, or royal residence, of the Pictish sovereign, the renowned King Brude himself, situated close by the modern Inverness. This man's name and fame are thoroughly historical. Adamnan celebrates him. A little later Bede describes him as "the powerful king of the Pictish nation,"[1] while again, the mediæval lives of St. Kenneth, or St. Canice, and of St. Comgall of Bangor, the friends and companions of St. Columba, equally bear traces of him.[2] Columba knew how important, and yet how dangerous, was his mission on that occasion. He had not yet attained sufficient command over the Pictish tongue; so he summoned to his help two of his friends and fellow-students at Clonard, St. Comgall, the founder of the celebrated monastery of Bangor, in the county Down, and St. Canice, the founder of Aghabo, in the Queen's county, and the patron saint of Kilkenny. Observe the reason of this. St. Columba was a genius in many respects. He was a poet, an artist, a teacher, but he was above all things great as an organiser and leader. One characteristic of all such leaders is knowledge of men, power of choosing

---

[1] Bede's *Eccles. Hist.*, iii., 4, where the following account of Columba's mission is given. "Columba came into Britain in the ninth year of Bridius, who was son of Meilochon, and the powerful king of the Pictish nation; and he converted that nation to the faith of Christ by his preaching and example, whereupon he also received of them the aforesaid island (Iona, or Hii, as Bede calls it) for a monastery. It is not very large, containing about five families according to the English computation. His successors hold the island to this day. He was also buried therein, having died at the age of seventy-seven, about thirty-two years after he came into Britain to preach."

[2] See the article on St. Cainnech in the *Dictionary of Christian Biography*, t. 1, p. 382, and on St. Comgall, p. 608; Adamnan's *Life of St. Columba*, ed. Reeves, pp. 28, 121 about S. Cainnech, pp. 93, 94 about St. Comgall.

fit instruments and assistants, specially qualified for their work. Now, why did Columba choose Comgall and Canice? Can we discover any peculiar fitness in these men for the dangerous mission to the very source and centre of Pictish Druidism? Yes, I reply, we can. Columba summoned Comgall and Canice to his help because they were Picts—Irish Picts by birth, and, therefore, possessed of that linguistic fluency which St. Columba as yet lacked.[1] Attended, then, by these friends, and followed by a number of his monks, St. Columba evangelised most diligently all along the great glen which divides Scotland into two parts, until he came to the palace of King Brude himself. The story of the king's conversion is very similar to that of Laoghaire's at Tara. Both kings at first were hostile, both were made hostile by Druidical influence, and both were overcome by the mighty wonders displayed by the missionaries. Adamnan's Life of Columba is more a record and laudation of our saint's miraculous gifts, than a history of his life and work. Yet, here and there, we gain glimpses of his missionary activity. Thus he relates that "when the saint made his first visit to King Brude, the king would not open his gates to him. When Columba observed this, he approached with his companions, and having first formed upon the closed doors the sign of the cross, he knocked and laid his hand upon the gate, which instantly flew open of its own accord, the bolts having been driven back with great force. The saint and his companions then marched through the gate thus wondrously opened. When the king learned what had

---

[1] For proof of the Pictish origin of Comgall, see note by Bishop Reeves, in his edition of Adamnan, p. 94; and his *Eccles. Antiqq.*, p. 337.

occurred, he and his counsellors were filled with alarm, and immediately setting out from the palace advanced to meet the holy man, with due respect, addressed him in the most conciliatory language, and ever after from that day the king held the saint in very great honour." The conversion of King Brude took place in A.D. 565, and, as was the case in most rude and Celtic communities, was rapidly followed by his tribesmen. Churches and monasteries were founded in every direction, an evidence of which is still extant in the vast number of churches and parishes in those northern regions dedicated to St. Columba,—a dedication preserved even by the most rigid Presbyterians. During the nine years which followed, that is, from 565 to 574, Columba devoted himself with all the enthusiasm of his character to evangelistic work. He had now gained complete mastery over the language, and was a frequent visitor at King Brude's residence. Columba, with that political tact which always marked his course, saw at once what a powerful instrument for the promotion of Christianity he possessed in Brude, whose influence and power extended to the farthest Orkneys. His own zeal and pious ambition reached even unto that distant spot. Adamnan tells us that, when visiting Brude, St. Columba on one occasion addressed him thus in the presence of the ruler of the Orkneys: " Some of our brethren have lately set sail, and are anxious to discover a desert in the pathless sea.[1] Should they happen, after many wanderings, to come to the Orcadian islands, do thou carefully instruct this chief, whose hostages are in thy hand, that no evil befall them within his dominions."

---

[1] For the meaning of this expression see the lecture on "Ireland and the East," note, p. 179, and Reeves' *Adamnan*, p. 366.

Columba did not, however, escape the hostility of the pagan party. The Druids, too, headed the opposition at the Pictish court, just as they had previously done at the court of Tara when Patrick preached. The various lives of Columba, that by Adamnan, the old Irish life of the tenth century,[1] and O'Donnell's life,[2] contain many notices of Druidical antagonism to our saint. One of the most notorious of his foes was a Druid named Broichan, the king's foster-father, a relationship which at every period of the Celtic race has been counted a specially sacred one. He opposed Christianity in every way. One day, when Columba and his monks came out of the enclosure of the fort where the king resided, to chant their evensong, according to monastic custom, the Druids attempted to prevent them singing, lest the sound should reach and attract the people. Columba, however, was equal to the emergency. He possessed a voice of the most magnificent compass, which could be heard like a trumpet, even to a mile's distance. So the abbat at once uplifted this voice in the words of the forty-fifth Psalm, " Eructavit cor meum verbum bonum : dico opera mea regi ;" "My heart is inditing of a good matter, I speak of the things I have made unto the king," with such effect that he caused all his adversaries to tremble. This same Druid is said to have raised a storm against Columba when the latter boldly launched his boat on Lough Ness, and victoriously sailed right

---

[1] Edited and translated by Hennessy, in an appendix to Skene's *Celtic Scotland*, and by Dr. Whitley Stokes, in *Three Middle Irish Homilies*, p. 90—125 (Calcutta : 1877).

[2] See O'Curry's *M.S. Materials*, i., 328—407, and Colgan's *Trias Thaumat.*, pp. 389—446, where O'Donnell's work is summarised. The original is in MS. at Oxford, see Reeves' *Adamnan*, Preface, pp. xxxiv—xxxvi.

in the teeth of the wind,—a fact which Adamnan duly reckons among his miracles. Another incident strikingly illustrates the tenacity with which the Celtic race retains its most ancient superstitions. This Druid possessed an Irish captive maid. Columba's national feelings were stirred on her behalf. He asked the Druid for her liberation, which he refused. "Be it so," said the saint; "but know that if thou refusest to set free this foreign captive, thou shalt die before I leave this province." When he had spoken thus he left the king's residence, directing his steps towards his boats, which were moored on the river Ness. He was soon overtaken by messengers from the king, saying that the Druid had met with a terrible accident from which he was dying, and was now quite willing to set the captive free. Columba stooped down, took a pebble from the shore, blessed it, and sent it back with the assurance that water in which it should be dipped would heal the sick man, the girl being first set free. The cure, we are assured, duly took place, and the blessed pebble was carefully deposited among the king's treasures as an infallible remedy against disease. The king himself had occasion, some years afterwards, to test its powers; he fell sick and lay dying. He remembered his pebble, and ordered it to be brought; but, unfortunately, it had disappeared, and King Brude died for want of its aid.[1]

---

[1] This incident can be illustrated from superstitions and customs still existent among the Irish peasantry. No belief is more widely spread among them than a belief in pebbles as charms against diseases of man and beast. The use of crystal pebbles for similar purposes still continues in the south of Ireland, instances of which have been given by Windele in a paper on "Irish Medical Superstitions," *Journal* Kilk. Archæol. Society, vol. v., p. 306, 2nd series; in a paper on the "Imokilly Amulet," by G. M. Atkinson, in the *Journal* of the Royal Histor. and Archæol.

One of the most notable and authentic circumstances in the life and work of St. Columba is the Synod or National Assembly of Drumceatt, A.D. 575.[1] Let me very briefly state the facts thereof. Brude, the first Christian king of the Picts, died in 584, twenty years after his conversion. He was duly succeeded by a Christian prince, under whom Christianity continued its career of conquest among the Picts. But all this time Columba had never forgotten his kinsmen of Dalriada, to whose aid he had originally come. He had successfully used his influence with King Brude on their behalf. He also reorganised the internal condition of Dalriada. One king died. Columba, with the instinct of a statesman and the authority of a princely Churchman, recognised the incapacity of the legal successor to cope with such troublous times; so he set aside the incapable one, and appointed and consecrated a more energetic prince out of the regular order of succession according to brehon or Irish law.[2]

---

Association of Ireland for 1875, p. 440, and in the same journal for 1880, p. 347. See also a learned and exhaustive paper on the same subject by my friend Dr. Frazer, M.R.I.A., of Dublin, in the last volume of the *Proceedings* of the Royal Irish Academy. The Irish, in their superstitions and customs, are the most conservative of Western nations.

[1] See Reeves' *Adamnan*, p. 92.

[2] The prince whom Columba thus appointed was one Aidan by name. He was a descendant of Niall of the Nine Hostages. He was consecrated, according to tradition, upon the Stone of Fate, afterwards transferred to Scone, and thence brought to Westminster Abbey, where it now serves as the coronation stone. But this is not the only link between our present sovereign and King Aidan, this Hibernian prince. Queen Victoria is descended from him, and through him from Niall of the Nine Hostages, King of Ireland about the year 400. This may seem incredible, yet it is capable of most satisfactory proof. Aidan's descendants continued to reign over Dalriada alone till 842, when Kenneth MacAlpine, a prince of his house, united Picts as well as Scots, Highlanders and Lowlanders, under the

The princes of Dalriada chafed under their subjection to the kings of Ireland and the tribute exacted from them. So Columba determined to plead their cause before the supreme king of Tara. Other motives, too, led Columba to Ireland. Columba was a poet and a bard, qualified for such a profession by that intense love for nature, in all its aspects, whether grave and magnificent or soft and gay, which he ever displayed. The poets were threatened with expulsion from the kingdom on account of their exactions, and their fate now hung in the balance. To Drumceatt, therefore, St. Columba, the most saintly and venerated of all the bards, was duly summoned to plead their cause. Drumceatt, the scene of the synod,—or parliament rather, for it was an assembly of lay chiefs as well as of bishops and abbats,—is still pointed out. It is situated at Roe Park, near Newtownlimavady. The memory of this famous assembly lasted till the seventeenth century. Colgan, the famous writer of that age, tells us in 1645 that the site of this assembly was even then still frequented by numerous pilgrims, and that a procession was formerly celebrated there on All Saints' Day, with a great concourse from all the adjoining neighbourhood.[1] This synod, which made so deep an impression upon the popular mind, was no affair of a few days. The Irish lords and clergy encamped under arms during its entire duration, which lasted

---

same rule. The male line of these Celtic kings ended only with Alexander III. in 1285. But then came in the dynasties of Bruce and Stuart, which were descended in the female line from the Celtic kings, whence the blood of the Celts passed over to our present royal family.

[1] Colgani *Acta Sancti.*, p. 204 ; see p. 203 for Colgan's account of the poem said to have been composed in honour of St. Columba by Dallan Forgaill ; *cf.* O'Curry's *MS. Materials;* Reeves' *Adamnan*, p. 17 ; and next page below.

fourteen months. I cannot go into the details of it. Montalembert, in his *Monks of the West*, has done this at great length, and depicted its proceedings with all his French vivacity and brilliancy, making the ordinary reader feel as if the historian had been present at the synod, but leading the more suspicious student to fear that his imagination has carried him captive. It must suffice for me to state that Columba attained both his objects. He gained Home Rule for Scottish Dalriada, freeing it from subjection to the king of Tara, and he procured the revocation of the decree which had been issued against the bards. The bards proved themselves grateful for his mediation, and we still possess a poem in his honour, expressing their thanks to their sainted protector, composed by Dallan Forgaill, poet laureate of Ireland at that time. This poem has been at least twice printed and translated, once by the late Mr. O'Beirne Crowe, and a second time, by Mr. Hennessy, of the Record Office, in his life of St. Columba, attached as an appendix to the second volume of Skene's *Celtic Scotland*.

Time would fail me to give even a brief sketch of Columba's deeds subsequent to Drumceatt. He repeatedly visited the leading monasteries of Ireland. Adamnan gives us a lively picture of Clonmacnoise when Columba approached it. On every side, he tells us, the monks ran together. They left their out-door work, crossed the cashel or entrenchment, and came to receive him chanting hymns. When they met him, they prostrated themselves on the ground ere they embraced him, and then, forming in procession, carried him into the monastery under a canopy of branches. His greatest difficulty was, however, with the king of Tara, Aedh or Hugh, the same who threatened to expel the bards. He did not like St. Columba, and was jealous of his power. His eldest son, too, shared his feelings, and mocked the monks of Iona. But the second son was of a more devout turn, and revered them. There is an interesting story told of him which illustrates the social life of this, the golden age of Ireland's history. Columba was so pleased with his religious turn that he predicted for this young prince, not only a long and glorious reign, but also the very exceptional privilege that he should die in his own bed, on condition of receiving the Holy Communion every week, and of keeping at least one in seven of his promises, certainly not too exacting a limitation.[1]

But, as we all know, "to every man upon this earth Death cometh soon or late," and from this law St. Columba was not exempted. He had premonitions of the event, and he got himself back to his beloved Iona, there to meet the last enemy. Marvels cluster around the story of his departure, the natural outcome of pious but very simple souls. His death, we are told, was retarded four years by the prayers of his community. The brethren meanwhile often saw the angels of God conversing with him. A celestial light shone in his cell, rendering it a kind of antechamber to heaven, and diffusing therein somewhat of that Divine effulgence which lightens the city of God. At the end of four years the inevitable time came. He visited his monks at their labours in the fields, and blessed them. He visited the granary, and saw that the provisions were sufficient till the next harvest; then he turned home to die. Here Adamnan tells one of his most touching stories, illustrating Columba's keen poetic sympathy

---

[1] Reeves' *Adamnan*, pp. 36-38.

with nature and with animals.[1] Half-way between the granary and the storehouse is a spot still marked by one of the ancient crosses of Iona, called Maclean's cross. There St. Columba met the old white horse which had been employed to carry milk from the dairy to the monastery. The horse came and put his head on his master's shoulder, as if to take leave of him. The eyes of the aged animal seemed bathed with tears. His attendant would have sent the horse away, but Columba forbade him. "'The horse loves me,' he said; 'leave him with me; let him weep for my departure. The Creator has revealed to this poor beast what He has hidden from thee, a reasonable man.' Upon which, caressing the faithful brute, he gave him a last blessing." After this he went to his cell, and worked at the transcription of a psalter. When he came to Psalm xxxiv. 10, "Inquirentes autem Dominum non deficient omni bono," he stopped short, feeling his work was done. "I must stop here," he said. "Baithene will finish the rest." He then sent a last message to his followers, enjoining peace and charity. It was now Saturday night, June 9th, 597. As soon as the midnight bell rang for the matins of Sunday, he rose from his stone couch, ran to the church before the other monks, and there was found by his attendant prostrate before the altar. Columba opened his eyes once, turned them upon his brethren with a look full of serene and radiant joy, raised his right hand in an effort to bless them, and so passed away, says Adamnan, with a face calm and sweet, like that of a man who in his sleep had seen a vision of heaven.

---

[1] Reeves' *Adamnan* l. iii., c. 23, p. 233.

Such was the life of the apostle of Caledonia, a mixed life, like all human lives, chequered, wild, and passionate at times, but ever consecrated to the one great object of evangelising the masses of Paganism, and always advancing in charity, gentleness, and the Divine life, until he came to God's everlasting kingdom.

## LECTURE VII.

### COLUMBANUS.

THE golden age of the Irish Church was at its earliest age. From 500 to 700 was the period when most of those missionaries appeared whose names have made the fame of the early Celtic Church,—Columba, Columbanus, St. Gall, St. Colman, Adamnan, and a host of others. The missionary activity of the Irish Church did not then cease utterly and at once. It was prolonged for centuries later, till the time of Marianus Scotus, of Ratisbon, in the eleventh century.[1] But after the seventh century it was no longer the one all-absorbing national thought and passion. Other interests had arisen. The Roman controversy about Easter, and the ever-increasing claims of the Roman see, helped to distract attention. Controversy then, as now, led men's minds from practical work, and hindered the advance of the Gospel. The incursions of the Danes, too, deprived the Irish Church

---

[1] See Dr. Reeves on Marianus Scotus in the *Proceedings* of the Roy. Ir. Acad., vii., 290, where he notices the achievements of the following Irish missionaries, SS. Cataldus, Fiacra, Fridolin, Colman, and Kilian, none of whom find place in our Annals. St. Cataldus laboured in Southern Italy, where San Cataldo, near Otranto, is called after him; St. Fiacra in France; St. Colman is patron saint of Lower Austria; Kilian taught in Franconia; Fridolin at Glarus, where his figure finds place in the cantonal arms and banner. *Cf. Mittheilungen der Antiquarischen Gesellschaft* in Zurich, vol. ix., part I., tab. 12, No. 10.

of that internal tranquillity needful for missionary enterprise. The boldest spirits, which used to seek the post of danger and the crown of martyrdom in foreign missions, could now find that position much nearer home. It is to the sixth and seventh centuries I must, therefore, again direct your attention when describing one who in many respects was the greatest, bravest, most thoroughly national, and most representative of all the warriors of the Cross sent forth from Irish shores.

Columbanus is quite distinct from Columba or Columcille. It is necessary to bear this most carefully in mind, for Columba and Columbanus are very often confounded, and have been so confounded even by eminent scholars. Let me briefly distinguish them. They were both Irishmen, indeed, and both born in the sixth century. Columba was an Ulster man, however, Columbanus a Leinster man. Columba was born in 521; Columbanus was more than twenty years his junior, having been born in 543. Columba was the apostle of Scotland or Caledonia; Columbanus never set foot in Scotland. He was the apostle of Burgundy, Switzerland, and Northern Italy. Columba spent his life among the Pictish pagans of North Britain; Columbanus laboured among the pagans of Central Europe. Now, some may say, or secretly think, as ignorant people are wont to do, "Is not his whole history legendary, with just as much historical truth in it as in the Arthurian legends, and not nearly so much as in Homer's account of the destruction of Troy?" This, indeed, is the real view of many who write in newspapers, whose political or national spleen leads them to confound the miserable squabbles and degradation of the mediæval Church of Ireland with its earlier and purer period. They seem to think there are no real authentic records of early Irish Church history, and they really class Columba and Columbanus with the legends and myths of a poetic people. With such persons I have neither patience nor sympathy, because they are wilfully and inexcusably ignorant. I have already shown you the folly of such a notion about Columba, and pointed out that we have as good reason for believing the leading facts of his life as for believing any others in history. St. Columbanus is in a still more favourable position. Let me, then, briefly tell you first of all what are the authorities for his life. They are of the highest value and character. First, we have his own writings. These consist of his *Monastic Rule*, in ten chapters; a book on the daily penances of the monks; seventeen sermons, all of them very short; a book on the measure of penances; an instruction concerning the eight principal vices; a considerable number of Latin verses; and five epistles, two addressed to Boniface IV., one to Gregory the Great, one to the members of a Gallican synod, upon the question of Easter, and one to the monks of his monastery of Luxeuil, wherein he gives us various details of his life. Besides his own writings, we have his life, written by the Abbat Jonas, a contemporary of St. Columbanus and a monk in his Italian convent of Bobbio. From these documents, aided by the general history of the age wherein Columbanus played a leading political as well as religious part, we can construct a strictly historical life of this great missionary.

Columbanus was born in Leinster, A.D. 543, the same year in which Benedict of Nursia, his great monastic predecessor and rival, died at Monte Cassino. He was educated first of all on one of the islands of Lough

Erne, which in those early times was studded with sacred retreats, of which the island of Devenish, the home of St. Molaise, now presents the only remains. From Lough Erne Columbanus migrated to Bangor, on Belfast Lough, which was then at the height of its fame as a place where the greatest attainments in learning and sanctity were possible.[1] We are apt to undervalue the studies of these ancient monasteries, just as we, in our intellectual conceit, are apt to undervalue all mediæval learning, because the men of those times knew nothing of the daily press, photography, electricity, or gunpowder. In monasteries like Bangor, the range of studies was a wide one. Take up the works of the Venerable Bede, produced at the monastery of Jarrow by a man who never travelled farther than the neighbouring city of York, and then you will have some idea how extensive must have been the range of monastic studies. Listen to one of the latest and most competent judges upon this point. Bishop Stubbs, writing of Bede in Smith's *Dictionary of Christian Biography*, says, "The attainments of Bede were very great. He certainly knew Greek, and had some knowledge of Hebrew. Among the classical writers of antiquity he knew Virgil, Ovid, Lucian, Lucretius, Terence, and a host of smaller poets. Homer he quotes once. He knew nearly all the second-rate poets, using them for the illustration of the *Ars Metrica*. The earlier fathers were, of course, in familiar use. The diversity as well as the extent of his reading is remarkable: grammar, rhetoric, poetry, hagiography, arithmetic, chronology, the holy places, the Paschal controversy, epigrams,

---

[1] See Reeves' *Eccles. Antiqq.*, pp. 93, 199, about the foundation and celebrity of Bangor. St. Comgall, the friend and companion of St. Columba, was its first abbat.

hymns, sermons, pastoral admonition, and the conduct of penitents; even speculations on natural science, on which he specially quotes Pliny, furnished work for his pen, beside his great works on history and the interpretation of Scripture. He must have had good teachers, as well as a good library and an insatiable desire of learning." Bede was, indeed, a century later than Columbanus, yet all this description might be transferred to Columbanus and to Bangor, which must have been a thoroughly equipped and vigorous seat of learning in the latter half of the sixth century, when it could despatch such a trained and even elegant scholar as he was to convert the pagans of France. The proofs of his learning are evident to the student of his writings. The scholarship of them is manifest. He writes good Latin verses, full of quaint metrical conceits, both in the classical and monkish rhyming style. Allusions to pagan and Christian antiquity abound in his poems.[1] Where did he get this scholarship? His life on the Continent was one of rough, vigorous, all-absorbing practical effort, leaving no time for such studies. His age, too, forbids the idea. No man ever, I should think, gains the facility in Latin versification

---

[1] At sixty-eight he addressed to a friend, named Fedolius, an epistle in Adonic verse, which everywhere bears the impression of those classical studies which the Irish monks of that period cultivated. He prays him (Opp., ed. Migne, *Pat. Lat.*, lxxx., 291) not to despise those little verses by which Sappho, the illustrious muse, loved to charm her contemporaries in lines like the following:—

"Inclyta vates,
Nomine Sappho,
Versibus istis
Dulce solebat
Edere carmen.
Doctiloquorum,
Carmina linquens
Frivola nostra
Suscipe lætus."

which Columbanus possessed unless he begins the study in youth. Even did time and leisure permit, the opportunity was wanting, as the Continent was then plunged in utter darkness, literary as well as spiritual. St. Columbanus, we therefore conclude, gained his extensive knowledge and elegant scholarship at the abbeys of Bangor and of Lough Erne. About the year 585, he was seized with a desire to preach the Gospel. The triumphs of Columba and of the Caledonian mission were then rousing the holy ambition of the Irish monasteries, and Bangor, within sight of the Scotch coast, must have felt a special call to such work. Some circumstances—what they were we know not—determined Columbanus and twelve companions to seek the shores of France. They crossed to Great Britain, and thence reached Gaul.

France was, towards the end of the sixth century, a bye-word throughout Europe for immorality and irreligion. When we think of the Gaul of that period, we must not think of it as it was in the fourth and fifth centuries, the age of a Hilary of Poitiers, of a Martin of Tours, or a Germanus of Auxerre. For a hundred years and more it had been the prey of every invader; and, though the country was struggling on towards better things, these better things were yet far distant. Let me quote from Milman a vigorous passage illustrating the dangers and obstacles our countryman had to face as he went forth to call the Franks and Burgundians to the obedience of Christ.

"It is difficult," says that historian, in his *Latin Christianity*, lib. iii., cap. ii., "to conceive a more dark and odious state of society than that of France under her Merovingian kings, the descendants of Clovis, as described by Gregory of Tours. In the conflict of coalition of barbarism with Roman Christianity, barbarism has introduced into Christianity all its ferocity, with none of its generosity or magnanimity. Its energy shows itself in atrocity of cruelty, and even of sensuality. Throughout, assassinations, parricides, and fratricides intermingle with adulteries and rapes . . . . That King Clotaire should burn alive his rebellious son with his wife and daughter is fearful enough, but we are astounded even in these times with a bishop of Tours burning a man alive, to obtain the deeds of an estate which he coveted. Fredegonde sends two murderers to assassinate Childebert, and these assassins are clergymen. She causes the Archbishop of Rouen to be murdered while chanting the service in church; and in this crime a bishop and an archdeacon are her accomplices. Marriage was a bond contracted and broken on the lightest occasion. Some of the Merovingian kings took as many wives, either together or in succession, as suited either their passions or their politics. Christianity hardly interferes even to interdict incest."

It was into a country where all the bonds which bind society together were thus totally dissolved, St. Columbanus flung himself, with all the headlong courage of his race, to be the champion of morals, the apostle of civilisation, the fearless soldier of the cross of Christ. He landed in the north of France. The two languages used by him, the Celtic and the Latin, would, of course, carry him everywhere. He at once set out on a course of apostolic wanderings, which at last led him to Burgundy, at that time ruled by Gontran, who may be described as the least immoral of the grandsons of Clovis.[1] This king received

---
[1] Gontran was son of Clotaire I., the youngest of the four sons

him gladly, offered him riches and honour, which the missionary declined, and settled upon him the old Roman castle of Annegray, where the first Irish monastery ever planted on the Continent raised its head.[1] There he laid the foundations of his system as he had learned it in Ireland. These foundations were plain, aye, the very plainest, living, high thinking, and hard work. His biographer Jonas describes the simple life led at Annegray. Columbanus lived for weeks without any other food than the herbs of the field and the wild fruits yielded by the forest around. We trace in him the same love of nature and of natural objects which we find in some of the beautiful stories told of St. Columba. Everything is said to have obeyed his voice. The birds came to receive his caresses. The squirrels descended from the tree-tops to hide themselves in the folds of his cowl. One day, when wandering in the depths of the woods, meditating whether the ferocity of the brutes, which could not sin, was not better than the rage of men, which destroyed their souls, he saw a dozen wolves approach and

---

of Clovis, among whom his kingdom was divided in 511. See the articles "Clotaire I." and "Guntramnus" (2) in the *Dict. Christ. Biog.* Gontran has been canonised, and his memory is celebrated in the Roman martyrology on March 28th. The article just cited will show what a strange saint he was.

[1] Columbanus drew up a rule for the use of his monasteries. It was of the sternest kind, and doubtless represents the discipline of Bangor, Clonard, Iona, and the Irish monastic system of his day. It punished the slightest fault with fasting or corporal chastisement. See *Regula Cœnobialis* and *De Pœnit. Mensurâ.* in Migne's *Pat. Lat.*, t. lxxx., 209, 223; Wasserschleben, *Die Irische Kanonensammlung*, p. lxxvi., and his *Bussordnungen der Abendländ. Kirche*, pp. 52-60. The rule has also been made the subject of a monograph by Dr. Otto Seebass, styled *Ueber Columba von Luxeuils Klosterregel und Bussbuch* (Dresden: 1883), where the author uses of set purpose the name Columba instead of Columbanus (*cf.* p. 3).

surround him on all sides. He remained motionless, repeating the words, "Deus in adjutorium." The wolves touched his garments with their mouths, but seeing him fearless, passed upon their way. The example of a quiet Christian household, shedding the blessings of civilisation, education, and religion all around, proved a very powerful one, even upon men more ferocious than wolves. Crowds flocked to the Irish teacher to learn the secret of a pure and happy life, and the great foundations of Luxeuil and Fontaines followed one another in rapid succession. They were all successful ventures, and among the disciples of Columbanus were numbered by hundreds the children of the noblest Franks and Burgundians. For twenty years the great missionary thus laboured, till the crisis of his life came, and his activity was changed to a new direction.

You must bear with me while I go somewhat into detail about this event, as the details alone will enable you to realise the state of religion and of morals with which Columbanus was obliged to deal. About the year 600, Gaul, in its widest limits, from the British Channel to the Vosges and Jura mountains, was subject to the government of two Jezebels,—Fredegund, called the enemy of God and man, who ruled, roughly speaking, the north; Brunehault, who ruled the south and east, and of whom the best that can be said is this: she was not quite as bad as the other.[1] Now fix your attention on Brunehault, for it is with her St. Columbanus came into conflict in defence of the plainest principles of Christian morality. Brunehault ruled Burgundy as regent for the young king Thierry, her grandson. To preserve her own power, and to prevent

[1] See the article "Fredegundis" in the *Dict. Christ. Biog.*

a rival standing near the throne, she for a time successfully encouraged him in the utmost licentiousness, and opposed every attempt to replace his numerous concubines by a legitimate queen. Her ambition overcame even her national and patriotic feelings. She was herself a Visigothic princess. Thierry at last chose a lawful wife from the same house. But.Brunehault so worked upon him, that at the end of twelve months he repudiated her, and St. Didier (Desiderius), Bishop of Vienne, who had arranged the match, was murdered by the agents of the queen-mother.[1] She was utterly shameless, too. Thierry, her grandson, was a man of strong passions, indeed, but still was not devoid of religious instincts, and always bore most respectfully those sharp reproofs Columbanus bestowed upon him. On one occasion the saint was thus visiting him, when he came into conflict with the queen regent. Brunehault presented to Columbanus the four sons Thierry already had by his concubines. "What would these children with me?" said the uncourtly monk. "They are the sons of the King," said the queen regent; "strengthen them by thy blessing." "No," replied the fearless saint; "they shall not reign, for they are of bad origin." From that moment Brunehault vowed war to the death against Columbanus. Another cause hastened his fall. He never would abandon his Celtic peculiarities and national customs in religion. Here we come upon the first symptoms of those controversies which were so soon to rend asunder the Celtic Church in all its branches. Columbanus would never surrender his Celtic tonsure and his Irish method of celebrating Easter. The Gallic bishops followed the custom of Rome in both respects, and strove to reduce the fearless Irishman to confor-

---

[1] See "Desiderius" (9) in *Dict. Christ. Biog.*

mity with their own practices. It was all useless. He not only refused obedience, but addressed a long epistle to the bishops in synod, in which he deals very plainly with them, and then touchingly sets forth his own case thus :—" I am not the author of this difference ; I have come into these parts a poor stranger for the cause of Christ the Saviour, our common God and Lord. I ask of your holinesses but a single grace : that you will permit me to live in silence in the depths of these forests, near the bones of seventeen brethren whom I have already seen die. Oh, let us live with you in this land where we now are, since we are destined to live with each other in heaven, if we are found worthy to enter there. I dare not go to you for fear of entering into some contention with you; but I confess to you the secrets of my conscience, and how I believe, above all, in the tradition of my country, which is besides that of St. Jerome." Both Church and State were thus arrayed against the undaunted Irishman, who dared to maintain the traditions of his forefathers, and to champion the laws of immutable morality. Columbanus had soon to pay the penalty of his bravery. His monastery was regularly boycotted. The inhabitants were forbidden to have any dealings therewith. He was himself arrested and confined at Besançon, whence he soon escaped to Luxeuil. Thither a royal officer and a strong detachment of soldiers were sent to arrest him. They found him, as Athanasius was found, in church, chanting the service with his community. "Man of God," said they, "we pray you to obey the King's orders, and to return from whence you came." "No," answered Columbanus ; "after having left my country for the service of Jesus Christ, I cannot think my Creator wishes me to return." Parley was, however, useless. The soldiers treated him with every respect, but if they did not execute their commission, their lives would have been forfeited. He was, therefore, arrested, bade a final adieu to his beloved Luxeuil, was hurried across France, and placed on board a ship of Nantes bound for Ireland. Brunehault and Thierry thus freed themselves of their enemy, but his future work lay not in Ireland, whither they thought they had despatched him. The Bishop and Count of Nantes hastened his departure, according to the royal wishes. But though man proposes, God disposes. The Irish vessel in which Columbanus was embarked was flung back upon the sands at the mouth of the Loire. The captain, with a true sailor's superstition, imbibed the notion that Columbanus was an unlucky passenger, landed him and his Irish companions who had been exiled with him, and at once continued his voyage. Columbanus was permitted to go where he would. Thus ended his struggle and woik in Burgundy. And now, when more than sixty, he began with indomitable energy to carve out a new career for himself. The prospect, however, was not inviting. His quarrel with Brunehault and Thierry shut him out from the greater part of France. For a time he took refuge with Clotaire II., son of Fredegund, but his heart was set upon the evangelisation of Northern Italy, which was even yet filled with Arian heresy and with pagan superstition.[1] But how was he

---

[1] The Arianism of North Italy was persistent. Some of the most authentic and interesting information about the Arian Ulfilas has been thence derived. See Scott's *Ulfilas*, pp. 38, 117 (Cambridge: 1885) and Card. Mai's *Scriptt. Vett. Nov. Coll.*, iii., 186, where Arian documents have been printed, derived from Bobbio, Columbanus' own monastery. The library of Bobbio proves the scholarship and research of the Irish missionaries. The Muratorian fragment, a MS. of the age of Columbanus, was derived

to get there? The usual routes down the Rhone and by sea, or through the passes of the Western Alps, were all cut off by the dominions of Burgundy. He, therefore, chose another road, destined to be rich in spiritual trophies which still perpetuate the fame of these devoted Irish missionaries.

Clotaire's court had no charms for Columbanus. He was in very deed no fit subject for a courtier. He was not a man clothed in soft raiment, neither did his tongue easily frame those soft and honeyed words which alone suit the tone and temper of kings' palaces. Clotaire received him generously, and protected him effectually. Yet Columbanus felt not at home. The atmosphere was tainted, heavily laden with that miasma of immorality and vice which ever haunted the descendants of Clovis. Columbanus, fearless as a John the Baptist, reproved the king for all his wicked deeds, and the king took the reproof mildly and well, and promised reformation, but never fulfilled his promise.

Columbanus longed, however, for freedom. He was, like Columba, a child of nature. The moan of the storm, the murmur of the ocean, the rustle of the forest, spoke to these men of purity, of power, and of God, and Columbanus ardently desired to regain those wilds and forests where he had laboured and conquered for Christ. One path of escape alone remained open to him. The Rhine presents a waterway often traversed in later times from the shores of the German Ocean to the very border of Northern Italy, and it lay wholly beyond the realms and power of Brunehault and

---

from thence; see *Canon Muratorianus*, by S. P. Tregelles, LL.D., and Dr. Salmon's article on the "Muratorian Fragment" in the *Dict. Christ. Biog.*; see below, note on p. 146.

Thierry.[1] He, therefore, embarked upon that river, and traversed a large part of the beautiful defile between Mayence and Bingen which has made the name of the Rhine famous. It must have been very hard work pulling against that stream. Those who have not seen it, or, still better, tried to swim against it, have no idea of the force and power wherewith the river rushes from the tableland of Switzerland to the sands of the Dutch coast. It is hard work even for the powerful express steamers which daily strive to overcome it. They descend the stream from Bingen to Cologne in almost half the time which they take to ascend it; but what must have been the exertions used by St. Columbanus and his companions as they slowly battled their way in their coracles all up the defile of the Rhine, and then along through the calmer waters between Heidelberg and Strasbourg, and thence by Bâle, and Schaffhausen, and the falls of the Rhine, till they emerged into the great broad expanse of the Lake of Constance? There they halted for a time, evangelised, preached, taught, and established the monasteries of Reichenau, and above all of St. Gall, a monastery which to this day is one of the richest repositories of Irish MSS. and Irish literature on the continent of Europe. St. Gall was a companion of Columbanus; he has given the name to the town and canton of St. Gall. In preaching the Gospel to the Swiss, Columbanus displayed all the impetuosity of his temper. Sometimes he broke the boilers in which the pagans prepared the beer they offered—a truly national sacrifice—to Woden.

---

[1] Even so late as two centuries ago, about the year 1659, the Rhine formed the route traversed by the followers of Johannes Bollandus on a famous literary journey to Rome. *Cf.* the "Life of Bollandus," capp. xiii.-xx., in the first volume of the *Acta Sanctorum* for March; *Contemp. Review*, January 1883, p. 75.

At times he burned their temples or broke their images. Such conduct naturally provoked opposition. The Irishmen were driven from place to place with violence, and refused food by the inhabitants. But such sturdy missionaries were no way disconcerted. They erected their huts of timber, planted their gardens, snared the wild fowl, fished like apostles on the Lake of Constance. Columbanus made the nets. Gall, the learned and eloquent preacher, flung them into the lake with no small success. A fine legend illustrates the difficulties they so long encountered and so bravely overcame in Helvetia. One night St. Gall was in his boat, silently watching his nets, when he heard the demon of the mountain calling to the demon of the waters. "Here I am," answered the water demon. "Arise then," said the other, "and help me to chase away the strangers who have expelled me from my temple; it will require us both to drive them away." "What good should we do?" answered the demon of the lake; "here is one of them upon the water-side whose nets I have tried to break, but have never succeeded. He prays continually, and never sleeps. It will be labour in vain; we shall make nothing of it." Gall made the sign of the cross, and said to them, "In the name of Jesus Christ, I command you to leave these regions without injuring any one." Then he hastened to land, awoke the abbat, and rang the bell for nocturns; but before the first psalm had been intoned, they heard the yells of the demons echoing from the tops of the surrounding hills, at first with fury, then losing themselves in the distance, and dying away like the confused voices of a routed army.

Success attended the labours of Columbanus in Switzerland, and even greater success attended his disciples, but his soul was not yet satisfied. He felt as if he had not yet attained the great end for which his spirit panted. Columbanus, in truth, was made to rule, and to rule a large community. He felt the need of a sphere where his activity could find scope for its exercise, as at Luxeuil and Fontaines. Other influences, too, combined to lead him from Switzerland. King Thierry had been extending his dominions, which now embraced the very district where Columbanus was living. The inhabitants had got tired of him and his preaching. They stole his cows; they slew his monks. They complained to the duke of the province that these strangers scared away the game of the royal chase, by infesting the forest with their presence and their prayers. It was necessary to depart. Columbanus put it vigorously: "We have found a golden egg, but it is full of serpents." He set out, therefore, with one companion, painfully crossed the Alps, probably by the route of the St. Gothard pass, and arrived at the court of Agilulf, King of the Lombards. There he was received with the greatest respect, and endowed with the church and territory of Bobbio, in a retired gorge of the Apennines between Genoa and Milan. An old church, dedicated to St. Peter, was in existence there. Columbanus undertook to restore it, and to add to it a monastery. Despite his age, he shared the workmen's labours, and bent his old shoulders under the weight of enormous beams of fir-wood. This abbey of Bobbio was his last stage. He made it the citadel of orthodoxy against the Arians, lighting there a lamp of knowledge and instruction which long illumined Northern Italy.[1] The monastery

---

[1] Even modern learning owes something to it. The school and library of Bobbio rank among the most celebrated of the

existed till suppressed by the French in 1803, while the church still serves as a parish church. Bobbio was in one sense his last stage. It was his final scene of work, whence he evangelised the pagans and Arians all around. In another sense it was not. Columbanus ended life by seeking a solitude more profound still. Upon the opposite shore of Trebbia he discovered a cavern, which he transformed into a chapel, and there, like other Irish anchorites, he spent his last days " in a desert" till God called His faithful and fearless servant home, on November 21st, 615.

Did time permit, we might devote, and with much profit, a whole lecture to consider the ecclesiastical position of Columbanus. It has been a great crux for modern Ultramontanes. In Columba's life there is not one trace of the pope or the slightest acknowledgment of his claims. There is silence, however, and this is at most only a negative argument. In the Life of Columbanus there is many a mention of the pope and several epistles to popes, but there is also an express rejection and denial of their claims, and a use of plain language to them which no Irish priest of the Roman obedience would now dare to use. For an Ultramontane's explanation of this phenomenon I must refer you to Montalembert in his *Monks of the West*. It is very amusing. For instance, striving to explain away his letter to Pope Boniface IV., Montalembert says: "Doubtless some of the expressions he employs would be now regarded as disrespectful, and justly

---

middle ages. Muratori has given a catalogue of seven hundred MSS. which the monastery possessed in the eighteenth century. Thence, for instance, came the famous palimpsest from which Cardinal Mai published the *De Republica* of Cicero. See Tregelles, *Canon Murator.*, part i.; Muratorii *Antiqq. Ital. Medii Ævi*, t. iii. (Mediol. MDCCXL.), coll. 809-880; and note, p. 142, above.

rejected. But in those young and vigorous times, faith and austerity could be more indulgent." Let me, however, give a brief extract from his epistle on the Easter question, written to one of the greatest popes, Gregory the Great, in defence of his own Irish rites and ceremonies, and in opposition to the Roman mode. The unbiassed student can then draw his own conclusions. "How is it that you, with all your wisdom, you, the brilliant light of whose sanctified talents is shining abroad throughout the world, are induced to support this dark Paschal system? I wonder, I confess, that the erroneous practice of Gaul has not been long since abolished by you. . . . You are afraid, perhaps, of incurring the charge of a taste for novelty, and are content with the authority of your predecessors, and of Pope Leo in particular. But do not, I beseech you, in a matter of such importance, give way to the dictates of humility or gravity only, as they are often mistaken. It may be that in this affair a living dog is better than a dead lion" (or Leo). "For a living saint may correct errors that have not been corrected by another greater one."[1]

I do not think that the reverence of Columbanus for the pope or his belief in papal infallibility can have been very great, when he would use such language.[2]

---

[1] The full force of the play upon words in this passage only comes out in the Latin. It was not very complimentary to Pope Gregory to call him a living dog.

[2] A full analysis of the life and letters of Columbanus will be found in Ceillier, *Hist. des Auteurs Ecclesiast.*, vol. xi., pp. 612—630. Migne's *Patrologia Latina*, t. lxxx., offers a convenient edition of his works, including his Latin poetry. See also Fleming's *Collectanea Sacra* (Lovan.: 1667); and for the bibliography of the subject "Columbanus" in the *Dict. Christ. Biog.*

# LECTURE VIII.

## *THE PASCHAL CONTROVERSY.*

I HAVE now endeavoured to sketch the histories of Patrick the apostle of Ireland, of Columba, the apostle of Scotland, and of Columbanus, the apostle of Burgundy. These three men represent the early Celtic Church in its origin and development, during the fifth and sixth centuries. In considering their careers I have omitted many interesting questions. The organization, the liturgy, the government of the Church have merely been alluded to. Our attention has been fixed on men, not on measures.[1] The period which elapsed from the seventh to the twelfth centuries, or, broadly speaking, from St. Columbanus to the Anglo-Norman conquest, is an unknown time for most people. Men have heard of Brian Boru, and perhaps of Cormac of Cashel, and they have a vague idea that they lived some time in that period; but in their secret hearts regard them as mythical personages. And when we pass beyond them there is no other personality which stands out dominating the whole horizon and calling attention to his work as does the

---

[1] A French historian has well remarked that "history studies not merely facts and institutions. Its true object is the human soul. It ought to seek to know what that soul has believed, thought, and felt during the different ages of the life of the human race." Fustel de Coulanges, *Cité Antique*, pp. 103, 104; *cf.* Jean Réville, *Religion sous les Sévères*, Pref., p. i.

personality of a Patrick or of a Columba. Yet the period of five hundred years we have now to study is an extremely interesting one, and no more mythical or dark than the same period in the history of England. Original Irish documents, original Irish works, and original Irish records of that age abound. They lie concealed, sometimes in manuscripts, sometimes in the ponderous volumes of a D'Achery, a Canisius, a Colgan, the *Four Masters*, or the tomes, even more ponderous still, of the Bollandists; but there they are, to reward the diligent student with a contemporaneous glimpse of the ways and doings of the ancient Celtic Church. There are two distinct methods in which we might study this period. I might present you with a record as voluminous, minute, and accurate as I could make it of the successions and struggles of the multitudinous chieftains and ecclesiastics who lived in Ireland. I might, in fact, copy out and read to you the annals of the *Four Masters;* but I fear you would not be much the better, but rather the worse for such a style of treatment, as you would have the feeling intensified—which too often prevails already—that Irish history is intensely stupid and intensely uninteresting.

There is another and more useful method of dealing with our subject. I may avoid burdening your memory with bare lists of names, and present you instead with a series of pictures of great movements, or of leading characters, which will illustrate the whole spirit of the times and shed light upon the course which the development of the national life followed. This latter is the method which I shall adopt, and in doing so I shall begin with the first great external movement which impinged on Irish national life, modifying at first, and then radically altering, its whole tone and character.

That movement I call the Paschal Controversy. Let me explain this for you, and in doing so I must preface a few words. The feast of Easter has been a subject of controversy since the second century. Polycarp of Smyrna and popes Anicetus and Victor of Rome, held diverse views as to the proper time of its observance.[1] Polycarp and the Churches of Asia followed the Jewish method of computation, while all other Churches observed the Christian style. This caused the celebrated Quartodeciman Controversy. With that controversy the Irish Church had nothing to say, though its adversaries, to give it a bad name, designated it by the opprobrious name of Quartodeciman. Irish churchmen agreed with their opponents in celebrating Sunday and Sunday alone as the feast of the Resurrection. But they differed from them as to the method of computing the Sunday. Let me explain how this happened. You will see that my explanation will throw some light upon the vexed question of the age and period at which Irish Christianity first arose. The earliest Easter cycle of the Christian Church was naturally identical with that used by the Jews. It was called the eighty-four year cycle.[2] During the debates of the second century this cycle was discovered to be faulty, whereupon the celebrated Hippolytus, bishop of Portus, devised his cycle of one

---

[1] See art. "Anicetus" in the *Dict. of Christ. Biog.*, p. i., 116.
[2] The Jews at the time of our Lord's crucifixion probably used an eight-year cycle (*Octaëteris*). After the fall of Jerusalem they adopted the eighty-four year cycle. See on the whole question the article on Easter in the *Dictionary of Christian Antiquities*, and Dr. Salmon's articles on the Chronicon Cyprianium and Hippolytus in the *Dict. of Christ. Biog.;* Hefele's exhaustive treatise on the Easter question and the Nicene Council in his *History of the Councils*, vol. i., pp. 298-341 (Clark's trans.); Bingham's *Antiq.*, xx., c. 5.

hundred and twelve years, which we find inscribed on the chair of his statue, discovered in 1551, and now in the Lateran. The Fathers of Nice took up the question. They laid great stress upon the true time of keeping Easter. They placed their ban upon the Quartodecimans and all who followed Jewish customs, and to ensure uniformity entrusted the duty of calculating and announcing the true time of Easter to the bishops of Alexandria, as living at the great scientific centre of the existing world. However, even in such a slight matter Rome was not willing to be second to Alexandria; so the Roman Church fell back, with that conservative instinct she has always displayed, upon the original Jewish cycle of eighty-four years, while the Alexandrian Church used the ancient metonic cycle of nineteen years, as arranged by Anatolius, Bishop of Laodicea, about the year 284. Now mark this point. During the fourth and first half of the fifth centuries the Alexandrian Church used the nineteen-year cycle; the Roman Church used the old Jewish cycle of eighty-four years. This divergent use at last caused great inconvenience. Thus from an epistle of St. Ambrose[1] we learn that in the year 387 Easter was observed at three distinct dates: by some on March 21st, by others on April 18th, and by others on April 25th. The popes of Rome, with their old imperial notions of accuracy and uniformity, chafed at this. It was bad enough to be subject to Alexandria on such a topic, but it was still worse when Alexandria seemed unable to give a certain, or at least an accurate answer.[2] The uncertainty which prevailed

---

[1] Quoted in Bingham's *Antiq.*, bk. xx., ch. v., sec. 4.
[2] There is no formal canon or decree of the Council of Nice now extant committing the function of calculating Easter to the Alexandrian patriarch. Pope Leo I. refers, however, to some such decision in an epistle addressed to the Emperor

in the fifth century may be illustrated by one fact. Pope Leo the Great wrote to St. Cyril of Alexandria, the very last year of St. Cyril's life, to inquire concerning the true date of Easter. The Roman calculation made it March 26th, while the Alexandrian fixed it to April 23rd. The Roman Church determined at last to shake itself free from this thraldom, and to assert its competence to determine all such questions for the entire Western world, of which the Roman See was now becoming more and more visibly the guide and leader. So Rome determined to have a reform of the calendar. For this purpose Pope Hilary, in the year 463, employed Victorius, an abbat of Aquitaine, who framed a new cycle. Hitherto, as I have said, the Roman Church used the old Jewish cycle of eighty-four years. Henceforward they used the new cycle of Victorius and Dionysius Exiguus, which embraced a period of five hundred and thirty-two years. But the Irish Church had received with St. Patrick and its first teachers the old Jewish and Roman cycle of eighty-four years. Barbarian invasions and wars and distance separated them from Rome and its new fashions. They knew nothing of the new cycle of five hundred and thirty-two years. Their whole energy was concentrated on study and missionary effort, and so continuing faithful to the practices of their forefathers, they found when St. Augustine and the Roman mission came to Canterbury, about the year 600, that Rome and Ireland

Marcian, where, speaking of Easter, he says: "Studuerunt itaque Sancti Patres occasionem hujus erroris auferre, omnem hanc curam Alexandrino episcopo delegantes (quoniam apud Ægyptios hujus supputationis antiquitus tradita esse videbatur peritia) per quem quotannis dies prædictæ solemnitatis Sedi Apostolicæ indicaretur, cujus scriptis ad longinquiores ecclesias iudicium generale percurreret." See Hefele's *Councils*, vol. i., p. 327 (Clark's trans.)

differed very considerably about this important question.[1]

Now observe two facts: (1) The mission of Augustine, about A.D. 600, first raised this question; (2) As I shall afterwards show you by contemporary evidence, the Irish Church never heard till then of the new Roman cycle introduced for the first time in 463. And from these two facts I conclude that Christianity must have been introduced into Ireland prior to 463, or, in general, about that epoch, the first half of the fifth century, to which St. Patrick's mission is usually attributed. But why, you may say, did they make so much fuss about such a trumpery matter as the proper method of calculating a date? The answer is easy. We all know from our own experience that the bitterest quarrels in religion rage over apparently the pettiest details. What can seem to an external observer more insignificant than the proper position of the celebrant at the Holy Communion, whether he should look towards the south or towards the east? and yet two parties in the English Church have fought most bitterly, threatening even at times to rend that communion in twain, over this point. And why have they done so? Not that they saw any special virtue in either the south or the east, but because this position symbolised for both parties views they either cherished or abhorred with equal vigour. So it was with the question of Easter. The Council of Nice and the Church of the fourth century regarded the Quartodecimans as heretics, and cut them off from Christian communion. The Roman Church transferred

---

[1] The Irish Church came, as we shall see, into contact with the Roman missionaries from the very outset. See Bede, *H.E.*, ii., 4; *cf.* Baron. *Annal.*, A.D. 601, sec. 25, and contra Migne's ed. Greg. Mag. *P.L.* lxxvii., 1203.

the same penalty to all those who would not conform themselves to her calculations. She regarded them as Judaizers and Jews, and Judaizing and the Jewish controversy were still a real terror and a real danger to the Christian Church.[1] Let this suffice upon the importance of the question. We shall now proceed to the history of this bitter strife.

St. Augustine landed in England towards the close of the sixth century. His mission was twofold : first, to preach to the pagan Saxons ; secondly, to correct and instruct the members of the old Celtic Church. In the year 603, or thereabout, Augustine assembled the bishops of the Celtic Church to a conference at a spot near the Severn, afterwards called Augustine's Oak. There he propounded three points upon which he demanded conformity with the customs of Rome : (1) The use of chrism in baptism;[2] (2) The new Easter cycle ; and (3) The fulfilment of the primary duty of every Christian Church, the preaching of the gospel to the pagan Saxons, which the British Celts in their national hatred refused to do. Augustine failed, and failed utterly, to bring the Celts over to his view. Augustine died the very next year, and was succeeded by Archbishop Laurentius, who soon discovered that the British Celts were supported in their controversy by the Scots, the Irish Celts, who held precisely the same views as the

---

[1] The Theodosian Code, bk. xvi., title viii., treats of the privileges, disabilities, offences, etc., of the Jews, and shows how actively hostile to Christianity they still were in the fifth century. Gebhardt and Harnack in their *Texte und Untersuchungen zur Geschichte der altchristlichen Literatur*, Bd. i., Hft. 3, Leipzig, 1883, have given us a specimen of the Jewish controversy of the fifth and sixth centuries in a dialogue called "Altercatio Simonis Judæi et Theophili Christiani." Their Introduction shows what a burning question it then was.

[2] See note on p. 318 concerning the difference between Rome and Ireland about chrism.

Celtic Church of England. He wrote, therefore, an epistle to the bishops and abbats of Ireland about the year 605. It is most important, for it is the earliest document, save one, connecting Rome and Ireland, and places us at the very fount and origin of this prolonged controversy. We find it in Bede, Bk. ii., ch. 4. "To our most dear brothers, the lords, bishops, and abbats throughout all Scotland, Laurentius, Mellitus, and Justus, servants of the servants of God." You will observe what a convincing proof we here have of the episcopal character of the Celtic Church of that period. Some persons have endeavoured to make out that its government was presbyterian. Laurentius has many faults to find with it. But neither he nor any subsequent controversialist ever impugned its church government as defective, which they undoubtedly would have done had it been presbyterian. This letter then proceeds: "When the Apostolic See, according to the universal custom which it has followed elsewhere, sent us to these western parts to preach to pagan nations, we came into this island which is called Britain without possessing any previous knowledge of its inhabitants. We held both the Britons and the Scots in great esteem for sanctity, believing that they had proceeded according to the customs of the universal church; but becoming acquainted with the errors of the Britons, we thought the Scots had been better; but we have been informed by Bishop Dagan coming into this aforesaid island, and by the Abbat Columbanus in France, that the Scots in no way differ from the Britons in behaviour; for Bishop Dagan coming to us not only refused to eat with us, but even to take his repast in the same house where we were entertained."

It is quite clear from this epistle that hostility and

separation between the Roman and the Irish party were bitter, clear, and distinct when an Irish bishop would not even eat in the same house or beneath the same roof as his Roman opponents. Yet the Roman party soon made extensive conquests in Ireland. Ireland from its earliest history had been divided into two great sections, separated broadly by that curious chain of sandhills which takes its rise at the Green Hills near Tallaght and terminates at Galway Bay. The southern half of Ireland was of course very conveniently situated for intercourse with southern England and with France. Harbours like Cork and Waterford and Wexford offered abundant opportunities for intercourse with the Continent, of which the monks largely availed themselves. This continental intercourse helped rapidly to undermine the old Irish customs. Pilgrimages to Rome became the fashion, and Rome soon gained the affections of the Munstermen, while then, as still, the heart of Ulster remained sternly anti-papal. It is easy to see how it was so. The untutored Irish, accustomed to their own humble homes, crossed the Bay of Biscay, and there came into contact with the Roman Church in all its majesty. They beheld its liturgical service developed by the genius of a Gregory the Great, its magnificent churches, its hierarchy ever growing in power and dignity, and dominating the rough and rude though powerful princes of that age, and then, contrasting their own mean circumstances at home, they were prepared to hear and to acquiesce in the argument of a Pope Honorius when he wrote to these Munstermen, as he did about the year 634, "exhorting them not to think their small number placed in the utmost border of the earth wiser than all the ancient and modern churches of Christ throughout the world;

and not to celebrate a different Easter contrary to the Paschal calculation and the synodical decrees of all the bishops upon earth." Active negotiations now were set on foot between Rome and Munster. The principal agent in this transaction was St. Laserian, Abbat or Bishop of Old Leighlin, where to this day the old cathedral marks the site of his seventh-century monastery.[1] He was one of those Irishmen who had travelled to Rome and been seduced by its charms from allegiance to his national rite. He is said to have been ordained priest at Rome by Gregory the Great, and bishop some thirty years later by Pope Honorius, who sent him as his deputy to bring the Irish into submission. He called a synod for this purpose, but was defeated for a time by the interposition of St. Fintan, Abbat of Taghmon, near Wexford, the most famous saint of that time. Fintan was an Ulster man, an adherent of the Columban order, and a thorough Irishman, opposed to all foreign notions and interference. Fintan's action was characteristic. It reminds us of St. Patrick on Tara. He challenged Laserian to the proof, and offered him a threefold choice. "You have three options given you, O Laserian. Let two books, one of the old order, another of the new, be cast into the fire, and let us see which of them will escape from the flames; or, let two monks, one of yours and another of mine, be shut up in the same house, and let the house be set on fire, and we shall see which of them will escape unburnt. Or let us both go to the sepulchre of a dead monk and raise him up to life, and he will tell us which order we ought to observe in the celebra-

---

[1] See art. "Laserian," in *Dict. Christ. Biog.*, vol. iii., p. 625; Ussher's Works, ed. Elrington, iv., p. 342, vi., pp. 503—505, 604, 605.

tion of Easter." All of which proposals the Roman deputy declined, on the ground that Fintan's holiness was so well established that if he prayed " that yonder mount," pointing to the cliffs of the neighbouring Slieve Margy, " were to change places with this white field," pointing to the site of Old Leighlin, " God would at once grant the request."[1]

But notwithstanding all opposition Rome rapidly gained ground in the south, till at last the whole province yielded obedience. We have a historic document of the most clear and satisfactory character, which certifies us of this fact, and at the same time illustrates the state of learning and the intercourse with Rome and the Continent, as then existing in the Church of Ireland. That document is the letter of St. Cummian[2] to Segienus, Abbat of the Columban monastery of Iona. The Columban monks and monasteries were the great opponents of Rome, and the supporters of the Irish Easter. Cummian had been trained as a Columban monk in their celebrated monastery at Durrow, in the Queen's County. He now joined the Roman party, and sent an epistle, preserved for us by Ussher,[3] which is a wonderful monument of Irish learning in that age, and at the same time sheds most important historical light on the events of the time. The epistle begins by an apology on Cummian's part for daring

---

[1] See Ussher's Works, ed. Elrington, t. vi., p. 504, where this story is told.
[2] See "Cummian" in *Dict. Christ. Biog.*, i., p. 723. The name in various forms was very common in ancient Ireland (see "Cumin" in *Dict. Christ. Biog.*) Mr. Bradshaw attributes the collection of Irish Canons called Hibernensis, to an abbat Cummian, of the south-east of Ireland, living early in the eighth century (see Wasserschleben's *Irische Kanonensammlung*, zweite Aufl., Einleit., S. lxxii.)
[3] *Sylloge*, ep. xi., Works, ed. Elrington. iv., pp. 432—444.

to differ from the Abbat of Iona. "What I have here to say in defence of my conduct I do not presume to thrust upon the notice of your holiness in an offensive manner, but I desire that you should as a father accept of my apology; for I call God as a record upon my soul that it is not from disrespect towards you, nor from a conceit of my own moral wisdom, regardless of what others may think, that I have not adopted the mode of celebrating Easter which is used by other sensible men." He then proceeds to discuss the question from the scriptural point of view, beginning with the first institution of the Paschal feast in Exodus. In doing so he quotes commentators like Jerome and Origen. Then he proceeds to later authorities and the views of the Fathers, where he discusses the calendars of the Macedonians, Egyptians, and Hebrews, the opinions of Augustine, Cyprian, Cyril, Pachomius, the head and reformer of Egyptian monasticism, and of Gregory the Great, whom he reverenced most of all, and describes as one "qui etsi post omnes scripsit, tamen est merito omnibus præferendus." He refers to the views of ancient Irish saints which he had investigated during the previous twelve months. He quotes St. Patrick as "Sanctus Patricius noster papa." He mentions names that are now regarded as shadows or myths; Ailbe of Emly, Kieran of Clonmacnois, and Brendan of Clonfert. He balances the decrees of Councils like those of Nicæa and of Arles, and sums up his case very neatly and very epigrammatically by asking, "Quid autem pravius sentiri potest de Ecclesia matre, quam si dicamus, Roma errat, Hierosolyma errat, Alexandria errat, Antiochia errat, totus mundus errat, soli tantum Scoti et Britones rectum sapiunt?" (What can be thought worse concerning the Church, our mother, than

## THE PASCHAL CONTROVERSY. 161

that we should say Rome errs, Jerusalem errs, Alexandria errs, Antioch errs, the whole world errs; the Scots and Britons alone know what is right?) This letter is well worth study. It bears the most interesting notes of time and of historical truth evident upon its face. It repeats the very language of Pope Honorius' letter, as described by Bede. It ridicules the claim of the Celts to set up for themselves, "being but an eruption on the very chin of the world." It mentions an embassy sent to Rome some three years before on this point, and finally notices a circumstance which completely establishes its own authenticity. Cummian points out that the Irish deputies found during their stay at Rome that the Roman Easter was divided by a whole month from the feast celebrated by the Irish Church, which happened in the year 631, when Easter fell on March 24th at Rome and on April 21st in Ireland.

Munster yielded to the Roman customs within the first half of the seventh century, though no formal Roman connection or supremacy was thereby established. But a much harder struggle remained. More than half a century was yet to elapse before the Columban monasteries and northern Ireland would consent to abandon their ancient usages. To their subjugation the Roman party now bent every effort. The point round which the battle first raged was the Irish mission in the north of England. Aidan at Lindisfarne had inaugurated that great work about the year 635, when the Roman party had already gained the victory in southern Ireland. But what the Columban party lost in one direction they gained in another, and soon the Northumbrian kingdom acknowledged the sway of the Cross through St. Aidan's labours, while his friends and disciples Finan and Cedd and Diuma pushed the borders of the Irish Church far down into the Midland Counties (Bede, Bk. iii., ch. 21).[1] During St. Aidan's life the controversy concerning Easter was not raised. The Roman party had quite enough to do to hold its own in the south, leaving the Columban party to pursue in quietness the work of northern evangelisation. But they soon came into contact. Just as Russia and England are daily drawing closer to each other's boundary limit in Central Asia, so during the middle of the seventh century Rome and Iona drew daily closer to each other in central England. The contest between them must be therefore settled. The crisis came, as far as England was concerned, in 664. That year was marked by a celebrated conference held at Whitby between the Roman and the Irish parties. St. Aidan and his successor St. Finan had been allowed to celebrate the Irish Easter, and to retain Irish customs in northern England.[2] But now great inconvenience was ensuing. The Roman party too was cleverly utilizing an agency which they still manage with great effect. Mixed marriages were playing into their hands. The Northumbrian King Oswy had married a Queen Eanfled[3] who had been converted to the Roman view in Kent, and had imported Roman clergy to act as her private chaplains. Great trouble soon followed. Nothing brings a man round quicker than to find all his

---

[1] I lately heard of an English ecclesiastic, holding a high official position, who when visiting Dublin scoffed at the idea of England owing any of its Christianity to Irish missionaries. It is thus evident that a man may gain great ecclesiastical promotion in the English Church and yet never have opened his Bede.

[2] See art. "Finan" (7) in *Dict. Christ. Biog.*, t. ii., p. 516.

[3] See art. "Eanfled" (2) in *Dict. Christ. Biog.*, t. ii., p. 15.

domestic arrangements upset by a difference with his wife. Thus it was with Oswy. He held to the Irish custom of Easter, but one year he found himself in an ugly predicament. The king had ended his fast of Lent and was celebrating his Easter, while the queen, who calculated with the Romans, was still fasting and observing the lengthened services of Palm Sunday and of Passion Week; and you may be sure she felt bound, as an ardent Roman, to bring Oswy round to a more catholic frame of mind, by putting him on the same meagre allowance she was herself enjoying in that penitential season. An appeal to the dinner table is usually very effective, so King Oswy determined to bring the contending parties to an interview, and to have the question threshed out. You can see the debate fully reported in Bede, Bk. iii., ch. 25. The speeches are very interesting. The conference was held in a monastery ruled by the royal Abbess St. Hilda, where the king's own daughter had taken the veil.[1] King Oswy presided, like Constantine of old at Nice, and listened attentively to the speeches, though all his prejudices were with his own bishop Colman and the Irish clergy. The priest Wilfrid for the Roman party urged the authority of the Roman See founded by SS. Peter and Paul, and of the Universal Church. Colman, the Irish champion, defended himself by the example of St. John, whose authority he pleaded, and of St. Columba. The Roman divines scorned St. Columba however. Listen to the concluding words of Wilfrid's speech : "As for you and your companions, you certainly sin if having heard the decrees of the Apostolic See and of the Universal Church you refuse to follow them ; for though your fathers were holy, do

---

[1] See art. "Hilda" in *Dict. Christ. Biog.*, t. iii., p. 77.

you think their small number, in a corner of the remotest island, is to be preferred before the Universal Church of Christ? And if that Columba of yours was a holy man and powerful in miracles, yet, could he be preferred before the most blessed Prince of the Apostles, to whom our Lord said, 'Thou art Peter, and upon this rock I will build My Church, and the gates of hell shall not prevail against it; and to thee I will give the keys of the kingdom of heaven'?" This last was a triumphant stroke. When Wilfrid had spoken thus the king said, "Is it true, Colman, that these words were spoken to· Peter by our Lord?" He answered, "It is true, O king." Then said Oswy, "Can you show that any such power was given to your Columba?" Colman answered "None." "Then," replied the king, "Peter is the doorkeeper, whom I will not contradict, but obey in all things his decrees, lest when I come to the gates of the kingdom of heaven there should be none to open them, he being my adversary who is proved to bear the keys." Whereupon the assembly was dismissed, and the hopes of the Irish party vanished for ever in England. The struggle, however, was prolonged in Ireland and Scotland for half a century longer. The Columban order died hard. Colman resigned his bishopric at Lindisfarne, but he retired into Ireland, and sought its western shores.[1] He established with his adherents, partly English and partly Irish, a monastery on the island of Inisbofin, off the coast of Mayo. Colman, however, afforded a curious example, showing the perpetuity of national tastes, customs, and affinities, for Bede tells us that the Saxons and Celts, though agreeing in opinion, could not live there in peace and unity. Listen to Bede's words:

---

[1] See art. "Colman" (23) in *Dict. Christ. Biog.*, t. i., 599.

"Arriving at Innisbofin, he built a monastery, and placed in it the monks of both nations, who not agreeing among themselves by reason that the Scots in the summer season, when the harvest was to be brought in, leaving the monastery, wandered about through places with which they were acquainted, but returned again the next winter and would have what the English had provided to be in common."[1] So he removed the English monks, and placed them in a new monastery called Mayo, which long continued to be the site of a Saxon monastic settlement in the extreme west. But all resistance was in vain. The Roman view gained every day fresh accessions. Every year saw the adherents of the Columban rite become fewer and fewer, till at last the monks of Iona itself yielded to the persuasions of St. Egbert in the year 716, and consented to celebrate Easter after the universal rule. But though the Celtic Church by the beginning of the eighth century had thus consented to the universal practice of the Church both east and west alike, this consent involved no submission upon other matters to the supremacy of the See of Rome. Nay, rather we shall see hereafter that down to the twelfth century the Celtic Church differed from Rome on very important questions, which indeed formed a pretext for the conquest of this country by the Normans.[2]

---

[1] The annual migrations of Mayo harvest-men, as they are called, is thus shown to have a very respectable antiquity.

[2] The supremacy of Rome over Ireland would doubtless have been established much sooner but for the Danish invasions. The pagan Danes cut Ireland off from the Continent just as, three centuries earlier, the Saxon irruption completely isolated the British Islands. Rome in both cases gained access through the invaders. *Cf.* above, p. 50, note [2].

# LECTURE IX.

## *IRELAND AND THE EAST.*

THE distinguishing feature of the Celtic or Irish Church in the earliest centuries was its monastic character. This may strike you as strangely at variance with notions popular in some circles. With many it is a favourite idea that St. Patrick, St. Columba, and the other worthies who adorned the early days of Irish Christianity were Protestants of the most approved modern fashion, while with others these Irish saints were Roman Catholics of the most devout and obedient kind. Now in my opinion these early Irish Christians were neither Protestants nor Roman Catholics. Many of their practices and doctrines would horrify an ordinary Protestant; others of them would scandalize the ordinary Roman Catholic. Their communion in both kinds would be a stumbling-block to the latter, while their monastic and ascetic practices would be a rock of offence to the former.

I propose to take this one point, the monasticism of the early Irish Church, and thoroughly to investigate it; for I have some ideas about it which, as I hope to prove, are based upon the most solid foundations, and are supported by the latest investigations in very various branches. There is, I repeat, then, no fact more patent on the face of history than this—the early Irish Church was thoroughly monastic. Monasticism pervaded every department of the Church, and was the secret of its rapid success. The question then naturally arises, how did monasticism arrive in Ireland? To answer this I must first of all explain how monasticism arose in the Catholic Church of Christ. The early Church was not monastic. Ascetic practices and ascetic lives found place in the Church from the beginning. The life of a James the Just struck the early Jews from its ascetic devotion. He never used the bath, as Eusebius tells us; while his knees were worn hard and flat as a camel's, from his protracted prayers. Lives pledged to celibacy, too, found a place in the earliest Church organisation. The widows mentioned in the Epistles to Timothy were plainly analogous to a band of deaconesses, or sisters of mature years. But there was no separation from common life, with its every day duties, in any of these cases. The introduction of the monastic life arose first about the close of the third or beginning of the fourth century in Egypt and Syria. It arose quite naturally. The Decian persecution in the middle of the third, the Diocletian at the beginning of the fourth, drove vast numbers of Christians into the deserts of Egypt. There they learned the sweetness and consolation of a solitary life devoted to the one object of saving their own souls. The climate too made them the more inclined to such a career. Extreme heat always makes men inclined to meditation and disinclined to active exertion. It has always seemed to me a natural result of the climate that the Buddhists of the East make their heaven to consist in Nirvana, absorption into the one absolute Being, and consequent cessation of all individuality and individual effort. At any rate, as a historical fact, it is only after the Diocletian persecution and the triumph of

Christianity under Constantine that the monks and monasticism emerge distinctly upon the field of history.[1] However, they rapidly grew and extended themselves in every direction. Athanasius patronized and utilized them. Jerome joined them, and as the result, before the fourth century terminated monastic institutions had spread to the most distant regions of Gaul, Arabia, or Persia. Egypt, however, as it was the original seat, so it continued to be the model and pattern of every true monastery and for all true monks.

The first monks soon divided themselves into two classes. One kind led a solitary or anchorite life; these were the original monks. The others united themselves in communities, and lived the cœnobite or common life under the rule of an abbat. The earliest convent or monastery was established near the Nitrian lakes, some forty or fifty miles from Cairo. It will give you some idea of the fixity and perpetuity which mark the East and eastern character when I tell you that this earliest monastery,—the pattern after which every monastic society, eastern or western, those of Basil, Benedict, Dominic, or Francis, have been formed —is still in existence, and still, after fifteen hundred years, preserves the same rule and the same manner

---

[1] See the article "Monastery" in the *Dictionary of Christian Antiquity*. I would be disposed to date the origin of monasticism a little earlier than the writer of the first section of that article. The Decian persecution conjoined with the influence of Jewish monastic societies must have developed the system during the latter half of the third century. This alone can explain its sudden up-growth in every direction during the first half of the fourth century. Buddhist ideas and influences may also have been at work. See my article on "Manicheism" in the *Dict. Christ. Biog.*, t. iii., and Baur's *Das Manichäische Religions System*, S. 334—481 (Tübingen: 1831). Pagan monks, too, existed in Egypt before Christian times.

of life.[1] Now let us take a considerable step forward. One of the earliest offshoots from Egyptian monasticism was planted in Gaul. The communication between Marseilles and Alexandria was as vigorous then as now. Christians of the Eastern rite abounded in Marseilles and all along the Rhone, and naturally looked to Egypt far more than to Rome as their spiritual teacher. In fact, monasticism for long enough found no favour, among the men at least, in Rome. St. Jerome, the great advocate of monasticism, had to fly from Rome because the men were so enraged against him on account of his success in persuading the best-looking and richest ladies to become nuns.[2] But it was otherwise in France. In southern Gaul the monastery of Lerins was founded, between which and Syria and Egypt a very active intercourse was constantly maintained. Perhaps, however, the liveliest picture of the constant communication which existed between Marseilles and Egypt will be found in two circumstances which I shall now relate.

One of the best known writers of the time of St. Patrick, the beginning of the fifth century, was John Cassian. His life was a varied one. He was educated in Bethlehem, trained among the monks of Syria and Egypt, and ended his life in southern Gaul, where he helped to propagate and develop his monastic views. For the first forty years of the fifth century he was one of the most influential men in that district. He wrote a book called the *Collations of the Monks*, wherein you will find a picture of the sayings, doings, and daily life of

---

[1] A good account of it will be found in Curzon's *Monasteries of the Levant*.
[2] See art. "Hieronymus" in Smith's *Dict. Christ. Biog.*, t. iii., p. 34.

the Nitrian ascetics of that day held up as a model for the monks of St. Patrick's time. Now tradition represents St. Patrick as connected with Lerins and living for many years in the district where John Cassian was thus teaching the laws and practices of Egyptian monasticism. In fact, Cassian made Egypt so well known in France that whenever a bishop or presbyter desired a period for spiritual retreat and refreshment he retired to Egypt, to seek in Nitria the development of his higher spiritual life.

Here, then, is one channel through which the ideas of the East may have passed over to the extremest West.[1] Take another case. It has often astonished me that no one has ever translated the letters of St. Jerome. The letters of St. Augustine have been translated, and are in many parts very entertaining reading, but they are nothing in point of living interest when compared with St. Jerome's.[2] These letters illustrate life about the year 400 as nothing else can. They show us, for instance, what education then was, what clerical life consisted in; they tell us of modes and fashions, and they teach us how vigorous and constant was the communication at that same period between the most distant parts of the Roman empire. We are apt to think of the fifth century as a time when there was very little travel, and when most certainly the East and West—Ireland, England,

---

[1] See the articles on "Cassianus and Palladius" in the *Dict. Christ. Biog.* The monastic works of Cassian and Palladius seem to have been well known in Ireland in the seventh century. Professor Atkinson of Trinity College has shown me some mediæval Irish homilies which he is publishing, full of references and names drawn from them.

[2] This want will soon be supplied, as Dr. Schaff of New York proposes to include Jerome's letters in a library of patristic translations, the first volume of which will appear this autumn.

Gaul, and Palestine—were much more widely and completely separated than now, when steam has practically annihilated time and space. And yet such an idea is very mistaken. There was a most lively intercourse existing between these regions, a constant Church correspondence kept up between them, and the most intense and vivid interest maintained by the Gallic and Syrian churches in the minutest details of their respective histories. Mark now how this happened. St. Jerome at Bethlehem was the centre of this intercourse. His position in the Christian world in the beginning of the fifth century can only be compared to, but was not at all equalled by, that of John Calvin at the time of the Reformation. Men from the most distant parts consulted him. Bishops of highest renown for sanctity and learning, like St. Augustine and Exuperius of Toulouse in southern France, deferred to his authority. The keen interest he took in the churches of Gaul, and the intimate knowledge he possessed of the most petty local details and religious gossip therein, can only be understood by one who has studied his very abusive treatise against Vigilantius or his correspondence with Exuperius.[1] Let me give you a specimen. Vigilantius was a Gallic divine of that period. He was reported to Jerome as an opponent of relics, the cultus of the saints, and the celibacy of the clergy, all of which doctrines Jerome held very dear. Jerome, therefore, launched a treatise against him filled with the most unfounded and foul-mouthed abuse. Jerome knew everything about Vigilantius just as well as if he were living in Gaul. He reviles him for his birth. Four hundred years before, his

---

[1] See the articles "Hieronymus," "Exuperius," and "Vigilantius" in the *Dictionary of Christian Biography*.

ancestors had been brigands conquered by Pompey. His father had been an innkeeper,—none of the honestest, too, as Jerome declares. Vigilantius himself—like George Whitefield in the last century—had drawn the wine and watered it well in his earlier days. Who could expect sound doctrine from this Pyrenean brigand and cheat? But how, it may be asked, was this correspondence carried on when there was no postal system? Here it was that the organization of monasticism supplied a want.[1] Jerome's letters tell us the very name of his postman. He was a monk named Sysinnius. He was perpetually on the road between Marseilles and Bethlehem. Again and again does Jerome mention his coming and his going. His appearance must indeed have been the great excitement of life at Bethlehem. Travelling probably *viâ* Sardinia, Rome, Greece, and the islands of the Adriatic, he gathered up all kinds of clerical news on the way—a piece of conduct on his part which seems to have had its usual results. As a tale-bearer, he not only revealed secrets, but also separated chief friends, and this monk Sysinnius with his gossip seems to have been the original cause of the celebrated quarrel between Augustine and Jerome.[2]

But it was not only with Palestine and the Holy Places that the clergy and Church of Gaul kept up an intercourse. Sysinnius always pressed on from Bethlehem to the monasteries of Egypt to visit the solitaries of Nitria and the Thebaid, bearing with him

---

[1] This is abundantly evident from the correspondence of Augustine and Jerome. See Letters of St. Augustine, i., 129, 255, in Dod's edition of St. Augustine (T. and T. Clark, Edinb., 1872).

[2] See Jerome's letter to Augustine, in *Letters* of S. August., Clark's trans., i., 255, ep. lxviii.

the alms of the faithful in France. I have enlarged upon this point to impress upon you how close and intimate was the contact between Syria and France when Christianity passed over from France to Ireland. About the year 450 Syrian monasticism was flourishing in southern Gaul, and the Syrian language and Syrian practices and Syrian colonies continued to flourish there for two centuries later. The extent to which Syrian customs prevailed, and the Syrian language and even the Assyrian language were spoken in Gaul during the sixth and seventh centuries, can only be appreciated by those who have studied the original authorities for the Merovingian period. Let me give you a few specimens illustrating this point. In A.D. 589 the council of Narbonne passed a decree for the observance of the Lord's Day. On that occasion it included within its scope the Goths, Romans, Syrians, Greeks, and Jews living in Narbonne. In the fifth century again Sidonius Apollinaris records the epitaph raised over a St. Abraham, who was born on the Euphrates, was a sufferer in the persecution raised against the Persian Christians by King Isdegerdes, then migrated to France and died abbat of a monastery there. Here was a veritable eastern monk flourishing in France. At Treves again, in eastern Gaul, Chaldean and Syrian inscriptions have been found dating from the same period, while an interesting incident in the life of an Irish saint shows us Ireland and Syria coming into immediate contact. St. Columbanus, about the year 600, as I have shown in a previous ecture, came into deadly conflict with the ruling sovereign of Burgundy. The sovereign expelled him, and ordered the audacious Irishman back to his own wild island. Columbanus was entrusted to a guard whose duty it was to convey him to the mouth of the Loire, whence vessels sailed to Ireland. They executed their mission very faithfully but very roughly. St. Columbanus tells us they allowed no one to speak to him, and that the only sympathy he met with was from a Syrian woman at Orleans, who gave him food when well-nigh starving, saying, "I am a stranger like yourself, and come from the distant sun of the east, and my husband is of the same race of the Syrians." Facts like these have only come to light of late years, principally through the labours of the eminent French scholar and archæologist, Le Blant;[1] yet it is they alone which will explain many oriental ideas, the existence of which in the west has puzzled historical students. They explain, for instance, the wild fantastic orientalism of the Albigenses and Manicheans seated round Toulouse in the Middle Ages. They explain, too, some peculiarities of the Celtic Church and of Celtic monasticism. In Gaul, as I have just said, Syrian and Eastern monasticism was flourishing when Christianity passed over to Ireland. In Irish monasticism we should therefore expect to find traces of Syrian and Oriental practices, and such, I believe, we do find in the constitution, the customs, the learning, the art, and the architecture of the early Celtic Church.

Some peculiarities of Irish monasticism, for instance, can only be explained by a reference to Syrian ideas and customs.

You have all heard of Simeon Stylites. Tennyson has made him celebrated, even were he not already so, in that poem where he introduces him, saying,

"Altho' I be the basest of mankind,
From scalp to sole one slough and crust of sin,

---

[1] See on this point Le Blant, *Inscript. Chrét. de la Gaule*,

Unfit for earth, unfit for heaven, scarce meet
For troops of devils, mad with blasphemy,
I will not cease to grasp the hope I hold
Of saintdom, and to clamour, mourn, and sob,
Battering the gates of heaven with storms of prayer,
Have mercy, Lord, and take away my sin."

Simeon Stylites is no mythical character. His life and career are thoroughly historical. His life was, however, more like that of an Indian fakir than of a Christian saint.[1] Let me briefly sketch it. Simeon was a Syrian by birth. He joined a monastery about the year 400, while yet a very young man, and at once pushed asceticism to its extremest limits. He dug a hole in the garden of the monastery, where he secluded himself for a whole summer, exposed to the heat by day, and to the dews and cold by night. His ascetic abstinence was so extreme that the monks requested the abbat to expel him, as his ultra-piety made the others feel uncomfortable. He then joined another monastery. Here he simply asked for a cell wherein he might be walled up or immured without food the whole of Lent. The monk to whom the work of walling up was entrusted kindly left with him a few loaves and a jug of water. When the cell was opened at the end of Lent, Simeon was found entranced in devotion and the food untasted. Simeon soon after separated himself from monasteries and monastic life, and became an anchorite. He immured or enclosed himself in a cell, depending for subsistence on the chance kindness of the traveller. But

---

Diss. 211, 225, 557, 613. I have discussed this point at some length in two articles on "Greek and Latin Christian inscriptions," in the *Contemp. Review* for June 1880 and January 1881.

[1] See the art. "Simeon Stylites" (1) in the *Dict. Christ. Biog.*, t. iv., or S. E. Assemani, *AA. MM.*, t. ii., where his life is given in full.

the fame of such sanctity could not be hid. Disciples gathered round him and established a monastery under his direction. Simeon, however, must live above the world if he could not live hidden from it. So he caused the cell, in which he was immured, to be raised first a few feet, then by degrees higher and higher, till at last the enclosed cell rested on the top of a pillar sixty feet high. I may just mention that the perfect authenticity of this story has been established within the last few years, as the ruins of the church of St. Simeon and the remains of this very pillar have been discovered by the Count De Vogüé, in Northern Syria, some miles from the site of Antioch.[1] I have described Simeon's life and state, not with a view of dwelling on his pillar life. Pillar saints were not very numerous among ancient ascetics. But I have introduced him because he was so long an enclosed anchorite. Anchorites of this description were frequent and numerous among Eastern Christians. There was one of them in Constantinople about the year 431, the time of the Nestorian controversy, Dalmatius by name, whose influence gained the day for orthodoxy as against heresy.[2] He was of such weight that so great a man as Cyril, Patriarch of Alexandria, made every effort to win him over to his side. And what gave him his influence? It was simply this. He had been for fifty years an enclosed anchorite, and during that time had never left his cell. The writings of Cassian and Palladius teem with instances of hermits who made it a matter of conscience

---

[1] See De Vogüé's *Architecture of Central Syria*, t. i., pp. 141—153 (Paris: 1877). The plates are simply magnificent.
[2] The life of Dalmatius will be found in Banduri's *Imperium Orientale*, t. ii; see Neander, *H.E.*, Bohn's ed., iv., 164, 165; art. "Dalmatius" (4) in *Dict. Christ. Biog.*

never to leave their cells even to receive the Holy Communion. Some of them, therefore, never communicated sometimes for half a century.[1] Now this Anchorite institution was a peculiar mark of Eastern monasticism. Western monasticism, as taught by Benedict, was much more practical. It devoted its efforts to agriculture, study, teaching, preaching. The monks of St. Benedict were indeed the great civilisers of the Middle Ages. It is to them we owe the arts of agriculture as well as the remains of Christian and classical antiquity we still possess.[2]

But come to Ireland, and there we find the enclosed anchorite flourishing side by side with the agricultural or learned and artistic monk. We have the proofs of this before our eyes, and in our own neighbourhood. You have all heard of St. Doulough's church. It is situated within a few miles of this spot, and there you can find a connecting link between Ireland and the

---

[1] See also Cotelerii *Monumenta Ecclesiæ Græcæ*, which contains some extraordinary instances of this kind.

[2] The Anchorite life sprang up in Egypt. Cassian and Palladius both recommended retirement to a "desert" as the highest type of the spiritual life. I cannot delay to prove this, but any one who will refer to the following passages will see abundant demonstration thereof. Cassian's *Collations*, xi., 2, xviii., 4, 6, 9, 10, xxiv., 3, 4, 19; *Institutes*, v., 36; Migne's *Pat. Lat.*, t. xlix; *Vitæ Patrum*, lib. i., Vit S. Onuphrii Eremitæ, and iv., 15, 36 in Migne, *Pat. Lat.*, tt. lxxiii., lxxiv. The *Vitæ PP.* prescribe the minutest rules for Anchorite dress, including a sheepskin, their only protection from the cold. The Anchorite life passed from Egypt to Gaul, where it abundantly flourished from the fifth to the eighth centuries (see Mabillon, *AA. SS. Ord. S. Bened.*, ii., 130, 133, v., 36). In the earliest ages the Anchorites always lived in a "desert," whether in Egypt, France, or Ireland (see next note). The Roman Church modified this custom, and attached the Anchorites to churches and communities, till at last, as I notice below, enclosed anchorites were found in the middle of the city of Dublin. The father of the Anchorite life compared a hermit living near a town to a fish out of water (Soz., *H. E.*, i., 13).

far-distant Syria. St. Doulough's church dates from about the year 1200. It was not always a parish church as it is now. It was originally the cell of a recluse or anchorite like St. Simeon Stylites. Anchorites of this kind were imported from Syria to Gaul and from Gaul to Ireland, where this institution flourished in greatest vigour, because it just fell in with that tendency to extremes which ever marks the Celtic race.

Let me explain about St. Doulough's. Just as Simeon Stylites walled himself up in a cell, separated himself from all human intercourse, so did the Celtic anchorites from the year 600 down to the year 1700. The earliest monastery in Iona had its anohorite who lived secluded in a separate cell, and the name of a bay in Iona still bears witness to this fact. This was about the year 600. To this day there are the remains of such anchorite cells in the ruined Columban monasteries of the west of Scotland. In fact, from the earliest times the anchorite system formed an essential part of Celtic monasticism; an interesting proof of which still exists in the nomenclature and topography of Ireland. One of the commonest names of townlands and parishes in this country is Disert, or Desert. We have, to take a few instances, Desertmartin in Londonderry, Desertserges, a parish in Cork; Killadysert in Clare, Disert-Nuadhan (Nooan) or Eastersnow near Boyle, Disert the name of a parish in Westmeath. This word Disert is a corruption of the Latin word Desertum or Desert, and signifies the solitary place where the anchorite took up his abode, free from all distracting and secular influences. Thus Desertmartin was Martin's Desert. Desertserges was Saerghus's desert, Desert Ocnghus in Limerick was the desert of

Oenghus, the celebrated Culdee of Tallaght.[1] Now this literally corresponds to the account given us by Evagrius, an ecclesiastical historian of the fifth century, when writing of the monks of his time. Thus, in book i., cap. 21, he describes the different classes of ascetics: "the Cœnobites, who lived in common; the Boskoi, or grazers, who cast off all clothes save the merest shred, and fed upon grass; and, thirdly, a class which individually seclude themselves in chambers of so limited a height and width that they can neither stand upright nor lie down at ease, confining their existence to dens and caves of the earth, as says the Apostle. Some, too, take up their dwelling with the wild beasts, and in untracked recesses of the ground, and thus offer their supplications to God." Now, if you will turn to

---

[1] Ussher's opp., ed. Elrington., t. vi., p. 478, *Brit. Eccles. Antiq.*, cap. xvii., quoting an ancient catalogue, notices as a peculiarity of the third order of Irish saints that they dwelt "in desertis locis et oleribus et aqua et eleemosynis fidelium vivebant." In fact, to one reading the lives of the early Irish saints, no circumstance occurs oftener than mention of their departure in search of a desert; an expression which indicates their abandonment of a community in favour of the anchorite or hermit life. In Reeves' *Eccles. Antiq.* the names Disert and Desert often occur, generally in connection with the great monasteries of Connor and Down, which formed the germs of the dioceses so called. The Irish monasteries usually had such a desert or solitude for anchorites connected with them. There were deserts and anchorite residences at Iona, Bobbio, and at Lindisfarne, where St. Cuthbert died in the desert (Bede, *H. E.*, iv., 27-29). Bishop Reeves in his *Adamnan*, additional notes, p. 366, gives other instances; see also Joyce's *Irish Names*, p. 313. The custom was kept up after the English conquest by the Roman orders which were then introduced, but in a modified shape, as I showed in the last note. In Sweetman's *Calendars of Documents belonging to the XIIth, XIIIth, and XIVth centuries* we find frequent notices of payments to the anchorites or recluses connected with the great conventual establishments of Dublin, St. Mary's Abbey, the Priory of the Holy Trinity, etc.; e.g., *Cal. Doc.*, 1252-1284, pp. 150, 181, 317. The art. "Hermits" in the *Dictionary of Christian Antiquities* may also be consulted.

Dr. Reeves' Memoir on St. Doulough's, or visit St. Doulough's church for yourselves, you will find the fittest commentary on the text of Evagrius. St. Doulough's church was originally an anchorite's residence. It comprises seven apartments, and three stone staircases. The most curious portion is a small cell or chamber at the west end, where the original anchorites lived and in which they were buried. It was the rule, in fact, for the anchorite to be buried in his cell. One of the most celebrated Irish scholars and writers of the Middle Ages was Marianus Scotus of Maintz. He was an enclosed anchorite, and tells us himself that he daily said mass standing on the grave of his predecessor, and with his own grave open beside him.[1] The institution of anchorites flourished to such an extent that a rule was drawn out for them which gives the details of their existence, many of which can be traced in the construction of St. Doulough's. Let me quote some of it. "An anchorite's cell should be built of stone, twelve feet long, and twelve broad. It should have three windows, one facing the choir through which he may receive the Body of Christ, another on the opposite side through

---

[1] Colgan, *AA. SS.*, p. 205. "Anno 1043 Amnuchadus Scotus et inclusus obiit 3. cal. Febr. In monasterio Fuldensi super ejus sepulcrum visa sunt lumina et psalmodia audita; super quem ego Marianus Scotus decem annis inclusus super pedes ejus stans, quotidie missas cantavi." In the story of Pelagia, the converted actress of Antioch, told by the Deacon James, ed. H. Usener, Bonn, 1879, p. 14, chap. xiv., we read a description of an anchorite's cell on the Mount of Olives, which would exactly suit an Irish one. It had no door, and only one small window securely fastened. The exact words are, ὡς δὲ εἶδον τὴν κέλλαν ὅτι θύραν εἰσόδου οὐκ εἶχεν, ἀλλὰ πανταχόθεν περιπέφρακτο, μικρὰν δὲ μόνον μίαν θυρίδα εἶχεν καὶ αὕτη ὑπῆρχεν ἠσφαλισμένη· Pelagia's history was written in the fifth century. See Memoirs by Dr. Reeves on St. Doulough's Church and on Marianus Scotus (Dublin, 1860).

which he may receive his food, and a third for light. The window for food should be secured by a bolt and have a glazed lattice, to be opened and shut, because no one should be able to look in except as far as glass will allow, nor should the anchorite have a view out. He should be provided with three articles, a jar, a towel, and a cup. After tierce he is to lay the jar and cup outside the window and then close it. About noon he is to come over and see if his dinner be there. If it be, he is to sit at the window and eat and drink. When he has done, whatever remains is to be left outside for any one who may choose to remove it, and he is to take no thought for the morrow. But if it should happen that he has nothing for his dinner he is not to omit his accustomed thanks to God, though he is to remain without food till the following day. His garments are to be a gown and cap which he is to wear waking and sleeping. In winter he may, if the weather be severe, wear a woolly cloak, because he is not allowed to have any fire save what his candle produces."[1] Such was the type of individual for whom St. Doulough's was built, and who inhabited it till the Reformation. But the type was scattered all over Ireland.[2] Many of the cathedrals of Ireland had anchorite cells attached to

---

[1] See *Memoir of the Church of St. Duilech, commonly called St. Doulough's*, read before the Royal Irish Acad., April 11th, 1859, by Wm. Reeves, D.D., p. 9; Raderi *Bavaria Sacra*, t. iii., p. 117 (Monachii, 1704). The woolly cloak is a remnant of Egyptian customs. The only extra garment permitted to Egyptian anchorites was a sheepskin (μηλωτή); see *Vitæ Patrum*, iv., 15, in Migne, *Pat. Lat.*, t. lxxii., col. 818-825. St. Antony left his sheepskin by will to Serapion, Bishop of Thmuis, and friend of St. Athanasius; see " Serapion " in *Dict. Christ. Biog*.

[2] The word "anchorite," in various forms, enters into the composition of the names of several townlands. Thus, outside Athlone there is a hill and townland called Anchors-bower or Ankersbower. Mr. Hennessy tells me this is an evident corrup-

them; St. Canice's, at Kilkenny, and Cashel cathedral were notable instances. You have all heard too of the beehive cells of Ireland; they are found here and there on the mainland, but are most numerous on the islands off the west coast. These were all inhabited by enclosed anchorites, and correspond most accurately to the cells described by Evagrius, wherein their inhabitants could neither comfortably stand nor lie. But you might say to me, how possibly could such an institution be perpetuated through so long a period of time? Can it possibly be conceived that an Oriental custom should not only extend from Ireland to Syria, but maintain its existence through all the storms of the Middle Ages till the sixteenth or seventeenth century? To such an objection I would reply that modern research has conclusively proved that the Celtic race is endowed with a marvellous tenacity. Its race customs, its tribal organizations, its tales and traditions, all embody oriental ideas carried with them from the most distant East. The investigations of Dr. Whitley Stokes, for instance, have clearly shown that many of the popular tales and traditions—the folklore of Ireland—are identical with those of India. While, again, I can give you a proof of this tenacity in regard to this very institution of enclosed anchorites. Take up Sir Henry Piers' *History of the County Westmeath*, published by General Vallancey in the last century. Sir Henry Piers wrote it in the reign of King James II., and there you will find that so late as the year 1682 there existed at Fore, in the county Westmeath, an enclosed anchorite whom the worthy baronet carefully describes, without

---

tion for Anchorboher, the anchorite's road, and certainly the old road to the parish of Disert (Desertum) in Westmeath led over it.

the slightest idea that he was drawing the portrait and describing the condition of the last follower, the true lineal descendant of Simeon Stylites.[1]

You should remark, however, still further, that not only the constitution of the monastic system, but even the very form of the early Irish monasteries displayed their oriental origin. When we speak of an early Celtic monastery we must modify very considerably our ordinary conceptions. The usual notion of a monastery is that of a society united together in one building, under one common roof. Now, none of the Celtic monasteries were of this type. The monastery of Iona under St. Columba was a true Celtic monastery, and there every monk, from the abbat down, had his own cell, or hut of timber or wattles, where he lived. "We must not suppose," says Mr. Skene (ii., p. 57), "that the primitive Irish monastery at all resembled the elaborate stone structures which constituted the monastery of the Middle Ages. The primitive Celtic monastery was a very simple affair, and more resembled a rude village of wooden huts. We find from the Irish Life of Columba that when he went to the Monastery of Glasnevin, on the banks of the river Finglas, where no fewer than fifty scholars were assembled; their huts, or bothies, were by the water or river on the west, and there was a church on the east side." The type of the early Celtic monastery is to be sought not among the Latins, but among the Greeks and Orientals. Some of you will remember Charles Kingsley's vivid presenta-

---

[1] See also Harris' *Ware's Works*, ii., 134, 237, where a list of the celebrated anchorites of Ireland is given, with an account of the anchorite of Fore as he flourished in Ware's time; compare also Rev. J. Graves' *History of St. Canice's Cathedral*, p. 71. The Anker's Land is still the name of a townland at Fore. Ordnance Survey, *List of Townlands*, 1861.

tion of the wild, weird, yet devoted lives of the monks of the Egyptian Thebaid, leading a lonely existence in caves and cells planted high in the most inaccessible cliffs. Go to Mount Athos, that mountain of monasteries, and there you will find the same system still prevailing. Visit the most distant East; there the Laura of St. Sabas, founded in the fifth century and still flourishing near Jerusalem, and the monastery of Mosul, for fourteen hundred years the seat of the Eutychian primacy, are both of this type.[1] Then transport yourself to the shores of the county Sligo, and six miles off the coast you will find the island of Inismurray, where, safeguarded by the waves and storms of the Atlantic, stands the monastery of St. Molaise, organized and built on identically the same principle, a number of beehive cells surrounded by a cashel or fortification, and grouped round a central church. A visit to that distant island will be fruitful in many results; it will bring you in contact with the finest sea breezes in Europe; it will give you a glimpse of magnificent mountain scenery, the whole range of the Donegal, Sligo, and Mayo mountains lying exposed to view in all their stately grandeur. It will give you, too, a true idea of an eastern monastery, without putting you to the expense and danger of an Eastern tour; and it will enable you to realise, as otherwise you could not, what the appear-

---

[1] In the convent of St. Matthew at Mosul we find a fortified monastery of scattered huts or cells, "propter imminentes barbarorum invasiones, castelli perinde ac asceterii speciem præ se fert." *De Vita et Scriptis Aphraatis*, ed. Jac. Forget, p. 79 (Lovanii: 1882). The Jacobite Patriarchs there have always continued to be monastic bishops like the ancient Irish ones (see *l.c.*, pp. 65, 80, 87-103); Wright's *Cat. Syr. MSS.*, ii., 401, col. 2; Rich, *Residence in Koordistan*, ii., 73; and Le Quien, *Or. Christ.*, ii., 1559.

ance of Iona, Clonmacnois, and Glendalough must have been in the seventh and eighth centuries. Let me give you a brief description of it, taken from the narrative of a visit lately paid to it. I take my narrative from a Roman Catholic magazine, the *Irish Monthly*, for November 1883.[1] Having described the journey and the exquisite scenery, the tourist tells us of Innismurray itself, that it is an island about seven miles from the mainland, about midway between Sligo Bay and the Bay of Donegal. As seen from *terra firma*, it looks like a long horizontal tongue of land, well-raised above the water, and ending in a vertical bluff on the other side. It is quite impossible to get into it or out of it in rough weather, such are the huge waves that surge around its ironbound coasts, devoid of haven, or breakwater, or any shelter whatever. The island is of red sandstone, which passes through every shade, from pink to white. The first thing the tourist meets is the women's burial ground, surrounding the Lady Chapel. But the crowning glory of the island is the men's enclosure, which you next approach. Fancy a wall, originally about fifteen feet high,[2] and about ten broad, built of red sandstone slabs of moderate dimensions, and without cement, just the same as the surrounding cottages of the peasantry. This is the original cashel, or fortification; like the cashel, for instance, surrounding the churches and round tower at Glendalough. This cashel is circular, and encloses about half an acre of ground. Inside the cashel are found the famous

---

[1] See also Lord Dunraven's *Notes on Irish Arch.*, i., 46-54.
[2] See Reeves' *Eccles. Antiqq.*, p. 182. This height will illustrate Bede's description (*E. H.*, iv., 28) of St. Cuthbert's cell as surrounded by a rampart so high that the resident could see nothing but heaven above. See note on Celtic monastic cashels, on p. 117, and Wakeman's description of Innismurray in a late number of the *Irish Archæol. Jour.*

beehive-habitations and the primitive old chapels. The beehive-habitations that remain are seven in number, and all pretty much alike, except that one of them is quite diminutive. These beehive-habitations, or hermitages, like the cashel and churches, are built of red sandstone; the entrance is low and narrow, covered by one flag, tapering inwards and upwards. "I entered them all," says the writer, " and had to crawl on hands and feet to do so; they are circular, or nearly so, inside, and one or two still retain a stone off-set about two feet above the floor to serve as a couch for the hermits. The roofing is formed by the slabs gradually overlapping one another, the courses thus drawing closer, till they are capped by one central flag; the builders being entirely ignorant of the principle of the arch, this was the nearest approach they could make to it. The churches are three or four in number, but all very diminutive, the largest being twenty-four feet by fifteen, while the chapel of St. Molaise is only ten feet high, twelve feet long, and eight feet broad. They are built of the same materials, and roofed like the cells with overlapping courses of flags." They are, like all the ancient Irish churches, rectangular and devoid of chancels, which was quite a mediæval fashion, as can be seen in the ruined Church of Dean's Grange, near Blackrock, which is so ancient that it was in ruins in the time of Queen Elizabeth. There you can see that the original church, built perhaps a thousand years ago, was rectangular and of rubble masonry; while in the later Middle Ages, say after the Norman conquest of Ireland, the eastern wall was broken through, and a chancel added of regular cut stone. I have dwelt on this monastery, Inismurray, and have described it minutely, because it is in all its features an exact reproduction of many an Eastern one.¹ In Central Syria, to this day, you can find dome-shaped cells, stone-roofed churches, roofed, too, on the very same system, each tier of masonry overlapping the one below, which we find in Inismurray, and walls, or cashels, thrown up to protect the whole community. And now, strange as it may appear, we can produce documentary evidence, proving, not only that Eastern monasteries were constructed on the same plan as that in the Bay of Donegal, but also that the Celtic clergy and architects of the seventh century knew that this was the case, and constructed their buildings designedly on Syrian models. The proof is easy. Adamnan, the biographer of St. Columba, in his book on Palestine and the holy places, informs us that the Monastery of Mount Thabor was built on this plan, with a cashel, or circular fortification, enclosing both the monastic cells, and three small chapels for their use.²

I have now taken you over a long journey. It is a far cry certainly from Syria to Donegal Bay, yet I trust I have been able to show you the line of march

---

¹ One of the most interesting monasteries of Ireland is found on Iniscleraun (Quaker Island), in Lough Ree, some fifteen miles above Athlone. It is built after the fashion of Inismurray. There is a lady chapel and female burial place outside the cashel, four churches inside it, and a sixth at some distance upon the loftiest point of the island. This last has a tower which marks the transition stage from the round to the square church tower. The sacristy of the largest church retains its waggon-shaped roof. Only one church has a chancel. St. Diarmit's Chapel inside the cashel is very small, eight and a half feet long, six and a half broad; the doorway is four feet nine by one foot eight. See O'Hanlon's *Irish Saints*, i., 152-158, and " Diarmaid " (4) in the *Dict. Christ. Biog.* Iniscleraun was rendered famous in pagan times by the adventures of Queen Meav or Mab.

² Adamnani, *De Locis Sanctis*, lib. ii., cap. 27, in Migne, *Pat.*

pursued by monasticism. I have already identified Oriental and Irish monasticism on several important points. I shall endeavour, in the course of my future lectures, to show how the early Irish Church owed to the same source many other leading peculiarities in art, learning, and architecture.

*Lat.*, t. lxxxviii., col. 801 ; Butler's *Ancient Coptic Churches of Egypt*, lately published by the Clarendon Press, has some very interesting illustrations of the views put forward in this lecture. It proves that the use of cashels, enclosing numerous churches and a conventual establishment, is common to Ireland and Egypt, the Egyptian churches having also waggon-vaulted roofs like the Irish (vol. i., p. 14). The second volume is full of notices of features common to the ritual of the Coptic and Irish churches, the most notable of which are the use of embossed metal covers for MSS. (vol. ii., p. 61), of hand-bells (p. 81), of book-satchels (p. 246), and of ecclesiastical fans; *cf.* Reeves' *Adamnan*, pp. 115, 359; Curzon's *Monasteries of the Levant*, p. 93 (London: 1849. Another striking illustration of the same fact may be derived from the *Saltair Na Rann*, a collection of mediæval Irish poems, lately published in the *Anecdota Oxoniensia* by Whitley Stokes, LL.D. (Clarendon Press : 1882). It is simply an Irish eleventh or twelfth century edition of the *Book of Adam and Eve*, composed in the fifth or sixth century in Egypt, known in no other European country save Ireland, and first published in English in London, 1882, by S. C. Malan, D.D. A glance at the two will show their identity; see more on this topic below, note, p. 216, and in Art. " Pseudepigrapha," in *Dict. Christ. Biog.*, t. iv. My friend Dr. Gwynne has called my attention to an illustration of book satchels from Milan in Ceriani's Introduction to the text of the Syriac Bible.

# LECTURE X.

## *THE SOCIAL LIFE OF THE EIGHTH CENTURY.*

NO period of Irish history is so profoundly buried in obscurity as the eighth century. Individuals like Patrick or Columba render previous ages conspicuous. Great national revolutions, like the Danish or English invasion, mark the following period; but the eighth century is unmarked and almost unknown. Yet it has its own history and its own interest. Let us investigate it, for it will reveal to us some of the secrets of Ireland's subsequent course. I shall take our subject under two heads: (1) The political life; (2) The ecclesiastical life; which, however, will run very much into one another.

Our first topic is, therefore, the political state of Ireland. What documents have we to rely on concerning this period? The reply is very easy. The compilations called the *Annals of the Four Masters*, the *Chronicon Scotorum*, and the *Annals of Ulster*, must be our great guides in political matters. In the ecclesiastical department we are much better supplied, as our references will show; and this is but natural. Soldiers and men of action have in every age despised the pen, and left it to ecclesiastics and men of peace, who have had in turn their revenge, for if they have not acted, they have at least had it in their power to immortalise the actors, or to consign them to a speedy and complete oblivion. Let me now set forth for you the political organisation of Ireland as it existed in the eighth century, when the storm of Northern invaders burst upon this island. Celtic civilisation had then reached its height. In the various arts of painting, illumination, metal work, the Celtic genius never surpassed itself at that time. It is, therefore, a fitting epoch from which to survey the entire field, and endeavour to get a collective view of the whole social life of Ireland during the Middle Ages. It is only right, too, that we should begin with the political state of the country. In every age the Church has largely modified the State, permeating it by a new spirit, and thus influencing it from within. In every age, again, the Church has largely received its form, the mould in which its outer organisation was cast, from without. Thus the Roman Empire was revolutionised by the Christian Church. Yet the Church received from the empire the external framework of her organisation,—patriarchs, metropolitans, archbishops, all correspond to officials in the Roman Empire, and, notwithstanding all the changes and revolutions which France, for instance, has undergone, we can trace to this day in the episcopal arrangements of France the ancient organisation of the empire.[1] As it was within the Roman Empire, so was it, too, outside its bounds. Ireland was never subject to Imperial Rome, and, therefore, in Ireland there were no metropolitans till the twelfth century, when they were introduced through Roman influences. The Church, indeed, retained in Ireland, as it retained all the world over, its ancient episcopal

---

[1] See a learned article by the Abbé Duchesne, styled "Les Documents Ecclésiastiques sur les Divisions de l'Empire Romain au quatrième siècle," *Mélanges Graux*, pp. 133-144 (Paris: 1884).

system. But this system took one shape when it came in contact with the wild Celtic tribesmen; it assumed quite a different one when subjected to the influences of Imperial Rome. The Celtic genius, in fact, impressed upon episcopacy its own political form.

Let us first inquire what that political form was. Ireland of the eighth century is for most of us a land of myth and fiction. The England of the same period is a land of historical reality. Yet England and Ireland were precisely similar as regards political development, and we have just as good information about one as about the other.

It is considered, for instance, a special mark of the barbarous state of Ireland at that time, that it was split up into five kingdoms at least. But England was split up into seven, not counting Wales or Cornwall. And as it was in England, so was it in all other countries of the West. Charlemagne may have consolidated his vast empire into the appearance of a united whole, but we soon see that he was in reality only a kind of supreme king over a number of inferior rulers, who claimed and exercised a real independence of the supreme monarch in all the great affairs of State. The same was the case among all the Teutonic nations, just as it even still continues in some degree in Germany, where the suzerainty of the German emperor represents somewhat the position of the presiding king in relation to the subordinate chieftains of ancient communities.[1] Ireland, then, in the eighth century was divided into five great kingdoms, which have left clear and distinct marks upon the civil and ecclesiastical divisions of our land. These five kingdoms were

[1] See on this point some judicious observations by Mr. Green, *Making of England*, pp. 278—281.

Ulster, Munster, Leinster, Connaught, and Meath. In civil matters the four provinces correspond roughly to the four great kingdoms of Ulster, Munster, Leinster, and Connaught, but there is no province of Meath.[1] It is, however, in ecclesiastical divisions we can trace most clearly the boundaries of the five kingdoms. Just as I have already pointed out that we can by the aid of the episcopal and archiepiscopal sees in Gaul reconstruct the Roman divisions of that country, so, too, we can reconstruct the ancient political divisions of Ireland by the help of our ecclesiastical arrangements.[2] You all know, of course, that till within living memory there were four ecclesiastical provinces in Ireland,—Armagh, Tuam, Dublin, and Cashel. These four provinces broadly answered to the kingdom of Ulster, ruled by the O'Neills; to the kingdom of Connaught, ruled by the O'Connors; the kingdom of Leinster, ruled by the MacMurroughs; and that of Munster, by the O'Brians. But there remains the kingdom of Meath, and what of that? The diocese of Meath appears in a peculiar position in the ecclesiastical hierarchy. It is called the premier bishopric of Ireland, and its bishop, though junior in consecration, takes rank before all other bishops, preserving thus a trace of the old political system, wherein Meath was a separate kingdom, taking pre-

---

[1] Simply because King John turned the Kingdom of Meath into a county, or Palatinate, which he bestowed upon the De Lacys, and united in civil matters to the province of Leinster. In John's time, and till the reign of Henry VIII., the shire of Meath embraced West as well as East Meath, together with portions fo Longford and King's County. It was defended on the west by the three great royal castles of Clonmacnois, Athlone, and Randon, or St. John's, on Lough Ree.
[2] See Dr. Reeves' *Analysis of the United Diocese of Dublin and Glendalough*, p. 7.

cedence of all other kingdoms in Ireland.[1] Meath formed the kingdom of the supreme sovereign of Ireland for the time being. It was, in fact, his mensal lands, the territory assigned for the support of his dignity, and it is a curious but interesting fact that the boundaries of the present diocese of Meath exactly correspond to the boundaries of the ancient Irish kingdom. We have a nice piece of evidence about the extent of this kingdom. The *Book of Rights* was published by the late Mr. O'Donovan, one of that great school of archæologists who in the last generation helped to shed light on the tangled pathways of Irish antiquity.[2] That book is a most important document for those who wish to understand the social state of this country in mediæval times. In its present state it dates from an ancient period. We have it in two MSS., either of which is five hundred years old. It is contained in the *Book of Lecan*, compiled in the year 1418 by MacFirbis, a celebrated professor of history in the county Sligo,[3] and also in the *Book of Ballymote*, compiled for MacDonough, another chieftain of that county, in the year 1390. It has all the marks of remote antiquity about it, and in O'Donovan's opinion shows us the manners and customs of the Irish as they existed during the period of which we treat. The contents of this volume

---

[1] Meath was for ages ruled by the Southern Hy-Nialls, represented in the eleventh and twelfth centuries by the O'Melaghlins, modernised into Molloy; see Dr. Petrie's pathetic story of the last of the royal O'Melaghlins in Sir Bernard Burke's *Vicissitudes of Families*, 2nd series, p. 359. Petrie found him fifty years ago living in a cottage in the outskirts of Athlone.

[2] *Book of Rights*, ed. John O'Donovan (Dublin: 1847). The preface contains valuable information about the chronology roads, and amusements of the ancient Irish.

[3] He belonged to the same family as the MacFirbis who, two centuries later, assisted Sir James Ware. See Mr. Hennessy's Preface to the *Chronicon Scotorum*, in the Rolls Series.

explain why it is called the *Book of Rights*. It gives an account of the dues of the monarchs of all Ireland, of the revenues they received from the inferior kings, and of the stipends paid by the monarchs to these same inferior kings for their services. It also tells of the tribute due from the tribes to the inferior kings, and of the subsidies paid by these kings in turn to the tribes for their services. It is, in fact, a handbook of the taxation of the country, and as such gives us a very lively picture of the manners and customs, the eating and drinking, the agriculture, the warfare, the whole inner life of Ireland at that time. It is such a book as would be prized above rubies if it dealt with the organisation and social life of ancient Greece, but which is neglected, because it deals with ancient Ireland, though the state of life depicted, the tribal organisation and customs, must have been very similar to those with which Homer, and Ulysses, and Achilles were familiar. This *Book of Rights* opens with a statement concerning the dues and privileges of the King of Erin, who was also King of Tara, or of Meath. I will give you a specimen of the book, which precisely marks the boundaries of Meath. The *Book of Rights* mentions, first, seven things which are prohibited to the king. Then the seven prerogatives of the King of Meath are enumerated. I will quote them, as they are given by O'Donovan, in a poetical shape.

> " Let the seven prerogatives be read. What harm ?
> For the King of Tara, if he observe them,
> The ready earth shall be fruitful for him,
> He shall be victorious in battle, wise of counsel.
>
> On the Calends of August, to the King
> Were brought from each respective district
> The fruits of Manann, a fine present,
> And the heath-fruit (bilberries) of Brigh-Leithe,

> The venison of Nas, the fish of the Boinn,
> The cresses of the kindly Brosnach,
> The water of the well of Tlachtgha too,
> And the swift deer of Luibneach."[1]

Now, observing the localities mentioned in these verses, and comparing them with those mentioned in the seven restrictions on the King of Tara, we find that his jurisdiction extended from the neighbourhood of Naas or Maynooth, or the line of the Liffey, on the east, to the Brosna, the Westmeath lakes, and the Shannon on the west, and from the Queen's County on the south to the point where Meath, Cavan, and Longford touch on the north,—a district which, roughly speaking, covers the present diocese of Meath. It is no wonder that this district became the dominant kingdom of Ireland. Its physical features mark it out for such a destiny. Where trade and commerce prevail, and a land is dependent for its supplies upon external sources, communication by sea is absolutely necessary for dominion. The possessor of the ports has the key of power in his hands, to open and shut as he pleases. But Ireland was then self-contained. The owner of the rich plains of Meath produced within his own boundary everything he needed. His kingdom lay touching the other four, and yet was so compact that a forced night's march would concentrate all his forces on any threatened point. It speaks volumes for the foresight and prudence of Niall of the Nine Hos-

---

[1] Brigh-Leithe is identified by O'Donovan with Slieve Golry, a lofty hill in the east of the county Longford; the heath-fruit was used to make beer. The Brosnach is a river in Westmeath and King's County, flowing into the Shannon, near Banagher; Tlachtgha is an ancient name of the Hill of Ward, near Athboy, in the north of Meath; Luibneach is situated near Portarlington, in the neighbourhood where the King's, Queen's, and Kildare counties touch one another, a district covered with forests till the reign of Elizabeth.

tages that he it was who selected this district as the special domain of the King of All Ireland, and at the same time determined that the selection of that potentate should be made from out of his own descendants. Ireland was thus split into five great sections. But this was not subdivision enough to satisfy Celtic taste. Each kingdom was again divided into tribes, and these tribes occupied territories corresponding to modern baronies, which often retain the names of the tribes which once dwelt in them.[1] Indeed, just as in the persons of Lord O'Neill and Lord Inchiquin we find the descendants of two at least of the ancient Irish royal families elevated to the English peerage, so too we have numerous instances of Irish chieftains still living and possessing estates where their ancestors lived a thousand years ago or more. It is a simple historical fact that, notwithstanding the numerous confiscations

---

[1] The tribal distribution of the population is still clearly recognisable in Ireland. The annual reports of the Deputy Keeper of the Rolls (Sir S. Ferguson) are very useful in this respect. He has been publishing for some years the fiants of Queen Elizabeth's reign. These record the tribal distribution of that time, which in many instances still remains the same. To take one case with which I am well acquainted. The barony of Brawny, in Westmeath, was the territory of the Brynes or Bryans, which still is a common name there. The barony of Athlone, in Roscommon, was part of O'Kelly's country or Hymany, and O'Kelly or Kelly is even still the most numerous name in the district. The publications of the various archæological associations of Ireland are full of information about the ancient tribal system of Ireland; the following may be specially consulted: O'Donovan's edition of the *Book of Rights of the Tribes and Territories of Ancient Ossory* (Dublin: 1851); of the *Tribes and Customs of Hymany;* of the *Tribes and Customs of Hy-Fiachrach*, and of the *Topographical Poems* of John O'Dubhagain; and of O'Daly's *Tribes of Ireland*,—almost all published by the Irish Archæological Society. The topographical appendix to O'Mahony's edition of Keating's *Ireland*, and O'Donovan's index to his own edition of the *Four Masters*, will also be found useful.

this country has experienced, if the descendants of the ancient Irish chiefs were removed from the ranks of the landed gentry, enormous tracts of Irish land would be devoid of owners. Thus about the middle of the tenth century The O'Donovan and his tribe perpetrated a foul murder on Mahoun, King of Munster, unwittingly contributing to seat the valiant Brian Boru on the throne of Ireland. The O'Donovans are still known in Cork; and then there are the Kellys, and the Cavanaghs, and the O'Connor Don, and the Fitzpatricks, and the Tighes, one of the most thoroughly Celtic of all our Irish families, and the Foxes and the Macnamaras, and dozens of other families, who perhaps in some cases are rather ashamed of the stock from whence they have sprung, and claim some fanciful English ancestry.[1]

Now, with a land so subdivided and cut up as I have just described, one result naturally followed. The wars and quarrels between the various kings and tribes were simply interminable. Their mode of life contributed to this. Agriculture was but little practised. Ireland then, as now, was above all things a pastoral country. The herds and flocks of sheep and cattle and goats constituted the staple possession of the tribes even in the third century, the age of Solinus, the Roman geographer. In the summer they were driven to the highlands, where they roamed at large, while their owners made themselves booths or bothies, and watched them, like the Alpine shepherds, or as the Achill and Belmullet peasantry did till within living memory.[2] In winter they sought more permanent

---

[1] See on this topic an interesting essay by O'Donovan, in the Introduction to *Irish Topographical Poems*, pp. 17-64 (Dublin: 1862).

[2] Sir W. Wilde said he quite well remembered the practice of living in mountain bothies in use in West Connaught.

dwellings both for man and beast. But yet at best their winter huts of timber or earth took neither much time nor money to erect. They were easily raised, and they were as lightly abandoned; and, therefore, the tribesmen, their owners, were ready for any fray, and only counted a plundering expedition one of the ordinary diversions or excitements of every-day life. Let me give you an instance or two. Plundering was regarded by the Celtic tribes of that day just as all nations in the same stage of development regard it—as a most honourable employment. Thus if we take up the *Book of Rights*, from which I have quoted, we shall there find solemnly laid down among the privileges of the King of Cashel or Munster that of burning Northern Leinster, and of plundering the cattle of Croghan (the rich plains of Roscommon), while the cuckoo sings. But it is only when you take up the *Annals of the Four Masters* you can at all realise what perpetual, unceasing quarrels and bickerings prevailed. The state of society was scarcely to be dignified by the name of war. It was just like the condition of affairs depicted by Sir W. Scott as existing in Scotland a century and a half ago upon the Highland line. The man who plundered another's cattle last night would meet the plundered person at a fair to-day, and joke and gamble and drink with him, though quite ready to cut his throat rather than surrender the cattle to the lawful owner. Those ravaging expeditions must have terribly thrown back the social advance of the country at large. They rendered life and property uncertain, and were conducted at times with an utter want either of mercy or of reverence.

What progress could Leinster make when we read that in the year 716 it was five times devastated by the O'Neills? The same terrible O'Neills were again in Kildare in 718, when they fought a bloody battle near the Hill of Allen, which forms a prominent object in the landscape as one looks south from the Curragh, and gives its name to the famous Bog of Allen, which covers so large a portion of Ireland's great central plain. In those expeditions the tribesmen spared apparently neither age nor sex; they regarded neither monastery nor church. Their notions seem to have been strictly tribal. They reverenced their own local priest and their own local sanctuaries, but they reverenced none other. Clonmacnois, Kildare, Clonard, Armagh, fared as badly at the hands of Christian Irishmen as at those of pagan Danes. These venerable shrines, whose history went back to the earliest ages, were again and again plundered and burnt to the ground.[1]

Let me give you an example of this. In the early part of the ninth century the King of Munster's name was Phelim (Feidhlimidh). He claimed to be sovereign of all Ireland, in opposition to the O'Neills, and proved his title to the position by the only law then recognised, the vigour of his sway. Like another monarch of the same kingdom, the famous Cormac MacCullinan, he was an abbat and bishop as well as a sovereign. His dual character, however, did not interfere with his warlike propensities. He did not hesitate, therefore, in the prosecution of his political designs, to plunder the most sacred places of Ulster, and to put to the sword their monks and clergy. In 826, and again in 833, he spoiled

---

[1] The Churches of St. Diarmit, on Iniscleraun, or Seven Churches Island in Lough Ree, bear to this day the marks of fire, as pointed out to me last summer by two architects, Messrs. Langrishe and Cochrane of Athlone, who visited them with me.

the termon lands[1] and sanctuary of Clonmacnois. On this last occasion, he slew the religious, and burned the sanctuary up to the very doors of the principal church. He treated in the same way the celebrated Columban monastery of Durrow. In 836 he stormed the sanctuary of Kildare, where the Archbishop of Armagh and his clergy had taken refuge. In 840 he burned Armagh, in 846 plundered and burned a second time the sanctuary of Clonmacnois, till finally this warlike priest died, in 847, of a disease supposed to have been miraculously inflicted by St. Kieran of Clonmacnois, in punishment of the outrages committed upon his own specially-loved establishment.[2]

But the bishops of Cashel were not the only offenders in this respect. The prelates of Armagh were just as bad. The *Four Masters* tell us of a terrible battle which took place at Fochart, the birthplace of St. Bridget. She was herself the patron saint of pity and mercy, yet but little of that spirit seemed to linger round her native soil. The Bishop of Armagh was the one who stirred up the strife, because, in one of the usual plundering forays, provisions had been forcibly taken from some church or monastery subject to his jurisdiction. The battle of Fochart was fierce, and the strife so bloody, that the King of Ulster was pursued to the shelter of a church, and his head cut off even in the sacred enclosure. Ireland gets credit for lightly estimating human life at the close of the nineteenth century. If so, she learned her lesson ages ago. The agrarian murders and the savage faction fights

---

[1] Upon the origin and meaning of "Termon" and "Termon-lands," see Ussher's treatise, Wks., ed. Elrington, xi., 419-445; Reeves' *Primate Colton's Visitation*, p. 3; see his index *s.v.*

[2] Todd's *Wars of Gaedhill*, Introd., p. xliv.; Reeves' *Colton's Visitation*, p. 93.

we sometimes hear of, and so graphically pictured by Carleton, are only survivals of ancient customs, proving how hard it is with nations as with men to eradicate a hereditary taint. Yet, bad as the nineteenth century may have been, it has never reached the fierce savagery of which we read in the year 755, when Bishop Eutighern, of Kildare, was killed by one of his priests at the very altar of St. Bridget in his own cathedral city.[1]

---

[1] See O'Donovan's note on the *Four Masters*, A.D. 755. The perpetual wars between the kingdoms of Connaught and Meath supplied many instances of sacrilege. In *Irish Christian Inscriptions*, by G. Petrie and M. Stokes, t. i., p. 47, we have an inscription commemorating Corbre or Corprius, the Bent. He was Bishop of Clonmacnois about the year 900, at which period his death is fixed by the *Four Masters*, the *Chronicon Scotorum*, and the *Martyrology of Donegal*. These annals mention the profanation of Inis Ainghin (Hare Island, near Athlone), in Lough Ree, as occurring in his time. Colgan (*AA. SS.*, p. 509) tells the story at length. An army of Connaught men invaded Meath, by crossing from one shore of the lake to the other. On their way they seized Hare Island, where were a church and burial-ground dedicated to St. Kieran, and connected with Clonmacnois. It was probably a hermitage belonging to that establishment. Bishop Corprius was just then holding a Synod of Seniors there. Notwithstanding the holy man's presence, the Connaught men plundered the shrine, and slew some prisoners before the eyes of the Synod, a deed which God avenged that same day, for the Meath men overtook the foe at the town of Athlone, and utterly defeated them. The ruins of St. Kieran's Church are still visible on Hare Island, one of the most beautiful of the many islands which stud Lough Ree. In 1822, Dr. Petrie, *l.c.*, p. 45, discovered a stone beside the ruined church which showed that some bishops of Clonmacnois were buried there. The legend was, "Pray for Tuathcharan." The death of Tuadhcar, Bishop of Clonmacnois, is recorded at A.D. 889, by the *Chronicon Scotorum*. See *Four Masters*, ed. O'Donov., i., 553. This stone has now disappeared, for nowhere else is there found so much theoretical respect and practical indifference to the remains of antiquity as in Ireland. Colgan, *l.c.*, p. 508, tells an extraordinary story about Corprius of Clonmacnois, and the spirit of Malachy, nephew of the King of Ireland. The spirit appeared one day before the bishop as he was meditating after evensong, all wretched and filthy on account of the punishments which he was enduring in the spiritual world. He besought the bishop's help

But now you may ask me, what function did those kings and chieftains fulfil? Did they govern in any sense of the word? The functions of government are various. They may be broadly divided into those of war and of peace. My reply then would be, those ancient Irish kings fulfilled one function of government. They managed war and all its various details, often well and vigorously too. But for the most part they disregarded all the matters pertaining to peace. Sometimes, indeed, a ruler of exceptional ability arose, who applied himself to the true functions of government, and strove to develop the resources of the nation, to improve its communications, and establish that internal peace and confidence absolutely needful for trade and commerce. A Cormac MacArt, in the third century, introduced mills; Cormac MacCullinan in the tenth, Brian Boru in the eleventh, built bridges, churches, round towers, and exercised a vigorous jurisdiction over the country. But in general such useful functions were utterly neglected.[1]

for himself and his confessor, who was in a similar plight. The bishop prayed for him for half a year, at the end of which he appeared, bright and clean in the upper part of his body, but in his former filthy state as regards the lower extremities. Corprius then prayed for another six months, when the spirit appeared, clear and radiant throughout. This tale may be compared with three others, drawn from very different quarters: the story of S. Perpetua and her brother Dinocrates in Tertullian's time; some stories about monks in purgatory, told by Dr. Salmon, in an article in *Contemp. Review* for October 1883, pp. 523, 524, on "Purgatory and Modern Revelations;" and Charles Lever's story about Micky Free and his father's sojourn in purgatory, in *Charles O'Malley*.

[1] Any improvements made by the ordinary Irish princes were only for military purposes. The O'Connors, kings of Connaught, repeatedly erected bridges of wicker work—such as still are found in mountainous districts—over the Shannon at Athlone, Lanesborough, and elsewhere, but merely to facilitate their invasions of Meath and Leinster. The only useful works were effected by the monks, who made bridges and roads for the

One of the greatest functions of the state is the administration of justice. One of the chief distinctions between the civilised and the barbarous state of society is this: among barbarians, law is a mere private matter; in a civilised community, it is an affair of state. Among barbarians, if a man is injured, he avenges his wrong as best he can; within the limits of civilisation the state steps in, takes the sword out of individual hands, and punishes with reason, deliberation, on fixed and known principles. Judged by this standard, Ireland was in a barbarous state during the eighth and succeeding centuries. I shall have occasion afterwards to show you that, judged by other tests, we should say she was at the same time highly cultured. Yet this undoubted fact, that a state-administered system of law and justice did not exist in the eighth century, simply proves that a community may have made great strides in one direction, while yet in another it may lag far behind. The princes of that age regarded the administration of law and justice as lying quite outside their jurisdiction. The Brehon law was the ancient Irish code. We have now ample materials to form a judgment concerning it, inasmuch as the learned labours of two professors of this University, Drs. Ritchie and O'Mahony, have rendered a large portion of the Brehon laws of Ireland accessible in an English shape to every student. Under the Brehon system law and justice were altogether private matters. Ireland, the Teutonic tribes, aye, and the Twelve Tables of ancient Rome too, were agreed on this point.[1] The Danes, for instance, used

---

accommodation of their sanctuaries. The princes, indeed, often became monks, when they at once became useful members of society.

[1] See Sir H. Maine's *Ancient Law*, chap. x., p. 370.

a code very similar to the Celtic, while some of its leading principles are even still employed by the English government in the Coercion Acts dealing with disturbed districts in Ireland. The essential principle of the Brehon law is this: Crimes are wrongs committed by individuals against individuals, with which the State has nothing to do. One man steals another man's cows, maims his horses, burns his house, kills his wife or child. With these misdeeds, the prince or chief has no concern, unless he is the person injured. The duty of revenge attaches to the individual injured, and a money payment can compensate the injured party.[1] But who is to settle the amount of compensation? This difficulty was solved by the institution of Brehons, who were a hereditary class of judges learned in the law, to whom the parties engaged in litigation voluntarily submitted themselves. But mark this, they were arbitrators merely. Their jurisdiction was purely consensual. They had no power of the sword, and if either party repudiated their decisions, they had no resources for enforcing them.[2] This was the fundamental weakness of the Brehon law, which lasted in Ireland in full force till the seventeenth century.[3] I have already said that the Northmen used a

---

[1] Exactly the same principle finds place among the laws of the Lombards transcribed into Latin so long ago as A.D. 643. See Muratorii *Scriptt. Rer. Italic.*, t. i., pt. ii., pp. 1-181; Gibbon, chap. xlv.

[2] The only penalty provided by the Brehons was like the famous Act of the last century, which punished a crime with a flogging of fifty lashes, half the penalty to go to the informer. Fasting on an offender was a penalty which told rather upon the plaintiff than the defendant. See Maine's *Early Institutions*, pp. 39, 40 (*cf*. pp. 297-304). He notices the sitting "Dharna" of the Hindoos as its exact equivalent.

[3] It is difficult for an outsider to discover the habits of the peasantry; still I have good reason to believe that in the distant

similar legal system in Denmark and in Scandinavia before they invaded the islands of the west. We have an interesting account of this matter in the Icelandic Saga of Burnt Nial, edited by Sir George Dasent some few years ago. There you can see how rapidly the Danes cast the Brehon code aside. The Danes in Iceland showed their Teutonic genius for business by developing legislation and institutions more consonant to the wants of civilised society, and by the time of the Norman conquest of Ireland, that is, within three centuries of their settlement in Iceland, they had constructed a very elaborate judicial system, with primary intermediate, and appeal courts, very similar in many respects to those which now exist in these kingdoms. I do not think the student of comparative jurisprudence could come across a more interesting incident illustrating the varying genius of tribes and nations for political development, than the very diverse fates which overtook the Brehon code in Ireland and in Iceland. The Celtic race clung to it. It suited their nature. It gave fine scope to their fighting capacities. If the decision suited the defendant, he submitted to it; if not he repudiated it, and fought it out with judge and plaintiff alike. The Teutonic race tried the Brehon code, found it wanting in all the elements of social stability, cast it aside, and developed one more suited to the wants of a commercial and a civilised community.[1]

mountain districts of the west the Brehon system is not even yet extinct.

[1] The best works on the Brehon Laws are, the general Introduction to the volumes of *The Ancient Laws of Ireland*, by the Editors; Sir H. Maine's works, *Early History of Institutions*, *Village Communities*, and *Early Law and Custom*. Sir S. Ferguson's article on "Brehon Law" in the new *Encyclopædia Britannica* is a convenient *résumé* of the whole subject.

But now some one might say, does not all this simply prove that the Irish princes and people of that date were a pack of savages? Such is clearly Mr. Froude's view. "The Irish," he says in the second chapter of his first volume of the *English in Ireland*, "when the Normans took charge of them were, with the exception of the clergy, scarcely better than a mob of armed savages. They had no settled industry, and no settled habitations, and scarcely a conception of property." There is much truth in this picture. Yet it is not all true. They had no settled habitations as far as stone buildings are concerned. The remains of all the royal residences of Ireland, at Tara, Armagh, Naas, and wherever else the various princes resided, are all of earth. When Henry II. received the homage of the Irish princes on our own College Green, he erected a palace of osiers or wattles upon clay, after the manner of the country, for this purpose. Yet the beauteous antiquities deposited in the Irish Academy, the gold work which cannot be surpassed for elegance and delicacy, the vast variety of articles mentioned in the *Book of Rights*, the garments of silk and satin, the coats of mail, the chessboards, the wax candles for the entertainments, all prove that a considerable amount of civilisation and knowledge of the arts must have existed side by side with a comparatively low state of political and social development. This, however, is rendered an absolute certainty when we turn from the political to the ecclesiastical side of our subject. We there find a most extensive culture. Art, learning, architecture, travel, were in a most advanced state. The proofs of this lie under your hands. The *Book of Kells*, which dates from the seventh or eighth century, exhibits the marvellous skill of the Columban monks of that period.  With all our modern resources we have never surpassed, nay rather have never attained, the marvellous beauty of its initial letters, which have elicited the admiration and wonder of judges, like Mr. Westwood, who have examined all the remains of ancient art.[1]  Compare, for instance, the illuminations in the *Codex Rossanensis* with those of the *Book of Kells*. The *Codex Rossanensis* was discovered some five or six years ago in southern Italy.  It is a magnificent volume in the Greek language, written in gold on a purple ground, enriched with pictures, executed perhaps by the imperial artists of Constantinople.  In it we have an example of Byzantine skill and taste in the time of its highest development, the period of Justinian and of the building of Saint Sophia.  Compare that, I say, with the Irish art of the *Book of Kells*, and a glance will show the immeasurable superiority of the Celtic artists both in design and in execution.  And the *Book of Kells* does not stand alone.  The *Book of Durrow* and the numerous other MSS. which Mr. Gilbert has made accessible to every student in his splendid facsimiles, all prove that a high state of artistic skill existed in the monasteries of Ireland.  All

---

[1] The reader should consult for a description of the *Book of Kells* Mr. Gilbert on the National MSS. of Ireland, pp. 12-21; in the letterpress attached to his *Facsimiles*. Prof. Hartley, F.R.S., read a paper before the Royal Dub. Society, in June 1885 (now published in its *Proceedings*), on the colouring matter used in the illuminations of the *Book of Kells*, where he showed solid reasons, from a chemist's standpoint, for believing that these colours were identical with those of the ancient Egyptians; offering another link in the connection I endeavour, all through this work, to establish between Ireland, Egypt, and the East. *Cf.* a paper, "Remarks on an Ogam Monument," read by Bishop Graves, in January 1885, before the Roy. Irish Acad., and published in its *Proceedings*.  On p. 280 he has some interesting remarks on this topic.  See also Westwood on *Book of Kells* (Dublin: 1887).

this, however, is well known and universally acknowledged. I wish now, however, to direct your attention more especially to the state of learning and of travel. Many of us have heard vague traditions of the learning of Ireland about the period of which I am treating, but I imagine that we have been in the habit of regarding it as somewhat mythical and devoid of the solid foundations on which its artistic claims rest. This, I can assure you, is a complete mistake. The scholarly claims of Ireland are as sound as its artistic.[1] In a previous lecture I have shown you how cultivated a taste Columbanus had in Latin verse. The education imparted in his day at Bangor can have been no limited one. The reputation of Irish schools at that period induced the highest ranks to send their children to our colleges. Let me give you a striking instance. One of the finest places for a day's excursion from Dublin is the Hill of Slane. It is the highest point of the county Meath. It dominates the whole country. Twice last summer[2] did I stand on its summit, once at five o'clock in the morning, when the mist was so thick in the valleys that we could see but little. Again towards the close of September, when a clear day showed me what a splendid prospect it commanded; as we could see from the Sugar Loaf on the south to the Mourne mountains on the north, and from the Irish Sea on the east to the hills of Westmeath and Cavan on the west. This spot is crowned by the ruins of the ancient monastery and College of Slane. The tower of the Abbey Church is still perfect, and can be ascended by a hundred stone steps. The ruins

---

[1] See more on this subject in my next lecture, on "Greek Learning in Irish Monasteries."
[2] The summer of 1884.

are indeed English in their character; thirteenth or fourteenth century in their date. But an ancient moat clearly points to the site of the ancient abbey celebrated by the Bollandists and in the *Annals of the Four Masters*. Now in this abbey of Slane, Dagobert II., King of France, was educated in the seventh century, when exiled by the enemies of his house for their own ambitious purposes. English and French alike resorted to our schools, and they did not forget the obligations they were under to their Irish teachers. Of this we have an interesting proof. Archbishop Ussher published, two hundred years ago, a valuable collection of letters concerning Ireland, dating from this period. I have often quoted them under the title of *Sylloge Epistolarum Hibernicarum*. There we find a correspondence between Colcu, the Senior Lecturer of the school of Clonmacnois, and Alcuin, the pride of Charlemagne's court, the glory of the school and Church of York, and the real author of those Caroline books, which repudiated on the part of the Gallican Church the decrees of the image worshippers of Nice. His letter to the worthy Senior Lecturer of that day is marked by two things: first, by profound reverence for the learning of Colcu; second, by a practical evidence of that reverence, since he sends Colcu a cheque, or its equivalent, for the pains taken with his Gallic and English pupils. Let me read a brief analysis of the letter, as it is the only proof which my time will now allow me to give of the debt then due from France to Ireland. He begins his letter with telling Colcu the news of the day; how Charlemagne had converted the Saxons and the Frisians, some (as he naïvely expresses it) by rewards, and others by threats. He narrates how during the previous year the Slavs,

Greeks, Huns, and Saracens had been defeated by his master's forces. He describes a quarrel which had broken out between Charlemagne and the Mercian king Offa. He laments that he had not received any Irish letters for a considerable time, and continues: "I have sent to thee some oil, which is now a scarce article in Britain, that you may divide it among the bishops for man's assistance and God's honour. I have also sent fifty shekels to my brethren from the king's bounty; I beseech you pray for him; and from myself fifty shekels. For the brethren in the south I have sent thirty from the king and thirty from myself, and for the anchorites three shekels of pure silver; that they all may pray for me and for King Charles, that God may preserve him to the protection of his holy Church, and the praise and glory of His holy Name." Words which clearly prove that a distant corner of the King's County which but few Irishmen, not to say English or Frenchmen, now visit, then excited keenest feelings of interest and of gratitude in the most powerful and warlike court which then existed in Europe.

This subject will receive some further illustrations in the course of my next lecture, on Greek Learning in the Irish Monasteries.

## LECTURE XI.

### *GREEK AND HEBREW LEARNING IN IRISH MONASTERIES.*

IN my last lecture I endeavoured to depict, as truthfully as I could, the political state of this land in the eighth century. I cannot hope to have pleased all parties in my sketch. There are two extreme views with respect to our past history. One paints Ireland previous to the Norman conquest as a very garden of the Lord, well watered, beautiful and fair. Another depicts it as a waste and howling wilderness, the abode of wild savage beasts, and of wilder and more savage men. Both extreme views are wrong, and the truth lies, as always is the case, in the mean between. The civilisation of Ireland was, as I have hinted, largely connected with the monasteries, which were strengthened during the eighth century by valuable accessions. The eighth century was a stirring and important time for Western Europe. The eighth century laid strong and deep the foundations of papal dominion. It consolidated the growing power of the Western Empire. It developed Western civilisation and Western art, and this it did through the iconoclastic policy of the emperors of Constantinople. Let me briefly explain this. The throne of Constantinople was occupied during the greater part of the eighth century by a highly Protestant race of emperors. The iconoclastic monarchs were able, vigorous, self-reliant. But they were narrow-minded and intolerant. They were determined to put down image worship among their subjects, which had largely eaten out the heart of religion among them. But they forgot that spiritual movements are only effected by spiritual motives and weapons. They strove to crush image worship by fire and sword, and they failed. Yea, even farther, they injured themselves in the vain attempt. They not only intensified the evil, but also drove the monks, who possessed all the best knowledge and skill, into the ranks of their opponents. The iconoclasts proclaimed war to the death against the monasteries, with the natural result that the monks fled for refuge to the West, and carried to Charlemagne, and to the Pope, and even to distant Ireland, the knowledge and culture of the Byzantine Empire. The Litany of Æengus the Culdee,[1] compiled at the monastery of Tallaght, expressly tells us of the numerous Eastern ecclesiastics who found refuge in Ireland during the eighth century; and the round towers which they built, and the Greek learning and the Oriental learning which they revived —if they did not found—prove the extent and variety of the benefits conferred by them upon the islands of the west.

You may be inclined, however, to object, surely it is impossible that Greek ecclesiastics should have penetrated so far west as Ireland. Now, *à priori* presumptions like this are most dangerous and misleading in history. We are apt to form a mental picture of the dangers and difficulties of travel in mediæval times, and

---

[1] Wh. Stokes, LL.D., has published the Calendar of Æengus among the *Transactions* of the Royal Irish Academy (Irish MSS. Series), 1880.

then to decide that no intercourse could have existed between nations so widely separated as Egypt, Greece, and Ireland. Yet the most distant East and the farthest West were never in more lively contact than in those times. A Jew or a Mahometan in Central Asia might start a novel theory. In a year or two it would be discussed amid the schools and synagogues and bazaars of Toledo and Seville. Justinian might issue his decree about the Three Chapters. It disturbed the theological repose of the Byzantine Empire, but was a still greater source of trouble to St. Columbanus and his monks at Bobbio, or to his still more distant brethren at Bangor or Lismore. To those again who have studied the history of the seventh and eighth centuries, I need scarcely mention the celebrated Greek ecclesiastic Theodore, who presided over the see of Canterbury, as an illustration of the unity and thorough communication which then existed throughout Christendom. But omitting well-known instances, let me briefly call your attention to a work which strikingly illustrates the wide travel, the extensive learning, the accurate geographical research of the Irish monks of the eighth century. Even if Greek ecclesiastics did not come to Ireland, Irish ecclesiastics sought out Greece and the East.

In the first half of this present nineteenth century, there lived in France one of the most learned and accurate Egyptologists of that day. The Egyptian expedition of Napoleon Buonaparte had raised a great scientific interest among French scholars. Napoleon, whatever his faults, formed magnificent scientific conceptions, and spared no expense in their prosecution. The investigations in Egypt, undertaken at his instance, were of a very thorough character, and have left their mark on European literature.  Among the scholars who devoted much attention to the Egyptian question was M. Letronne, whose great work on Greek and Latin Inscriptions in Egypt is still a standard authority.  About the year 1812, when Letronne was young and entering with all the enthusiasm of youth upon this study, he discovered in the French National Library two Irish MSS., brought from some unknown monastery.  They were copies of a work composed in the ninth century, about the year 825, by an Irish monk named Dicuil.  The subject of the work is geographical, and its title is *Liber de Mensurâ orbis terræ*.  Of its author we know practically nothing save what we can gather from a study of the work itself, which is indeed most interesting as a specimen of the geographies used in the Irish colleges of that day.  Letronne imagines that he was a pupil, either of Clonard or Armagh.  I rather think he must have been a student of the school of Clonmacnois, and for this reason.  Dicuil tells us that his master's name was Suibhneus or Sweeny, which occurs frequently among the lists of professors at Clonmacnois, and is to this day a common name in that locality.[1]

The book is interesting to us for many reasons.  It shows the knowledge and books then possessed by the Irish scholars.  Dicuil composed his work to a large extent out of the cosmography of Julius Cæsar, and out of those ancient geographers Pliny and Solinus.  He also quotes Pomponius Mela, Orosius, Isidore of Seville, and Priscian the grammarian.  He aims at the greatest

---

[1] A celebrated scholar of this name died at Clonmacnois in the year 891 (Ussher, vi., 278, 615; *Annals of Ulster*).  See Colgan, *AA. SS.*, p. 57, for a list of all the Suibhnei who distinguished themselves in ancient times.

accuracy. That accuracy can indeed only be realised by those who will take the trouble to compare it with a similar work produced elsewhere. Two hundred years before its composition, John Malalas wrote his well-known chronicle in the city of Antioch.[1] That chronicle made the fortune and established the reputation of the celebrated English critic Bentley, by affording him the opportunity of displaying his critical skill in its publication. Antioch about A.D. 600 was the centre of Greek culture and of Greek erudition, and the Chronicle of Malalas, as embodied in Niebuhr's series of Byzantine historians, is a mine of information on many questions. But compare it with the Irish work of Dicuil and its mistakes are laughable. The highest culture of Antioch was nearly as deficient as the highest culture of some of our most expensive public schools. Malalas was deplorably ignorant of Roman history and literature, and of the elements of geography. He calls Sallust and Cicero the wisest of the Roman poets, makes Julius Cæsar seize and kill Pompey in Egypt, and represents Claudius Cæsar as founding "Urbem Brettaniam" not far from the ocean. But now take up Dicuil's geographical treatise, and you will find the most accurate details about Iceland on the one hand, and about Egypt and the Pyramids on the other. It was, indeed, this latter point which led Letronne to edit and publish the manuscript. He was charmed to find in this Irish writer a description of the Pyramids, and measurements thereof which exactly tallied with his own investigations. And not only so, but Dicuil gives us in this treatise a statement of special interest at the present day. Dicuil describes, on the

---

[1] See the article "Malalas" in the *Dict. Christ. Biog.*, t. iii., p. 787.

testimony of a monk named Fidelis, the canal which Hadrian made connecting the Nile with Suez. Fidelis and certain priests and laymen from Ireland were making a pilgrimage to the Holy Places. They took Egypt on the way, and after visiting the Pyramids sailed to the Red Sea by this canal; a circumstance which demonstrates most clearly the accuracy of Dicuil.[1] This canal was made five hundred years before Christ, by one of the Pharaohs. It was cleared and repaired by Hadrian, whose devotion to Egypt is well known. Lucian, in the second century, speaks of a young man who sailed on it from Alexandria to Suez. This canal was open till the sixth century, when it silted up. The Arabs reopened it in 640, to send grain to Arabia. It continued in use till 767, when a revolt occurring at Mecca and Medina, it was closed, to hinder the rebels getting supplies from Egypt. This canal has again been reopened by M. Lesseps, and now forms the Sweetwater Canal, which carries the waters of the Nile to Suez.[2]

---

[1] Fidelis, or some monkish traveller like him, may have been the channel through whom the literature of Egypt and Syria passed over to Ireland, of which Dr. Whitley Stokes has published an interesting specimen, the *Saltair Na Rann*, in the *Anecdota Oxoniensia*, Mediæval Series, vol. i., pt. 3 (Clarendon Press: 1883). This volume contains a series of 162 Biblical poems or paraphrases attributed to Ængus the Culdee. The eleventh and twelfth are identical with the *Book of Adam and Eve*, translated by S. C. Malan, D.D. (London: 1882). This work was composed in Egypt about the sixth or seventh century, whence it was translated into Æthiopic. Some few years ago it was discovered in Æthiopia, and published in Germany by Dr. E. Trump, of the University of Munich. The identity of the tradition in both cases is fixed by one point. Both place Adam's skull or body in Golgotha, where it remained till Christ's cross was planted in it. Dr. Malan says the original work was unknown in the West, and presents no trace of Hellenic influence. If so, its presence in Ireland is very striking. See Dr. Hort on the Conflict of Adam and Eve, in an article on the Book of Adam in *Dict. Christ. Biog.*, i., 34; see above note p. 188.

[2] See Lucian's *Pseudomantis*, c. xliv., and Milman's note on the

But the researches of Dicuil and the daring of Irish travellers were not confined to the south. They reached to the farthest north as well. Dicuil describes Iceland long before it was discovered by the Danes. The Irish anchorites penetrated to it in the eighth century, and established Christian worship there. It was only in 874 that Iceland was colonised by the Northmen, and they have recorded that on their landing they found it had been previously inhabited by Irish Christians, who left behind them "Irish books, bells, and crosiers." Dicuil describes Iceland on the authority of persons who had lived there. Writing in 825, he says, "It is now thirty years since I was told by some Irish ecclesiastics who had dwelt in that island from the 1st of February to the 1st of August, that the sun scarcely sets there in summer, but always leaves, even at midnight, light enough to do one's ordinary business;" and then he gives an instance of its power, which does not speak much for the cleanliness of those ancient Irish anchorites, but shows the antiquity of a custom still prevalent in backward localities of this country. I can only give it to you in the original Latin. The light, continues Dicuil, is there so clear at midnight that one is able to perform such an ordinary piece of business as "Pediculos de camisia abstrahere tamquam in præsentia solis." But our time presses, and we must leave Dicuil. His book, however, proves completely what I have already maintained, that Ireland had in the eighth century a vigorous and living intercourse with the most distant East.

Let me now call your attention to some circum-

---

ancient communication between the Red Sea and the Mediterranean, in his edition of Gibbon, ch. li., where he collects the ancient authorities.

stances which show that a considerable knowledge of Greek and Hebrew, as well as a very extensive and critical acquaintance with patristic literature, existed in the ancient Irish schools. Every student of history knows that Joannes Scotus Erigena was summoned to France by Charles the Bald, where he alone was found capable of translating the Greek works of the pseudo-Dionysius.[1] John the Irishman was a truly erratic genius. He was brilliant, learned, heretical. He embodied in himself most of the virtues and vices of the Irish character, and to this alumnus of the monastery of Bangor can be directly traced the genesis of that Pantheistic philosophy which many moderns ascribe wholly to Spinoza. Through Joannes Scotus, the Irish schools indeed exercise a direct influence over the philosophic thought of modern Europe. But Greek was not confined to Bangor. The *Book of Armagh* bears witness to the existence of Greek studies in the Primatial city;[2] while again, to come to later times,

---

[1] A good account of the life and works of Joannes Scotus Erigena will be found in Ceillier, *Hist. des Auteurs Ecclesiastiques*, xii. 605—610. He wrote several brilliant works, one touching the question of predestination, where he opposed what we should call in modern language high Calvinism, and verges towards Pelagianism, which always seems to have had an attraction for the Celtic genius; another on the Eucharist, where he taught views opposed to transubstantiation; and another, *De Divisione Naturæ*, where he taught Pantheism. In this last he held that as before creation God alone existed, and in Him were the potential causes of all future existences, so too in the end all created existences would return to God and be swallowed up in the Divine nature; a doctrine which would practically be equivalent to the Buddhist Nirvana. Gieseler's *Eccles. Hist.*, t. ii. p. 284—299 (Edinb.: Clark, 1847), has a good analysis of these controversies.

[2] The Lord's Prayer in the *Book of Armagh* is written in Latin words, but in Greek characters; a tombstone has been found at Glendalough with a bilingual inscription, Greek and Irish; see *Irish Achæol. Jour.* (1883), p. 42.

we find that Cormac MacCullinan, A.D. 831—903, the supposed builder of that exquisite structure, Cormac's Chapel on the Rock of Cashel, wrote a glossary of Irish names, where he gives some very original derivations, which would not stand the tests of modern philology.[1] They prove, however, his knowledge of Greek. Thus, to give you a specimen, he derives Tara from the Greek θεωρεῖν, *to behold*,—influenced doubtless by the commanding position it occupies over the low-lying plains of Meath. In the year 986 again, we read[2] of Irish monks uniting with Greek ecclesiastics in performing service according to the Greek rite, at Toul in France. The memory of this Greek connection did not die out till after the Reformation and amid the troubles of the seventeenth century, as Archbishop Ussher tells us that even in his time there remained a church at Trim called the Greek Church.[3]

But now I must describe some of the works which establish the solid claim of the ecclesiastics of that age to a reputation for extensive learning. The latter half of the seventh century was a period when Clonard was a most flourishing establishment, very different from

---

[1] See Whitley Stokes' *Three Irish Glossaries*, where in the preface, ix.—xviii., he sets forth the reasons for and against Cormac's authorship. He admits, however, that it may have been written "if not in Cormac's time, at least within a century or so after his death."

[2] *Hist. Litt. de la France*, vi., 638.

[3] See Ussher's Works, ed. Elrington, t. iv., p. 462, where he calls attention to a Greek named Dobda, who went from Ireland into Germany, with Virgil the Geometer, an Irish monk, and first bishop of Salzburg, about whom see below. Ussher's comment on this story is a very pregnant one. "Mirarer veroex Hibernia nostra hominem Græcum prodiisse, nisi scirem in agro midensi apud Trimmenses, ædem sacrem extitisse, quæ Græcæ ecclesiæ nomen ad hunc usque diem retinet." *Cf.* Dean Butler's *History of Trim*, p. 141, in whose time, *i.e.* forty years ago, the site of it was still called the Greek Park.

the condition in which we now find it, when a national school alone represents its ancient college. About the year 660 Aileran was abbat of that place, as he died of the great plague which ravaged all western Europe in the year 665.[1] We have substantial evidence remaining of his attainments. He wrote a work on the mystical meaning of the names in our Lord's genealogy, which Lanigan describes as "small, but exhibiting, besides a great share of ingenuity, very considerable Biblical and theological learning." You can consult it for yourselves by turning to Fleming's *Collectanea*, where it is printed from a MS. of St. Gall.[2] In this work Aileran displays an acquaintance with Origen, Jerome, Philo, Cassian, and Augustine. He takes the names of our Lord's progenitors, investigates the meaning of the original Hebrew, and skilfully deduces lessons and applications which would afford valuable hints to some modern preachers. Have we not all heard preachers edifying congregations by interpretations not nearly so skilful or well-founded as the following specimens, which the Clonard abbat produced twelve hundred years ago? He finds prophecies of Christ or of Christ's attributes in every minute particular of His ancestors' names. Thus he takes the name Isaac, which means joy; this is a clear prophecy of our Lord: the angel said to the shepherds, "Lo, I announce to you great joy, which shall be to all people." Phares means a divider; for Christ separates the sheep from the goats, that is the fruit-bearing from the barren souls. Aram signifies the Elect One, and of Christ it has been said, "Lo my

---

[1] See Sir W. Wilde's "History of Epidemic Pestilences in Ireland," in the *Report of the Irish Census Commission of* 1851, p. 50 (Dublin: 1856). This report is very full of interesting illustrations of ancient Irish social life; *cf. Proc.* R. I. A., vi., 399.

[2] Reprinted in Migne's *Patrologia Latina*, lxxx., 328.

Servant Whom I have elected, Mine Elect upon Whom I have placed My Spirit." Aileran adopted the principle of the old divine, who explained that he always chose a long text so that, if persecuted in one verse, he might flee unto another. Aileran had three resources upon which to fall back. If Greek and Hebrew failed him, he tried the Vulgate. Thus Jacob offered a difficulty. Jacob means supplanter; and how could Christ answer to such a description ? Aileran fell back upon the Vulgate, however, where " supplantare " fortunately contains the word "planta," signifying either the sole of the foot, or else a young shoot or plant. The prophecy is then quite clear. The Lord is the plant of renown, and the foot thrusts things backward; and Christ supplanted Satan when He said, " Get thee behind Me, Satan," and thus thrust him backwards; and so on *ad infinitum*, quite in the style of a mystical teacher of our own day.

Augustine, an Irish monk of the seventh century, was a scriptural expositor whose writings will repay study. He composed a treatise on the *Wonders of Scripture*, which was long ascribed to the great St. Augustine of Hippo, and bound up with his works. It is worth notice, both on account of its historical references to Ireland, and also from the light it throws upon the theological position of this ancient Celtic writer. In the prologue, Augustine mentions two eminent Irish scholars of that age,—St. Manchan, of Lemanaghan, in the King's County,[1] and St. Baithen,[2] who lived near

---

[1] See a learned paper by the late Rev. James Graves on St. Manchan in *Jour.* Roy. Hist. and Arch. Soc. Ir., 4th series, vol. iii., pp. 134—150; art. " Manchanus " in *Dict. Christ. Biog.*, iii., 792; Ussher's Works, vi., 552. St. Manchan's shrine is still in existence (O'Curry's *Lectt.*, i., 337).

[2] *Dict. Christ. Biog.*, i., 237.

the remarkable hill of Usnach in Westmeath. He further displays his nationality by referring to the ebb and flow of the tides on the Irish coast, and the animals at that time inhabiting Ireland. He offers an explanation of their existence in Ireland wonderfully similar to that put forward by the latest investigators of geology. They arrived when there was neither Irish Sea nor German Ocean, and both England and Ireland formed a portion of the European continent. His work on the *Difficulties of Scripture* is divided into three parts: first, on the difficulties in the Historical Books; secondly, on those in the Prophets; and, thirdly, on those in the New Testament. I can only give brief specimens of them. He reconciles Gen. ii. 2, where God is said to have rested from all His work, with John v. 17, where our Lord says, "My Father worketh hitherto, and I work," by distinguishing between the work of direct and immediate creation, which has ceased, and the work of rule and guidance (" gubernatio "), which still continues. He has some curious notions about Enoch, teaching that he is still alive and reserved as one of the two witnesses who shall appear, according to Rev. xi., in the last age of the world's history. He must, however, then die, and thus, like the other sons of Adam, pass through the gates of death.[1] His explanations about the Deluge are very ingenious. Aquatic animals like fishes could not, of course, perish through water; nay, rather they are preserved through it, as water was the element through which regeneration and salvation

---

[1] Augustine derived these views from his patristic studies. See Tertull., *De Anima*, c. 50; Thilo's *Cod. Apoc.*, N. T., p. 765, and art. "Enoch" in Smith's *Dict. of the Bible*.

should be afterwards attained by the human race. The case of animals which gain their food in the deep, but rest on land, like otters and crocodiles, had to be considered. How did they escape? Irish ingenuity here came to the rescue, and he suggests that Noah may have made a ledge or broad platform all round the ark, on which such animals took their accustomed repose, and thus sustained existence. The whole work is interesting and instructive. It was evidently produced by a good scholar skilled in books, and with a wide experience in foreign travel. Thus in i. 28 he quotes the Chronicle of Eusebius; in i. 6 he refers to Egypt and the annual overflow of the Nile like one who had seen both. He often quotes Jerome; he shirks no difficulty; Balaam's ass, the walls of Jericho, the standing still of the sun, the swimming of the axe, Lot's wife, all come under review, and receive an explanation sometimes very modern in tone and sentiment. His theory of miracles is very ingenious. He maintains that in the case of a miracle nothing is done contrary to nature, but that some pre-existing law or principle is developed, and the result produced according to natural laws. Thus Lot's wife is turned into a pillar of salt, but this is in no degree irrational, or even contrary to nature. Salt is very largely diffused throughout the human system, as the tears which flow from the eyes clearly prove. Divine power simply permitted or caused an extreme development of this one element, and lo! the pillar of salt was produced. Perhaps the most interesting point for us about Augustine is this: he proves that the ancient Celtic Church of the seventh century held the same view upon the canon of Scripture as our own Church. He rejects the story of Bel and the Dragon "because it has not the authority of Holy Scripture,"[1] and declines to discuss the difficulties of the Maccabees on the same ground (ii. 34). " In the Books of the Maccabees some wonderful things are found, which might conveniently be inserted into this rank ; yet will we not weary ourselves with any care thereof, because we only purposed to touch in some measure a short historical exposition of the wonderful things contained in the Divine canon."[2]

Towards the end of the eighth century two great scholars flourished, Virgil the geometer and Sedulius the commentator. Virgil was a distinguished missionary as well as an able scholar. He evangelised Salzburg and its neighbourhood, and was the first bishop of that see. He was evidently well acquainted with the Alexandrian school of mathematicians and geographers. He wandered from Ireland to preach the Gospel in Central Europe, where he got into trouble through his Greek studies. From them he had learned the doctrine of the earth's sphericity and the existence of the antipodes. He had not learned, however, the great secret of all safe and of most successful men, never to startle one's hearers by advocating any novel or unpopular view. He proclaimed fearlessly all he knew about God's works either in nature or in grace, and as the result was accused to the Pope of preaching a theory very similar to that expounded in Lord Lytton's last work, *The Coming Race.* His opponents could not grasp the idea of the antipodes. So they

---

[1] A fact which gives much trouble to the Benedictine Sabatier, in his edition of the *Old Latin Bible*, ii., 883.
[2] See Ussher's *Religion of the Ancient Irish*, ch. i., in Works, iv., 250, ed. Elrington ; Reeves on Augustine in *Proc.* Roy. Ir. Acad., vii., 514. Augustine's works are in Migne's *Pat. Lat.*

accused him of heresy, and the Pope condemned him for teaching that there was a world inside the visible external world, with inhabitants who dwell there.[1]

The most striking monument of the erudition of that period is found in the commentaries of Sedulius, the manuscript proof of whose Greek scholarship still exists. If you turn to Montfauçon's great work *Palæographia Græca*, iii., 7, p. 236, you will find a specimen of a Greek psalter written by his hand, and preserved till the last century at the Convent of St. Michael in Lorraine. Sedulius was a man of wide erudition. Nothing came amiss to him. To-day he was copying a Greek psalter, to-morrow writing a political pamphlet, composing Latin verses, or compiling a learned commentary. He wrote a treatise on government, which Cardinal Mai discovered in the Vatican, and published in his *Nova Collectio Scriptt.*, t. ix. In this he discusses the power, conduct, and duties of princes, not in the dry style of a Hugo Grotius or of a Macchiavelli, but enlivens every page with Latin verses in various metres, grave and gay. He composed a grammatical treatise, using the older grammarians Priscian and Donatus as a basis. But his claim to fame rests upon his commentaries.[2] He explained

---

[1] See, for Virgil's history, Ussher's Works, ed. Elrington, iv., 324, 461-465; Pertz, *Mon. Ger. Hist.* (Scriptt.), t. xi., pp. 84-95; Mabillon's, *AA. SS. Ord. Bened.*, iii., 2, pp. 308-318; Potthast's *Bibliotheca*, *s.v.* Virgil flourished about 750-784.

[2] See his works in Migne's *Patrologia Latina*, t. ciii. Sedulius used Origen's writings very largely, sometimes copying whole pages. He also quotes Eusebius, Augustine, Chrysostom, Ambrose, Jerome, Aquila, the Gospel of the Hebrews, discusses, in connection with Rom. iii. 10-18, St. Paul's manner of quoting the Hebrew Scriptures, mentions deaconesses as existing in the East, and the Agape as still celebrated on the Sabbath in Egypt,— a fact he may have learned from Palladius and Cassianus; see, for instance, a curious story illustrating this in the life of the

Jerome's prefaces to the Gospels, and makes abundant use of the older writers. Ussher quotes these commentaries at great length in his treatise on *The Religion of the Ancient Irish*. Ussher and Sedulius were agreed on one important point: they were both devoted followers of St. Augustine about predestination, or what we should call extreme Calvinists. His teaching on this point is clear and distinct. Let me give you a specimen. Sedulius, commenting on the words of Rom. ix., "He hath mercy on whom He will have mercy, and whom He will He hardeneth," writes thus: "God has mercy with great goodness, and hardeneth without any iniquity, so that neither he that is delivered can glory of his own merits, nor he that is condemned complain but of his own merits, forasmuch as grace only maketh the distinction betwixt the redeemed and the lost, who, by a cause drawn from their common original, were framed together into one mass of perdition." Or, again, take the opening of his commentary on Romans. He is discussing St. Paul's words "Vocatus apostolus." He shows his Greek and Hebrew learning. He gives the Greek and the Hebrew for Apostle,[1] and then proceeds to state his views on the

---

abbat Nathanael, in *Vitæ Patrum*, Migne's *Pat. Lat.*, t. lxxiii., 1108; *cf.* Georgii, *Mirac. S. Coluthi*, p. 113, for a learned dissertation on the Agape in Egypt; Soz., *H.E.*, vii., 19; Soc., v. 22; articles "Agapæ" in *Dict. Christ. Antiqq.*, t. i., pp. 39-41, "Nathanael" and "Sedulius" in *Dict. Christ. Biog.* In his Commentary on the Romans, Sedulius has some noble thoughts on the nature, use, and end of law, and also on instant prayer. Our Irish Sedulius has been sometimes confounded with Sedulius, a fifth century poet, whose works have lately been republished in the Vienna *Corpus Scriptt. Eccles. Latt.*, t. x., ed. Joh. Hümer, 1885. From the Prolegom., p. iv., we learn that the poet Sedulius was a great favourite in the Irish monastery of Bobbio.

[1] Sedulius often refers to the Hebrew and Greek originals.

word "*vocatus,*" "*called.*" "Many are called, but few are chosen. Judas was called, but he was not chosen, because the elect cannot be separated from God." But you must understand that such extreme Augustinian views did not mark all the Irish scholars of that period, and the most distinguished of them, Joannes Scotus and his friends, repudiated and opposed them with all the energy and with all the genius they possessed. Sedulius and John were not, indeed, contemporaries. Sedulius belonged to an older generation. Like Joannes Scotus, he sought the French court, but it was in the days of Charlemagne, and the political treatise to which I have referred seems to have been compiled for the direction of that prince or his son. It sheds a flood of light upon a pressing danger which Sedulius feared. Charlemagne and his family were strong and determined. Like our own Tudors and Stuarts, they were addicted to theological studies, and were apt to legislate on Church matters. The Western use of the clause concerning the procession of the Holy Ghost from the Son in the Nicene Creed is due to the action and decree of Charlemagne in the teeth of papal opposition. Sedulius perceived the danger which might flow from this source, and was careful to lay down that kings are to be guided in theological matters by the advice and counsel of ecclesiastical assemblies. "The religious

---

Thus on Gal. iii. and Heb. vii. he commends the "Hebrew verity," and corrects the Latin N. T. by the Greek original. As to the Latin versions used in the early Irish Church, there is much room for investigation. The Old Latin and the Hieronymian Vulgate were both of them in use. Sometimes the same MS. will show their joint use by the one writer. Professor T.K. Abbott's learned work, *Evangeliorum Versio ante-Hieronymiana*, Dublin: 1884, specially Pref., pp. xiv., xv., and Ussher's *Religion of the Ancient Irish*, chap. i., should be consulted on this question.

king ought to be cautious, humble, and truly circumspect. Neither may he presume to determine anything on ecclesiastical matters until he know the decrees of his synod;" supporting this contention by many a reference to ancient authorities, Greek and Latin. Sedulius thus united high ecclesiastical claims with high predestination theology. His ecclesiastical views suited the age, and took root. His theology was repugnant to it, and faded away. He was the teacher and forerunner of a Gottschalk, who in the next generation pressed his principles to their logical conclusion. Gottschalk was met by Joannes Scotus in his celebrated treatise *De Predestinatione*, wherein, however, our brilliant countryman fell into some of those Pantheistic speculations which he developed in his still more celebrated work *De Divisione Naturæ*. Time would fail me to tell you of these speculations. Ueberweg, in his *History of Philosophy*, will give you, what I cannot now, a good sketch of John's theories and the influence exercised by them over modern thought. It must suffice for my purpose to show you that a thinker was educated in the Irish schools of those times who understood Aristotle in the original, who thoroughly grasped the system of Neoplatonism as expounded in the works of a Plotinus, an Iamblichus, a Simplicius, and thus forms in himself the great connecting link between that system and the speculations of the mediæval schoolmen.

Concerning the organisation of the schools and monasteries which produced such distinguished pupils we know but little. It was most probably very loose and simple. The modern university system can be traced back to the school system of Charlemagne, but scarcely farther. The Irish schools were most probably modelled after the form and rules of the Egyptian Lauras, the monastery of St. Mary at Nitria, and the school of Lerins, with which tradition connects the education of St. Patrick himself. These institutions were all closely united together, and, as I have already shown, pilgrimages from Ireland to Egypt were not unknown down to the close of the eighth century. Egypt furnished the original type, and imparted the original tone. The Irish schools then developed themselves in accordance with their own genius. They had one pre-eminent quality, distinguishing them from too many of their descendants: they pursued learning for its own sake. They did not require to be bribed by prizes and scholarships. They conceived, and rightly conceived, that learning was its own reward. The schools had moderate landed endowments, and their teaching was apparently free to all, or, at any rate, imparted at a very low charge. Bede[1] tells us that the Irish professors were in the habit of receiving English pupils, educating, feeding,

---

[1] *H. E.*, iii., 27, where speaking of the celebrated pestilence of A.D. 664, he says, "This pestilence did no less harm in the island of Ireland. Many of the nobility and of the lower ranks of the English nation were there at that time who in the days of the bishops Finan and Colman, forsaking their native island, retired thither, either for the sake of Divine studies, or of a more continent life, and some of them presently devoted themselves to a monastical life; others chose rather to apply themselves to study, going about from one master's cell to another. The Scots willingly received them all, and took care to supply them with food, as also to furnish them with books to read and their teaching, gratis." On the pestilence of 664—665 see Ussher's Works, ed. Elrington, vi., 515, 516, 538—541, 607, 608. Among those who died from its ravages were Dermit and Blathmac, kings of Ireland, Fechin, Abbat of Fore, Aileran the Wise, a commentator already mentioned, two abbats of Clonmacnois, Colman Cass and Cummene, and St. Cronan, the celebrated founder of the Abbey of Roscrea.

and supplying them with books, without making any charge at all,—a course which may be commended for imitation by English schoolmasters, as regards their Irish pupils at least. They lived under very simple conditions of society. They had no solid halls or buildings; a few wattled huts constituted their college. They lived an *alfresco* life. They taught and studied in the open air, just as in the hedge-schools of former days which Carleton depicts. Adamnan's *Life of Columba* tells us how he beheld a cruel murder as he was studying beneath a tree under the direction of Gemman, his master, at the school of Clonard.[1] Yet they had an organised system. They had usually a chief or senior lecturer.[2] They had professors of law, of poetry, of history, and of the other branches of education. They had an œconomus, or steward, who managed the temporal affairs of the institution. They had special schools, too, some of which lasted till modern times. The union of law and modern history, as in our own university, was not unknown there. MacFirbis, the annalist, who assisted Sir James Ware, the Irish antiquary, and was his chief authority on all questions of Irish language and history, belonged to a hereditary college of historians in the county Sligo; and that same MacFirbis studied Brehon law and Irish history, together with classics, at a school in the town of Tipperary, which lasted till two hundred years ago.[3]

---

[1] Reeves' *Adamnan*, p. 137.
[2] See Alcuin's Epistle to Colcu of Clonmacnois, in Ussher's *Sylloge*, ep. xviii., Works, ed. Elrington, iv., 466.
[3] Upon ancient Irish schools and the sad story of MacFirbis, the reader may consult Mr. Hennessy's learned Preface to the *Chronicon Scotorum*, to which work I, in common with all modern investigators of Irish history, am deeply indebted.

## LECTURE XII.

### *THE ROUND TOWERS OF IRELAND.*

THE science of historical criticism is largely a modern invention. The methods of inquiry pursued by, say, Tacitus, Livy, or Eusebius, were practically identical with those followed by a Burnet, a Robertson, or a Hume in the last century. But the extension of knowledge, the increased facilities for travel, the investigations of science, the accumulation and study of ancient documents, have worked a revolution in historical as well as other sciences, and have produced as the result the science of historical criticism, which, subjecting old and threadbare topics to a fresh examination, has thrown light upon many a darkened corner. Historical criticism attains this end by adopting simply the method of common sense, which is only another name for sound and true criticism. Goldsmith is a type of the old historian. You all remember how Lord Macaulay has described him in this character. Goldsmith compiled, for the use of schools, histories of Rome, of Greece, and of England, as well as a natural history. His qualifications for any of these were of the slenderest description. "If he can tell a horse from a cow," said Johnson, "that is the extent of his knowledge in zoology." In fact, instead of being qualified to write a natural history, he was profoundly ignorant of the subject. On one occasion, he, in defiance of the evidence of his own senses, maintained obstinately, and even angrily, that he chewed his dinner by moving his upper jaw. His qualifications for writing histories of England or Rome were not of any higher or profounder nature. He just acted as all his predecessors had done. He selected, abridged, translated into his own pure, clear, and flowing language, what he found in books well known to the world, but too bulky or too dry for boys and girls. But as for making independent investigations into a subject, he never dreamt of it. He committed, therefore, the strangest blunders, and was all but hoaxed into inserting in the *History of Greece* an account of a battle between Alexander the Great and Montezuma, ruler of Mexico when Columbus discovered America. Historical criticism has changed all this, and teaches that no one is qualified to write or to understand the history of a country till he has investigated not only the documents which directly bear upon it, but also its architecture, its art, its physical conformation, and its literature. Taught, then, by historical criticism, I ask you to follow me this day into a discussion of one of these subjects as illustrating the thesis I have so often urged, that Irish monasticism is largely due to Oriental influences, and still preserves clear evidence of its original. I shall take up for this purpose the interesting but oft-debated subject of the Round Towers.

First of all, however, I should perhaps tell some among you what a round tower is, though such ignorance in an assembly of Irishmen—and specially of Dublin men—is simply inexcusable, because we have in our own neighbourhood some half-dozen of the fine s specimens: at Clondalkin, for instance, within an easy afternoon's walk of this spot, and then at Glendalough, Kildare, Lusk, Swords, Kells, and Donaghmore, all within thirty miles of this city. There are upwards of one hundred round towers known in Ireland. The tower is a hollow, circular column, from fifty to one hundred and fifty feet high, usually capped by a short pointed roof of stone. From the base, which is frequently of Cyclopean masonry, and measures from forty to sixty feet in circumference, the tower is externally of ashlar or spawled rubble-work, and tapers upwards towards the summit. Occasionally, as at Ardmore, it is belted with string courses, which are, however, entirely ornamental, and not connected with the internal floors. The wall is pierced for a single door, which is always eight to fifteen feet above the level of the ground, and for windows, which are unfixed in position and number. The windows and doors are generally splayed. At a very short distance from the conical roof there are usually four windows. Internally, the tower is divided into storeys, varying in number according to the height, about twelve feet apart.

Few subjects have given rise to more debate than the round towers, simply because men have disregarded the principles of just criticism, and, instead of using rational methods of investigation, have evolved their history out of the depths of their own imaginations. The round towers have been attributed to fire-worshippers, to the original pagan inhabitants of Ireland, to the Firbolgs and Fenians, and, lastly, to the Danes, those roving sea-pirates, who, if they sorely harried this land a thousand years ago, have ever since been suffering the due reward of their deeds in bearing the burden of every action, good, bad, or indifferent, which could not be referred to any other cause. Let me mention some of the writers who have favoured these various views. Keane and O'Brien have maintained that they were the temples of a primitive religion among the Cuthites, though what brought the Cuthites to Ireland, I know not; General Vallancy, at the end of the last century, identified them with the pyreia, or fire-towers, of Phœnician, Persian, and other Eastern nations; Windele called them bell-towers; Walsh, Ledwich, and Molyneux called them Danish forts; Harris and Smyth determined that they were pillars for Stylite saints, like S. Simeon, whom I have already described. If so, our Irish saints had even a more uncomfortable and lofty position than the Syrian. Simeon stood at the top of a pillar, sixty feet high, in an erection like a pulpit, while the Irish saints had to stand or sit on the apex of a conical roof, a hundred feet from the ground, where the merest slip would consign them to certain destruction. The first person who undertook a rational investigation into their history was Dr. Petrie, in the great Memoir he compiled for the Royal Irish Academy, which you will find in the *Transactions* of that learned body for the year 1845. His investigations were continued and developed by the late Earl of Dunraven, in the magnificent volumes, well worth your study, with which he has enriched Irish literature, and by Miss Margaret Stokes, in her *Notes on Early Irish Architecture*. I shall now very briefly state the result of their investigations before proceeding to a further stage.

---

[1] The best modern works on round towers are Petrie's essay, *Trans. Roy. Ir. Acad.*, xx.; Lord Dunraven's *Memorials of Adare*, pp. 218, 232, and *Notes on Irish Architecture;* Miss Stokes' *Early Christian Architecture in Ireland.* Mr. Hennessy, in his *Chronicon Scotorum* (Rolls Series), p. 217, has fixed the date of the building of Tomgraney Round Tower at 964. This is

Their general conclusion is this. The round towers are not of pagan origin at all. The pagan Celts had no such knowledge of architecture as would enable them to build such very elaborate structures as they are. Their construction demanded, in fact, a very considerable knowledge of the principles and practice of architecture. The proof of this is easy enough. One can scarcely imagine that the pagan Celts of this country possessed more knowledge of architecture than an ordinary country builder of the present day. Now, if we were foolish enough to employ such a man to build us a round tower, like that of Lusk or of Clondalkin, without the guidance of a skilled architect, his work would probably tumble to the ground before it was fifty feet high.[1] Let me, however, as perhaps the best course of all, first tell you, in Dr. Petrie's own words, what his special conclusions were, and then set forth any modifications of his views at which more recent students have arrived. Dr. Petrie's work is styled *The Christian Architecture of*

---

the earliest historical notice of them in Ireland. The illustrations of Lord Dunraven's and Miss Stokes' works are admirable. Beautiful copies of them can be seen in the National Museum of Science and Art, Dublin.

[1] We are not devoid of a practical illustration of this argument. The Roman Catholic church of Slane has attached to it a round tower, built sixty or seventy years ago, when the present substantial church was built. It has, however, but a poor, ungraceful, stunted look when compared with the elegant tower of Donaghmore, which raises its head some four or five miles away. Several attempts have been made to build round towers of late years, but they are all comparative failures. The best I can now remember are those of Jordanstown Church, near Belfast, and of Kilcock Church, in Kildare. Mr. Drew, the learned architect of Christ Church Cathedral, Dublin, tells me that there are clear traces of classical influences in the construction of the round towers. The builders of them, he thinks, must have known the shape of the pillars in Greek temples.

*Ireland anterior to the Anglo-Norman Invasion.* It is well worth the study of every one who takes an intelligent interest in his country's antiquities. It is an ample refutation of such ignorant prejudices as I noted, for instance, the other day in a letter equally mischievous and ignorant, inserted in the *Daily Express*, signed "Irelander," which described the inhabitants of this island as simple barbarians prior to the invasion of Strongbow. I would commend, I say, this work of Dr. Petrie to your intelligent study, for you will find it, like his other work on the Hill of Tara, a most exhaustive, learned, and accurate discussion upon early Irish history.

Now Dr. Petrie's general conclusions, substantially adopted by every subsequent inquirer, about the round towers are these: (1) That the round towers are of Christian and ecclesiastical origin, and were erected at various periods between the fifth and thirteenth centuries.[1] (2) That they were designed to answer at least a twofold use; namely, to serve (a) as belfries, and (β) as keeps, or places of strength, in which the sacred utensils, books, relics, and other valuables were deposited, and into which the ecclesiastics to whom they belonged could retire for security in case of sudden predatory attack.[2] (3) That they

---

[1] This Christian origin seems proved by the fact that the Tower of Donaghmore has a figure of the Saviour sculptured over it, just as the round tower of Brechin, in Scotland, has a representation of the Crucifixion carved in relief.

[2] Towers were used by the solitaries of Mount Sinai for exactly the same purpose, under exactly the same circumstances; see an instance of this in the case of the monks of Mount Sinai and the Saracen queen Mavia, A.D. 373, in Combefis (*Lecti Triumphi*, p. 91, Paris: 1660); Ceillier (*Aut. Eccles.*, iv., 284); S. Sabas, in the *Dict. Christ. Biog.* Round towers are even still used for purposes of defence as well as ornament in Central Asia. See several instances of this in a series of articles and

were probably also used, when occasion required, as beacons and watch-towers. The only modification of these statements which recent investigators have offered is this: Lord Dunraven does not date them so early as Petrie. The latter fixed the fifth century, the time of S. Patrick, as the date of the earliest. Lord Dunraven fixes the date of the earliest as subsequent to the year 800 and the invasion of the Danes. Now let us accept the conclusions and dates of Petrie and Dunraven. They have formed them upon solid evidence. They carefully examined the towers themselves and the ecclesiastical buildings with which they are always found connected. They searched our ancient records thoroughly, and extracted every fact or notice which might throw light on their history. They compared them carefully with every vestige of early Christian or pagan architecture in Ireland, and they brought to bear on their investigations the most highly trained and skilled architectural and artistic knowledge, and, as the result, have presented us with conclusions which have never since been effectually disputed. Let us now see whether historical, architectural, and archæological inquiries of a still later date do not bear them out, and shed even fresh light upon conclusions at which men like Petrie, with the instinct of genius, have arrived. Petrie laid down that the round

---

illustrations on Bokhara and Khiva in the *Oesterreichische Monatsschrift für den Orient.*, Vienna: 1885, p. 264, and 1886, March and April, pp. 50 and 66. In De Vogüé's work, i., 58 (*cf.* plate 18), a tower attached to a church is depicted, which he considers was evidently for defensive purposes. It is divided into stories like the round towers, and has a door with a flat lintel in exactly the same position as those of the round towers. De Vogüé makes the church fifth century. The tower is very like the primitive square tower on Innisclothran (Quaker Island) in Lough Ree (see note on p. 187). *Cf.* Clarke's *Picturesque Palestine*, iv., 86.

towers were used as bell-towers for the churches beside which they always stood. Now whence did they come? *Ex nihilo nihil* is a motto of universal application. The law of cause and effect pervades our terrestrial world, whatever may happen in other worlds, and the more we investigate the more we find that no phenomena spring up spontaneously; they are ever the outcome of some foregoing conditions. Whence, then, did round towers connected with churches come to Ireland? The reply to this question will illustrate our thesis, that the Irish Church bears many marks of Oriental influences. To answer, however, this query aright, we must bestow a brief study upon the subject of Christian churches in general.

Church towers, either round or square, form no necessary or original parts of Christian churches. The earliest churches were simple basilicas. The basilica was the Roman modification of the Greek temple and of Grecian architecture. The Greeks knew nothing of the principle of the arch. This was the Roman contribution to the science of architecture. Now neither the Greek temple nor the Roman basilica had anything like a tower attached to it. The earliest Christian churches were, therefore, in the same condition. They were utterly towerless, and, to this day at least, a very considerable number of churches in the city of Rome are in exactly the same original condition.[1]

[1] The very ancient Irish churches had no bell-towers apart from the round towers. In my own neighbourhood, the old churches of Dean's Grange, Killiney, Howth, Bray, Ireland's Eye, Tullow, and numerous others are towerless. The only exception is the square tower on Innisclothran in Lough Ree (*cf.* Petrie's *Round Towers*, p. 360). Greg. Turon. (*De Gloria Marit.*, i., 65), mentions the building of a church with a tower and pharos. This is one of the earliest notices of such an erection. Lord Dunraven (*Notes on Irish Archit.*, vol. ii., p. 140) mentions a

This is a most important fact. It lies at the basis of our whole investigation, and should, therefore, be most carefully borne in mind. Whence, then, came the invention of church towers and steeples? They came, I believe, from Syria, the very same quarter whence came many other peculiarities of our early Celtic Church. Let me point out to you how this was. Napoleon III. was a man who committed great mistakes, and established a system of government which helped largely to demoralise the French nation; but though he had the vices of a despot, he had also some of the magnificent virtues of such a character, chief among which was the splendid assistance he lent to scholarship and to travel. It was under his patronage, for instance, that M. Renan produced the magnificent volume you will find in our library devoted to the archæology and history of Northern Palestine, the Lebanon, and Phœnicia. It was under his patronage, and at his expense, that M. Waddington investigated, as they were never investigated before, the antiquities of Asia Minor; and it was under the same discriminating patronage the Count de Vogüé produced an exhaustive and splendidly illustrated work called *Central Syria: its Architecture, Civil and Religious, from the First to the Seventh Century.*" This work has been strangely neglected by English scholars. I found on the first occasion on which I asked for it in the British Museum, some seven years ago, that it was unknown to the officials. But on making a search, they discovered it, unbound and uncut, as it came from the

---

suggestion of Mr. Freeman's, that the primitive small square churches of Ireland may have been ultimately derived from Italy in the fourth and fifth centuries, before the basilica and the apse were Christianised, or bell-towers required.

printers. Now it is this work, containing as it does a mass of information equally important for the classical or Semitic scholar, the architect, and the archæologist, which enables us to trace the genesis of the round towers of Ireland, and, indeed, also the genesis of Gothic architecture itself, a point which has hitherto eluded the investigations of antiquarians.

Let me first describe the ground which yielded those results. I shall do so in the words of Count de Vogüé himself: "Central Syria is the region which extends from north to south, from the frontiers of Asia Minor to those of Arabia Petræa, bounded on the east by the great Mesopotamian desert, and on the west by the rivers Jordan, Leontes, and Orontes. In this region we find a series of deserted cities almost intact, the sight of which transports the traveller back into the midst of a lost civilisation, and reveals to him all its secrets. In traversing those deserted streets, those abandoned courts, those porticoes where the vine twines round mutilated columns, we receive an impression like that experienced at Pompeii, less complete, indeed, but more novel, for the civilisation which we contemplate is less known than that of the age of Augustus. The buildings date from the first to the seventh century, and all seem to have been abandoned, as it were, on one day, upon the Saracen invasion, about A.D. 700. We there are transported into the very midst of the Christian Church of that time. We see its life, not the hidden life of the catacombs, timid, suffering, but a life opulent, artistic, spent in splendid houses with galleries and balconies, in beautiful gardens covered with vines. There we see winepresses, magnificent churches, adorned with columns, flanked with towers, surrounded with splendid tombs." Such is a brief analysis of De Vogüé's lengthened and enthusiastic description of an almost unknown region, a region which, as he says, has been only approached by a few travellers, and the most interesting part of which, the northern district, has been visited by two men only: Pococke, the distinguished Irish bishop and traveller, and Burckhardt, the former belonging to the last century, the latter to the early part of the present. Yet, says De Vogüé, it is one of the richest districts of the world in ancient monuments of every kind.

Now you will observe that in this district architecture received a new direction. Central Syria was the bridge, as we might call it, by which Greek and Roman architecture developed into Byzantine, and through Byzantine into Western architecture. Let me state how this was. In the year 105 of our era this district was made a Roman province. From that date it entered upon a career of great material prosperity. Architecture especially flourished. On every side were built houses, palaces, baths, temples, theatres. Christianity triumphed in this region in the fourth century, and at once a series of magnificent churches was raised, which still remain to attest the enthusiasm of that time. Now mark two special features of all this Syrian architecture. 1. Stone is the only material used. The country produces no wood. By ingenious contrivances, therefore, the inhabitants constructed edifices in which everything is of stone—walls, roofs, doors, windows. Necessity was, in their case, the mother of invention, and they evolved new principles of architecture in the adaptation of the arch to their varied and novel circumstances, an adaptation which found its highest perfection, its final application, in the Gothic architecture of mediæval times. 2. They first discovered the use of cupolas and of church towers, built upon pendentives or hemispheres. The earliest attempt at such a cupola, brought to light by De Vogüé, was that of Omne-ez-Tertoun, dating from the year 282, in the reign of the Emperor Probus. This method of construction reached its highest perfection in the Church of St. Sophia, built in the sixth century at Constantinople by the Emperor Justinian. Any of you that have ever stood beneath the dome of St. Paul's will remember a magnificent instance of architecture originally derived from the Hauran of Syria.[1]

Again, the first instance of a church tower is found in the same country. It is a very humble effort indeed. The Church of Tafkha is dated by De Vogüé at the fourth century, and in this lowly attempt he sees the prototype of those towers which have now become the most prominent feature in religious buildings. Such was Syrian Christian architecture in the fourth and fifth centuries; now let me very briefly trace its connection with the West. Syria was the great school for artists and for scholars in the fifth and sixth centuries. The school of Antioch at that time surpassed almost every other in scientific and literary repute, and its methods dominated all the East. Justinian, in the middle of the sixth century, wished to rebuild the cathedral of Constantinople, and from the school of Antioch he drew both his architects, Anthemus of Tralles and Isidore of Miletus.[2] Under their direction

---

[1] See Ch. Bayet's "L'Art Byzantin," in the *Bibliothèque de l' Enseignement des Beaux Arts* (Paris: 1883), pp. 39-61, 130-140, and especially 309-318. *Cf.* p. 311, where there is a picture which shows round towers in two different stages of development.

[2] Bayet, *l.c.*, p. 44.

was raised a church which set the fashions for the whole Byzantine or Oriental world.

The Church of St. Sophia gave, as Viollet le Duc, the great French writer on architecture, remarks, in his sixth lecture on this topic, the first example of a cupola raised upon pendentives upon so grand a scale, that when Justinian saw it completed, he exclaimed, " Glory be to God, Who has judged me worthy to complete this work. I have, indeed, conquered thee, O Solomon." From Constantinople Byzantine architecture rapidly passed westwards. Greek art was dead. Roman art was dead. In the sixth century, the only living, powerful, vivifying art was the art and the architecture of Byzantium. I have now to show you two things: first, how Byzantine art and architecture passed over to Gaul; and, then, how from Gaul it passed to Ireland. In the first place, as to the transition of Byzantine architecture from Constantinople to Gaul, the time and place of transit are easily determined. Justinian was a great builder. The age of Justinian was an age of earthquakes, and it was also an age of restorations. He renewed towns, theatres, and churches, and helped to impoverish and weaken the empire by the magnificence of his restorations. He rebuilt, for instance, the walls of Assos, which Schliemann has been elaborately referring to prehistoric times, though an extant inscription tells us they were raised under Justinian.[1] In every quarter of the empire, churches still existing, either as Christian temples or Turkish mosques, testify

---

[1] Archæologists sometimes make amusing mistakes by trusting to conjecture or *à priori* reasoning, without careful examination of the objects submitted to them. We have all heard how the Berlin archæologists were taken in a few years ago by Shapira and his Moabite pottery, which they assigned to the times of the kings of Israel, while in reality they had been made a short

to the magnificence of Justinian's conceptions. No city, however, in his wide domains enjoyed more of his generous munificence than Ravenna, where to this day his portrait can be seen among the frescoes of the Church of St. Vitalis, built by his order and at his expense a short time subsequently to the completion of St. Sophia, at Constantinople. Now fix your attention upon this Church of St. Vitalis, because it marks the point of contact between the new Byzantine architecture and the west of Europe. It is in connection with it, and five other churches of Ravenna, that the first round towers appear in Europe, being apparently a modification and combination of the two principles derived from the Syrian Hauran—the principle of the church tower combined with that of the cupola. I cannot now spend time in enlarging upon the churches of Ravenna, and I have the less hesitation in not doing so, because you can all refer to Mr. Freeman's Historical Essays on Ravenna, and to Lord Dunraven's and Miss Stokes' books on Irish architecture, where the subject has been exhausted. Lord Dunraven dwells at some length upon this point. He insists, in his work on Irish architecture, and in his *Memorials of Adare* (pp. 218, 232), that the towers of Ravenna are genuine round towers; and, indeed, no one can look for a moment at the tower of the Church of St. John the Baptist in that city, without seeing that it is in all essential details identical with the round towers of Ireland, which have given rise to so much discussion.

And now I have to advance further. Having traced

---

time before in Jerusalem, a circumstance well illustrated by the famous story of the archæologists who were expatiating enthusiastically upon the ogam mark on a piece of rock, which closer examination, however, proved to be simply the profound and suggestive words, "Bill Sikes, his mark."

Syrian and Oriental art from the Hauran to Constantinople, and from Constantinople to Ravenna, I have to take another step and to show you how the round towers, and with them Byzantine and Eastern art in every department, extended itself from Ravenna to Ireland.

From Ravenna, Byzantine art spread itself in every direction in the southern and central parts of Europe. We have to this day many specimens of genuine round towers in these regions. Miss Stokes remarks, " A number of towers, which bear more or less resemblance to those of this country, still exist or are known to have existed in other places beside Ireland. They are all high, slender, circular, with pointed roofs, and occasionally built of bricks. The examples on the Continent are, the tower of Dinkelsbühl in Bavaria, the belfries of San Nicolo at Pisa, San Paternian in Venice, one at Schoenen in Switzerland, two at the Church of St. Thomas in Strasburg, two at Gernrode in the Hartz, two at Nivelles, one at St. Maurice Epinal in Lorraine, and many other places." But the great influx of Byzantine architects and ideas into the West happened in the eighth century, just immediately preceding the period which Lord Dunraven fixes as the date of our own round towers.

Charlemagne was, to a great extent, the founder of our modern European system and civilization. To him are largely due all our modern institutions, political, religious, and social. Art, learning, and literature are under the profoundest obligations to a prince who, though he could scarce sign his name, and was in many respects a rude barbarian in heart, yet always displayed the keenest interest in, and sympathy with, subjects of which he was profoundly ignorant. Circumstances, too, favoured him. He was a patron of learned men, and learned men gathered round him. He was a patron of art and architecture, and the controversies of the time laid at his feet and placed at his disposal the choicest treasures of Byzantine art and intellect. It is well known that the iconoclastic movement of the eighth century exercised a paralysing influence upon the students of painting and sculpture within the bounds of the Greek Church.[1] But while this great movement paralysed art in the East, it revived and developed it in the West. The monks, who were the painters, sculptors, architects of that age, were driven headlong from the East. The iconoclastic Emperors were Puritans, and Puritans have ever been intolerant. You all know how modern Puritans hanged the Quakers in New England, and flogged a man if he dared to kiss wife or child on a Sunday.[2] The ancient Puritans, the iconoclasts of the East, flogged the artists till they were almost dead, and then burned the flesh off their fingers, to prevent them painting or sculpturing any more images.[3] Art, however, though crushed or repressed for a time, cannot be destroyed, because it is the expression of a Divine instinct; and so these iconoclastic Emperors, simply by their intolerance, drove away the choicest spirits of the East, and compelled them to seek

---

[1] See Didron's *Hist. de Dieu*, part ii., edited and translated by Margaret Stokes (London: 1886), about the strict rules laid down for painters under the Greek Church. Art can never flourish in such leading-strings. Miss Stokes' work, which has just appeared, contains translations of the Greek Manuscript of Dionysius, from Mount Athos, to which reference is so often made in works on the History of Art. It lays down the restrictions imposed on artists by the Church.

[2] See the notes to Hessey's Bampton Lectures on "Sunday."

[3] See the article "Iconoclastæ," in the *Dict. Christ. Biog.*, iii., 204.

a shelter with that rival power which was claiming the name and dominions of a Western Cæsar. Charlemagne's age and court were marked by a wondrous incursion of Greek artists, who brought their skill and knowledge and artistic taste to enrich Western at the expense of Eastern Europe, just as the Huguenots of later times brought their skill and knowledge to enrich England at the expense of France. Let me call your special attention to this point. It is one of the keys to the knowledge of the middle ages. Unless you grasp it you will fail to put yourselves at the true standpoint for understanding the evolution of modern civilization. All the best modern writers lay stress upon it. Labarte for instance, in his great work on the *History of the Industrial Arts in the Middle Ages*, has pointed out its effect in developing such very various departments as the manufacture of silk, the carving of ivory, and the production of goldsmith's work. Viollet le Duc, the greatest modern writer on architecture, has dwelt upon it as explaining the outburst of architectural art which marked the ninth and subsequent centuries.

Now, to come back to our more immediate subject; it is an interesting fact that we can produce a distinct proof that the round towers were known by the Greek architects of Charlemagne's court, and the mode of their construction thoroughly understood and commonly practised by them. You all have heard of the monastery of St. Gall. It is the greatest depository on the Continent of Irish MSS., and justly so, for, as I have already told, it was founded twelve hundred years ago by two great Irish monks and missionaries, St. Gall and St. Columbanus. The town and monastery of St. Gall form a happy contrast to some other people, who, although they may owe all they have and are to Ireland, yet have a quiet knack of forgetting this fact as soon as they get out of the country, and would fain be thought ignorant of even its very existence. St. Gall has always acknowledged its obligations to Ireland, and kept up a lively correspondence with this University as representing its learning and intellect. In the library of St. Gall is still preserved one of the most curious documents existing in the whole world. This document is the original plan drawn out by Eginhard, Charlemagne's chief architect, for the rebuilding of the great Church of St. Gall. The Abbat Gozpertus, in the year 829, desired to signalize his rule by some great architectural work, and applied to Eginhard, who sent him back this plan, where we see provision made for two round towers at the east end of the apse,[1] while in the cathedral of Aix-la-Chapelle, erected between 796 and 804, under Charlemagne and by the same architect, we find two round towers at the west end of the church.[2]

We have only to deal with one other point, and then we have completed our proof. How, it may be asked, did the round towers get from Charlemagne's court to Ireland? Now there is no fact more patent on the face of history, to any one who has studied the original documents of the seventh, eighth, and ninth centuries, than this: that Ireland and France were then in closest and most frequent correspondence. The proofs of this

---

[1] This plan was published originally by Dr. F. Keller of Zurich, and republished by the Rev. Robert Willis in the *Archæological Journal* for 1848, p. 85; see Lord Dunraven's *Memorials of Adare*, p. 225. It was nominally the work of Eginhard, but really that of his Greek assistants. Like many a modern departmental chief, he gets the credit due to his subordinates.

[2] See the article on Charles the Great in the *Dict. Christ. Biog.*, t. i., p. 457.

are ample. The Bollandists, for instance, discovered a French king, Dagobert II., who was sent to Ireland for his education; Colgan's *Lives* frequently mention Irish saints who travelled to France, resided there for a time, and then returned, while the number of Merovingian and other French coins found from time to time in Ireland show the commercial intercourse to have been very important indeed.[1] Foreign ecclesiastics came to Ireland in abundance in that age. Fifty Roman monks, we are told in the life of St. Senan, settled in Ireland for the purpose of leading a life of stricter discipline, and improving themselves in the study of Scripture, then much cultivated in Ireland.[2] In the Litany of Oengus the Culdee, which is said to have been composed about the time of Charlemagne, we learn that even Orientals sought the shelter of this island, driven hither by the intolerance of the Eastern emperors.[3] That litany commemorates vast numbers of strangers who came to this island, Italians, Germans, Frenchmen, and among others the seven Egyptian monks buried in Disert Ulidh.[4] There was direct correspondence, too, between the French court at that

---

[1] See Bolland., *Thesaur. Antiquit.*, Diss. on the Chronology of Early Merovingian Kings, for Dagobert; *Contemp. Review*, January, 1883, p. 79; Index to *Proc.* Roy. Ir. Acad., t. vii., *s. v.* "Coins," for numerous references about foreign commerce with Ireland, and above, note, p. 16.

[2] See Life of St. Senan, in *Acta Sanctt.*, Boll. *Mart.*, i. 760-779; and Colgan's *Acta SS. Hib.*, p. 530.

[3] Dr. Whitley Stokes shows good reasons for attributing the Calendar and Litany of Oengus to the close of the tenth century, nearly two hundred years after the time of Oengus; see the preface to his edition of the Calendar of Oengus, published in the *Transactions* of the Royal Irish Acad., 1880.

[4] See, for a list of the foreigners who sought shelter or repose in Ireland, Colgan's *Acta Sanctt. Hib.*, p. 539, where he gives an extract from the Litany of Oengus, and Vit. S. Senan, in the same volume, p. 533. O'Curry, in his *Manners and Customs of*

age and the leading Irish monasteries, as I have shown in the cases of Erigena and of Colcu the correspondent and friend of Alcuin; so that there was no difficulty in transmitting from Gaul to Ireland a type of architecture so exactly suited to the troublous times of the Danish invasions. With the causes and results of that great movement we shall deal in the next lecture.[1]

---

*the Ancient Irish*, t. i., inserts in an appendix an ancient poem about the fair or convention of Carman in the co. Wexford. Greek merchants are mentioned by it as frequenting that fair.

[1] Mr. W. M. Hennessy has kindly given me the following information about the Litany of Oengus Celi-Dé. This litany contains lists (or rather groups) of bishops, saints, and pilgrims, whom Oengus invokes "in auxilium meum." There are two old copies of the litany, which is particularly valuable as containing a large list of names of places identified with groups of *seven* saints, or bishops. The oldest copy of the litany is that contained in the portion of the *Book of Leinster* formerly preserved in the Franciscan Monastery of St. Isidore, Rome, but now in the Convent of the Order in Merchant's Quay, Dublin. The age of this MS. is not later than A.D. 1200. (See Facsim. *Bk. Leinster*, p. 373, col. ii.) The second old copy is in the well-known Irish MS. called the *Leabhar Breac* (R. I. Ac.), written in the end of the fourteenth century. This copy begins imperfectly; although O'Curry does not seem to have noticed the fact (*MS. Materials*, pp. 353, 615). A full copy is contained in the MS. H. 1, 11 (T. C. D.); but this copy was only written in the last century.

The litany, a translation of which has been published by Ward, in his *Life of St. Rumold*, is frequently quoted and referred to by Colgan, as a record of great value and authority. It is much to be desired that the litany should be edited by one so competent as Mr. Hennessy.

# LECTURE XIII.

## *THE DANISH INVASION OF IRELAND AND THE PAGAN CRUSADE.*

IF you are wandering through the remoter parts of Ireland,—a practice, by the way, to which Irishmen are too little inclined,—and in the course of such wanderings come across earthworks such as you can see in abundance at Tara, or Navan, or Armagh, the natural question rises to the lip: Whence came they? The reply is always the same, The Danes made them; an answer which, quite apart from its accuracy, conclusively proves the deep impression which the great movement called the Danish Invasion made upon the national memory. It is that movement with its far-reaching results, to be even still traced upon Irish life and history, which we propose now to study. In meditating thereupon we must always remember one great fact. The Danish invasion of Ireland was only a part of a great national upheaval. The Scandinavians hurled themselves, not only upon Ireland, but also upon England, Scotland, France, and sought openings for their energy even so far south as Italy and Constantinople. The Norman sovereigns of Naples and of the Balearic Isles, with whom the learned labours of the Bollandists have made us acquainted, were offshoots from the same stock which supplied the Scandinavian kingdoms of Dublin, of Man, of Waterford. and of

Limerick.[1] And here let me say, that in studying this subject we are not treating a question of merely local interest. The Danish invasions have engaged the attention and exercised the minds of our best modern historians. Stubbs and Freeman, to mention only two of our highest living authorities, have bestowed careful and learned investigations upon them; while among ourselves, Mr. Haliday's *Scandinavian Kingdom of Dublin* has shed a flood of light upon a dark corner of European history. Let us now strive to determine the date and the causes of this great movement.

The time when the Danes began to harass these islands is well known. All the chroniclers are at one upon this point. The Danes made their first hostile incursions in the last decade of the eighth century. Many causes conspired to effect this end. Chief among them was Charlemagne's military and missionary activity. Their arrival upon our own coasts exactly synchronises with it. Charlemagne had just then ravaged Saxony and Northern Germany with fire and sword to compel the inhabitants to become nominal Christians. The fugitives who escaped this military missionary fled into Denmark and Scandinavia, burning with hatred to the Christian name and cause. Witikind, chief or king of the pagan Saxons, was son-in-law of Sigefroi, King of Denmark. Witikind headed a revolt against Charlemagne in 782, and was driven by him northwards, together with the fiercest of the Saxon idolaters. They worshipped practically the same gods and professed the same religion as their Danish hosts, whom they inspired with the same desire for

---

[1] See Papebrock's Dissertation on the Palatine Laws of James II. of Majorca, in Bolland., *Thesaur. Antiquit.*, t. i.; *Contemp. Review*, January 1883, p. 79.

vengeance upon the Christian Church which possessed themselves. This fact accounts for the bitter hostility displayed by the Northmen against churches and monasteries and the clergy at large. Again, causes purely internal to the northern nations conspired to the same end. Their princes were struck with the power and conquests of Charlemagne. They saw the vast resources he wielded, and they desired a national union and a powerful military force, such as his empire possessed. The more ambitious of them endeavoured to gain a similar imperial position, and to assume a regal dominion which was very repugnant to the free Scandinavian spirit. Harold the Fair-haired was their leader. The Norwegians resisted him right boldly, till he gained a complete victory over the insurgents at Hafursfiord, in the year 872. The teeming North again has been at all times the fruitful mother of daring emigrants. The Scandinavians were bold and hardy traders too. To this day their ships are known in every port of these islands, manned by sailors who unite in their own persons the double character of farmers and of navigators. At that time they had their merchant ships built for trade on a different model from their war ships. Some of these traders may have brought back a report of the fertility of the lands which lay but a few days' sail from their coasts, and may have told their fellows of the internal wars and political divisions which invited the invasion of a hardy foe. Internal treachery—never wanting in Irish history—may have hastened the work. An Agricola in the first century was invited to invade Ireland by an Irish prince. A King of Leinster opened the way to Henry II. and the Normans. The Council of Kilkenny, the Parliament of 1690, the United Irishmen of 1798, all appealed to French assistance, and we think it highly probable that some chieftains of the eighth century may have invited the assistance and guided the ships of the most formidable foe that had as yet trodden the green sward of Ireland.

The report of the first comers, too, must have induced thousands to follow their example. They found the political and social state of the island more favourable to their designs than they had anticipated. I have endeavoured in a previous lecture to depict it. I need only now add, that the constitution of an Irish army, when assembled to resist a foe like the Danes, rendered it almost worthless. Treachery was not its only weakness. A still greater one lurked behind, and that was personal vanity. Scott, in his *Legend of Montrose* and in *Waverley*, has ably and truthfully shown how personal vanity spread division and strife through the Highland hosts of the seventeenth and eighteenth centuries. It was just the same among the Irish Celts of a thousand years earlier. "An Irish army was a rope of sand," says Dr. Todd in his *Wars of the Gaedhil and the Gaill*, pref., p. cxix. "It consisted of a number of minor clans each commanded by its own petty chieftain, receiving no pay, and bound by no oath or any other obligation of allegiance to the king or chief commander. Each clan, no doubt, adhered with unshaken loyalty to its immediate chieftain; but the chief, on the smallest offence, could dismiss his followers to their homes, even on the very eve of a decisive battle. He was ready at every personal insult, or supposed insult, to abandon the national cause, and for the sake of a selfish revenge, disguised under the name of honour, to expose the whole national army to inevitable defeat. Nor did his defection, however capricious or unreasonable, expose him to any loss of caste or of reputation, for all were conscious that under similar circumstances they would have done the same."

Professor Freeman, in his *Norman Conquest*, divides the Danish Invasion into three great portions. The first was for the sake of plunder. It lasted from 795 till about the year 850. The second was for the sake of settlement. It lasted from 850-950. During this period the Northmen were escaping from the tyranny of their princes. Like the Puritans of America, they were seeking new settlements and political freedom across the sea. During this period they settled where plain traces of them still remain, in Lincolnshire, the Orkneys, Ireland, France, and Iceland. The third period was that of political conquest, and extends from 950 to 1100. In this lecture I must be content to give you a brief account of the two former of these periods as we find them developed in Ireland.

All the Irish annals are agreed upon the year 795 as the time of the Danish arrival in this island. It is a striking mark of their historical truthfulness that our annalists exactly agree in this respect with the English and Continental chroniclers. The *Annals of Innisfallen* note under the year 795: "The Danes were first seen cruising on the coasts of Ireland, prying out the country." The *Annals of the Four Masters* speak thus of that year: "The heathen men burned the Island of Rechru, and broke and plundered the shrines." In 798 they burned St. Patrick's Island, or Holmpatrick, off the coast of the County Dublin. They soon penetrated to the west. In 807 they burned the churches of Inismurray in Sligo Bay, and in 812 plundered the romantic islands of Scelig Michel off the coast of Kerry, seized the anchorites and kept them captive till they perished for want of food. They were determined to avenge on the Christian clergy the wrongs inflicted upon their Saxon kinsmen by Charlemagne's missionaries. With these statements the English chroniclers exactly agree. On the English coast the Northmen appeared five years after Witikind had fled into Denmark and carried the story of Charlemagne's cruelties to the subjects of King Sigefroi. According to the *Saxon Chronicle*, the year 787 first saw three ships of Danish men seeking the land of the English race.[1] They came apparently as spies. Their report soon induced others to follow. In 793 and 794, the same authority tells us, "the Danes came with larger fleets and other objects, and dreadfully destroyed the Churches of Christ." Lindisfarne was totally ruined by them in 793, and in 794 they plundered and burned Ecgferth's monastery at Wearmouth. It was just the same in France, where Charlemagne is said to have wept as he beheld their fleets from his palace windows, and foresaw what miseries they would bring on his descendants. And yet it was only a measure of poetic justice. The Roman Church claims St. Peter as its head and founder. It was that same Peter who took the sword in Christ's cause, and received the prophetic warning, which the Roman Church, and the English Church, and the Covenanters of Scotland, and the Puritans of England, and all other Churches and sects have so often verified, a warning which Charlemagne, and Cranmer, and Zwingle, and George Walker of Derry have found true: "All they that take the sword shall perish by the sword." Yes, the Danish invasions of

---

[1] Anglo-Saxon Chron., in *Monum. Brit.*, p. 257; or in Bohn's Edition of Bede, *E. H.*, p. 341.

Christendom form a most apt and fitting commentary on those words, as well as upon these others, too often forgotten, "My kingdom is not of this world. If My kingdom were of this world, then would My servants fight. But now is My kingdom not from hence." "The weapons of our warfare are not carnal but spiritual."

The Danes came at first as simple pirates, and the islands and coasts, specially on the west, still bear marks of their presence. They sailed up the rivers, too, in search of shrines and monasteries. The broad bosom of the Shannon naturally invited them. They made their way to Clonmacnois, where the shrine of St. Kieran was reverenced then as his simple little primitive oratory is reverenced to this day by the peasantry of the district. They plundered the numerous monasteries of Lough Ree. Not a celebrated sanctuary in Ireland escaped these unpleasant visitors, Armagh, Kildare, Glendalough, Bangor, Lusk, Derry, Slane, Inisclothran. Nothing could evade their keen and searching eyes; they ascended the Boyne, and with northern instinct divined the secrets of those wondrous monuments of our early history, the pyramids of Newgrange, Dowth, and Knowth, situated on the northern bank of the Boyne, some four miles above Drogheda. The Danes, from their own experience, recognised them as the burial places of kings, and penetrated their inmost chambers in the year 862, that is, eight hundred years before Lloyd or Molyneux or Petrie or Wilde had seen them.[1] But the Danes were not mere pirates. The bolder spirits who began the invasions doubtless cared, like first adventurers of

---

[1] See Sir W. Wilde, in his *Beauties of the Boyne and Blackwater.*

every age, for nothing save war and plunder. The bulk of the nation, however, were vigorous, patient, laborious farmers and agriculturists, well accustomed to win a very spare subsistence from a barren soil and an inhospitable climate. Fiercer and more daring spirits always lead the way. The more thrifty, more industrious, and therefore more valuable emigrants, follow in their footsteps. So was it with the Danes. Let me sketch the career of the most celebrated of these early settlers. Turgesius was the first Danish leader who seems to have come with a fixed purpose of settlement. His exploits are detailed at length in the old Irish History concerning the wars of the Gaedhil with the Gaill, c. ix., published by Dr. Todd, in the English Master of the Rolls Series.[1] The Irish historian calls him Turgesius. He has been identified, however, with a celebrated Danish hero of the ninth century, Ragnar Lodbrok, whose descendants established towards the end of that century the Danish kingdoms of Dublin and of Northumberland. His history illustrates the new phase on which the Scandinavian invasion was entering.

Turgesius landed in the north of Ireland about the year 831. He brought with him a large number of ships which he divided into three great fleets. One entered the Bann at Coleraine in the extreme north, sailed up to Lough Neagh, and thence exercised dominion over Ulster. Another fleet was stationed in the bay of Dundalk, while a third, having ascended the Shannon, was stationed upon the broad waters of Lough Ree, whence the whole of Meath and Connaught was at their mercy. Turgesius was an active and

---

[1] See also Haliday's *Scandinavian Kingdom of Dublin*, pp. 19-36, and the Scandinavian and other authorities there quoted.

a skilful general. Armagh exercised supreme ecclesiastical dominion over the northern half of Ireland at least. It was a strong fort, too, and a royal residence, as the immense raths and moats in its neighbourhood still prove.[1] Turgesius directed his first efforts against that city. In 832, the Irish annals tell us, Armagh was three times assaulted in one month. Turgesius drove out the Christian primate, Forannan, and established himself in his stead.[2] The war became, in fact, a crusade directed against Christianity. Turgesius established the worship of Thor on the site of the most revered of Irish Christian sanctuaries, while the primate Forannan sought shelter for himself amid the southern Irish, where the invader's power could not as yet reach him.

But fleet after fleet was now arriving. "After this," says the chronicler (Todd, p. 13), "came threescore and five ships and landed at Dublin or Ath Cliath, and Leinster and Meath were plundered. The sea also vomited up floods of foreigners into Erin, so that there was not a point thereof without a fleet." Turgesius took bolder steps. You will easily note on the map how judiciously he stationed his forces to secure his conquests. His fleet on Lough Ree dominated Meath on the east and Connaught on the west. It sacked the monasteries and churches which marked the line of the Shannon and the lands bordering thereon. The monasteries of Clonfert,

---

[1] See Dr. Reeves' *Memoir* on the Ancient Churches of Armagh.
[2] See concerning Forannan, or Foranan, Ussher's Works, vi., 420, 613. Ussher fixes the date of Forannan's primacy to 834, and his expulsion from Armagh to 848, in which year Turgesius was slain, according to his calculation, though Todd and Haliday assign 845 for the latter event.

founded by St. Brendan, of Lorrha, founded by St. Rodan, and of Terryglass were ravaged. Two celebrated groups of churches were special objects of Danish hostility. Innis-Sceltra in Lough Derg, and Clonmacnois, some ten miles below Lough Ree, were famous sanctuaries. Clonmacnois, in fact, occupied a position second only to Armagh itself in popular reverence. To this day it presents us with some of the most genuine specimens of early Irish churches. Two round towers, numberless crosses covered with elaborate ornamentation, three of them still standing, an ancient castle, a well preserved cashel, the ruins of seven churches, all genuine Celtic monuments, with but few traces of English work, unite to make Clonmacnois a most interesting spot for the historian or the archæologist.[1] The churches all seem specimens of the true old Irish style. One alone out of the seven has a chancel attached. They are all oblong structures, and most of them very small. One is larger than any of the rest It was the Great Church or cathedral. It is still in a fair state of preservation, owing doubtless to some repairs executed during the wars and confusions of the Commonwealth. Clonmacnois now fell into Danish hands. Turgesius in the north had established paganism in Armagh, officiating himself as high priest. A pagan sanctuary was needed in the west. His wife Ota was a Pythoness, so she seized the Great Church of Clonmacnois, and from its altar, desecrated by foul and bloody pagan rites, amid the shrieks of butchered victims and the smoke of human sacrifices, the wild pagan priestess delivered her oracular

---

[1] Lord Dunraven's *Notes on Irish Architecture* will show the reader what the ruins are like. Clonmacnois can be reached by an hour's drive from Athlone.

responses.¹ But still the tide of paganism flowed on. Turgesius could not rest while Forannan, the successor of Patrick, was at large, carrying with him the shrine and sacred relics of the Apostle of Ireland, including that very *Book of Armagh* which fitly finds a lodgment in our own library. He despatched, therefore, a fleet to ravage the south-west of Ireland, where Forannan had taken refuge. The Danes stormed Limerick, and captured Forannan, together with the sacred shrine, which they smashed. Turgesius was not only a conqueror, he was an organiser as well. He recognised the necessity for securing his conquests. Armagh was a strong point of vantage for the ruler of Ulster; but it was most inconvenient for a conqueror whose forces were so largely naval. Limerick or Waterford, fine ports in themselves, were too far in the south. With a general's eye he recognised the importance of the ford of Ath-cliath or Dublin.² Hitherto it had had no existence as a city. Ecclesiastical writers of the twelfth century tell us tales of St. Patrick's visit to our city, and of its magnificence in his time. But they are simply tales. The real founders of Dublin were the Danes, and common gratitude should lead us—if we re-name our streets and squares—to remember, that the man who first laid our foundations and set up our gates was Turgesius, the first great Danish King of Ireland. Before his time it had been simply a ford where the great road from Tara to Wicklow, Arklow, and Wexford crossed the Liffey. A small village, doubtless, always existed at the ford, but nothing more

---

¹ See Todd and Haliday, *l.c.*
² See Mr. Haliday's work, Book i., chaps. 1 and 2, for a discussion of the early history of Dublin. The *Annals of the Four Masters* fix the year 840 as that of the building of the fortress of Dublin.

till the sagacious eye of Turgesius marked the spot and erected there the Dun or Castle of Dublin, which now for more than a thousand years has dominated the city and guarded the ford of the Liffey.

But I must not anticipate my next lecture, which will deal at some length with the subject of the rise of the city and kingdom of Dublin. It may well, however, be asked, What were the sovereigns of Ireland doing all this time? Turgesius landed in 831. He conquered Connaught and the distant west in 838, while Forannan, the exiled and persecuted Primate, was only captured in 845, the year when Turgesius was slain, after a fifteen years' sway reaching over the greater part of the island. The history of Turgesius illustrates the national weakness of Ireland, which for three centuries left it a prey to the Scandinavian invader, and then handed it over to their cousins the Normans, led by Henry II. and Strongbow. When Turgesius landed in Ireland, the King of Cashel, or of Munster, was the rising power in the land. The sovereign of Cashel at that time was Feidlimidh or Phelim.[1] He occupied the anomalous position of king and bishop. I have described, in a preceding lecture, the strange use he made of his power, ravaging the neighbouring lands with fire and sword, and pursuing his brother ecclesiastics with the most untiring hostility. The Danes came, headed by Turgesius. They were determined to overthrow Christianity. But the king was too strong for the bishop, and his ambitious instincts overcame his religious sympathies. He had an old feud with the O'Neills of Ulster concerning the sove-

---

[1] See Keating's *History of Ireland*, Mahony's edition, pp. 502—510 (New York: 1857), for the history of this king.

reignty of Ireland. The Danes attacked Ulster first of all. If the other kings of Ireland had had an atom of wisdom, they must have seen that their only hope of safety lay in joining hands and making common cause against the pagan invader. But vanity and jealousy had too strong a hold upon Feidlimidh's impulsive nature. He was delighted to see his northern rival worsted, even though that rival's defeat should only be the prelude of his own ruin. Treachery, however, effected what valour was unable to accomplish. Malachy (Maelsechlainn), King of Meath, had long felt the power of Turgesius, and had resisted him bravely, but in vain. Despairing of victory by honourable means, he resorted to guile. Turgesius had fallen in love with his daughter. It was arranged that she should receive him at a banquet upon an island in Lough Owel, one of the Westmeath lakes near Mullingar. There she appeared surrounded by fifteen beardless youths in female attire. Turgesius, suspecting nothing, appeared attended according to arrangement by fifteen of his friends. He advanced to embrace the lady, when the disguised youths drew their daggers, and after stabbing them all to death, flung their bodies into the lake.

And now a natural curiosity arises concerning this strange people whose name is so inextricably bound up with our own. Do we know anything of the Danes, of their social life, their everyday existence? I suppose the ordinary idea of the Danes is, that they were a very fierce, a very rude, and a very uncivilised pack of savages, whose only aim was bloodshed and plunder, and whose great abhorrence was civilisation in all its shapes and forms. Yet this is a very mistaken view. They were undoubtedly a brave, and even a fierce race.'

They made war vigorously and even ferociously, but then they had Christian examples to stir them up. Their friends had told them how Charlemagne, the great Christian prince, had beheaded in one day 4,500 of their Saxon kindred, who opposed his warlike efforts on behalf of the Church; and we can only wonder when we see them sparing, as they did, Forannan the captured Primate of Armagh, whose existence was a standing menace to their great leader Turgesius. The Danes we therefore conclude were bad enough, but yet not quite so bad as they are sometimes painted. We are not, however, left wholly to conjecture on this point. We have a more sure source of information in some contemporary records which good fortune has preserved for us. I have already mentioned Iceland as a Danish colony. It was originally an Irish colony. The Irish monks and hermits landed there in the seventh and eighth centuries. The Scandinavians discovered it only in the ninth. Harold of the Fair Hair was then consolidating his dominion at the expense of Norwegian liberty. His opponents, therefore, sailed to Iceland as well as to Ireland in search of freedom. In Iceland they found the field most favourable for their purposes, and there they founded a community which has preserved for us a copious literature, giving a picture of the everyday existence, down to its minutest details, of Norwegian and Danish life in the ninth century. Icelandic history and literature have received of late increased attention. If you take up, for instance, the article on Iceland in the new issue of the *Encyclopædia Britannica*, you will see what numerous interests centre round that distant northern island. The historian, the philologist, the jurist, the sociologist, all find there matter for fresh inquiry, and there we too shall find new light thrown on the dark spots of Irish history.

It will be impossible henceforth, I repeat, to understand or to write Irish history without a constant reference to Icelandic, because Ireland and Iceland were closely and intimately related for three centuries at least, in some of the most stirring and celebrated scenes of their respective histories. Time will not permit me to show this more at length on this occasion. Hereafter I shall be able to illustrate it by some interesting instances. It must now suffice to make the statement, and to refer you to the work of Sir George Dasent, *Burnt Njal*, where the learned author traces the connection of Ireland and Iceland in those early ages, and translates a charming Saga, in which a hero of Irish descent, bearing too the very Irish name of Nial, plays a prominent part. That work is well worthy of study if only for this reason. It shows that the Danes and Norwegians of those times were no mere savages. I shall mention one point merely. They were far in advance of the Celts of Ireland in the matter of house-building. They were in this respect in advance even of the Irish farmer of the present day. Sir George Dasent's book is most instructive on this subject. There you will find elaborate plans, elevations, and descriptions of the houses which the Danes built a thousand years ago when they landed in Dublin and in Iceland, derived from a careful study of the texts of the Sagas, compared with modern usage prevalent in Iceland. Their houses were very like the house described by Sir Walter Scott in *Ivanhoe*, where the old Saxon chief lived, guarding Rowena, the Saxon princess, with a jealous national care. There was a large central hall in every Danish house, with a high table across the hall for the head of the family, and tables stretched down from thence for the children and retainers. Off the hall were separate bedrooms for the men and the women, often elaborately decorated and carved, while numerous and extensive farm offices afforded shelter for the slaves and cattle. Their social life, too, was a very elaborate one. I have already said something about their judicial system, and in my next lecture I shall have occasion to notice at large their legislative and political ideas, which found a place in the Danish kingdom of Dublin, and which have left to this day, clear and distinct marks upon institutions still existing among us.

# LECTURE XIV.

## *THE DANISH KINGDOM OF DUBLIN.*

PROFESSOR FREEMAN has divided, as I noted in the beginning of my last lecture, the great Scandinavian movement into three parts. The first two, the eras of plunder and of settlement, I have now considered, so far as Ireland is concerned. The third division, the era of political conquest, remains for discussion. I shall treat it in connection with the national upheaval against the invaders, which found personal embodiment and heroic leadership in the great southern king, Brian Boru. Here let me offer a few words of explanation. This lecture may seem to have a purely political title. What has ecclesiastical history to say to Brian Boru? some objector may demand. Much every way, I reply. The ecclesiastical history of all nations is inextricably bound up with their politics. But with the Celts of Ireland this was specially the case. Their bishops and abbats were kings and chieftains, and secular advisers as well as spiritual guides, and it is impossible to follow the fortunes of the Church unless we understand their course of action. Let me give you an instance which illustrates very well the close union which existed one thousand years ago between Church and State. I have to discuss in this lecture the fortunes of Brian Boru and the rise of the great southern family of O'Brien. The foundations of the greatness of his kingdom were laid a century before his time, by one who united in his own person the highest ecclesiastical and the highest civil offices. Cormac of Cashel was both king and bishop. His history was a strange one. A brief outline of it will form a fit introduction to our subject.

Cormac belonged to the royal house of Munster. He was born in 831, trained for the ecclesiastical life, and duly raised to the episcopate, like two preceding sovereigns of Munster, who also had been bishops before they were made kings. Cormac's episcopal office, however, proved no hindrance to his military operations. He vigorously upheld the claim of Munster to supremacy over the other kingdoms of Ireland. He was called to the throne in 896, when an old man.[1] It was a time of most violent internal dissensions in this country. The Danes had long been ravaging the coast line. The chiefs were murdering and plundering one another, and every one of them ready to sell his country to the northern invader, if only he could himself be thus secure of a temporary triumph. Flann, King of Meath, and Cearbhall, King of Ossory, thought they saw their opportunity to crush the ambitious kingdom of Munster when it was governed by an ecclesiastic. Cormac, however, met them in the neighbourhood of the King's County, utterly defeated them, and then advancing through Meath received the submission of the northern half of Ireland. His triumph, however, was but shortlived. The Connaught men headed a revolt against the

---

[1] The dates of Cormac's accession and death vary. The *Annals of the Four Masters* place his death at 903; the *Annals of Ulster* at 907 or 908. There is at this period a fixed difference between these two *Annals* of three or four years. See O'Donovan's note on Cormac's death, in the *Four Masters*, A.D. 903.

bishop-king. They summoned the chiefs of Leinster and Ulster to their assistance, and under Cathal O'Connor, King of Connaught, attacked Cormac at Ballymoon, about two miles from the town of Carlow, where the site of the battle is still shown, and the very stone is pointed out where the warrior bishop was slain.[1] Cormac's reign was but a short one, from 896 to 903; yet it was long enough to enable him to leave us memorials of it far more permanent than the transient fame of military conquest. Cormac's Chapel on the Rock of Cashel is the most exquisite extant specimen of Irish architecture, and the man who has not seen it, is as yet unacquainted

---

[1] See a full account of this battle in Keating's *History of Ireland*, pp. 519-532; *Four Masters*, A.D. 903. Dr. Whitley Stokes gives a critical account of Cormac's life and literary labours, in the preface to *Three Irish Glossaries* (London: 1862). He notices the barbarous practice of cutting off the heads of fallen foes, on which the conquerors then seated themselves. Cormac's remains escaped this indignity. We are told that the triumphant Flann of Meath took Cormac's head and kissed it. Dr. O'Donovan, in *Three Fragments* (Dublin: 1860), p. 208, gives the following narrative of Cormac's death, from a MS. in the Burgundian Library at Brussels. It is evidently authentic. "King Cormac escaped in the van of the first battalion, but his horse leaped into a trench, and he fell from the horse. When a party of his people who were flying perceived this, they came to the king and put him up on his horse again. It was then he saw a foster-son of his own, a noble of the Eoganacht named Aehd, a sage in wisdom and jurisprudence, and history and Latin. The king said thus to him, 'O dear son, do not follow me, but escape as well as thou canst. I told thee before I should be slain in this battle.' A few remained with Cormac, and he came forward along the road, and abundant was the blood of men and horses along that road. The hind feet of his horse slipt on the slippery road in the track of that blood, the horse fell backwards and broke Cormac's back and his neck in twain, and he said when falling, 'Into Thy hands I commend my spirit, O Lord. And he gave up his spirit, and the impious sons of malediction came and thrust spears into his body and severed his head from his body." O'Donovan, *l.c.*, p. 211, notes that a great many clergymen were killed at this battle. It was very hard to eradicate the old fighting habits of the Irish ecclesiastics.

with the most beautiful effort of Irish architectural genius. The architect who planned that building, and the artificers who raised it, must have been profoundly skilful.[1] Cormac left us a more abiding monument still. He is numbered among the ancient writers of Ireland. We possess Cormac's Glossary, where he derives Irish names from Latin, Greek, and Hebrew. His philological speculations are not indeed very correct,[2] but neither were Cicero's, nor those of Firmicus Maternus, or the Fathers of the fourth century, whenever they ventured on such topics. His Glossary, however, proves that Greek and Hebrew were known and studied in the schools of the south of Ireland in the earlier years of the tenth century. Cormac's character was a strange mixture. A fighting bishop seems to us almost a contradiction in terms, but did not seem so to the men of that time. It was only in the previous century that the Irish clergy were formally exempted from compulsory personal service in war. A Bishop-King of Cashel, Phelim by name, some fifty years earlier than Cormac, had, as I have already shown you, penetrated as far as Armagh, slaying priests and bishops wherever he caught them, and then, when he had captured the primatial city, he quietly resumed his clerical office, and preached every Sunday for a whole year to the people of Armagh.[3]

---

[1] *Four Masters*, ed. O'Donovan, A.D. 1134, attributes it to a Cormac of the twelfth century.

[2] See Dr. Wh. Stokes' estimate of them, in his preface, quoted above, pp. xviii.-lix., where the many valuable elements of the Glossary are pointed out.

[3] I may add that Cormac was not only a fighting bishop; he was also a married bishop. His wife's name was Gormlaith. Upon his death she married at once, as it would seem, his opponent Cearbhbal or Carroll of Leinster, who defeated Cormac. Carroll himself was slain the very next year, A.D. 909, whereupon she consoled herself with Nial, monarch of all Ireland. It cannot be pleaded that Cormac lived separate from his wife when he became a bishop, simply because as he was a bishop before he

The kingdom of Munster was founded by a race of bishop-kings. But it possessed one great physical advantage which must have largely contributed to its rapid rise during the ninth and tenth centuries. The Rock of Cashel is one of the most striking natural objects in Ireland. Its position is most striking. It rises a precipitous crag out of the great central plain of Tipperary, the golden vale which successive travellers have admired and successive conquerors have appropriated. The legend of the neighbourhood is, that the Rock of Cashel exactly answers to the curious natural gap called the "Devil's Bit," in the mountain which overlooks Templemore. It is at any rate the most prominent object in that great and fertile plain which extends from the Slieve Bloom Mountains on the north to the Galtees and Cummeraghs on the south. It furnished the Kings of Munster with a natural stronghold of an almost impregnable character, enabling them to exercise the same dominion over their neighbours, which David exercised in virtue of his possession of the stronghold of Zion, or the Philistines through the fortress of Michmash. And the King of Munster recognised this. The noble mass of ruins which crown the rock are to a great extent Anglo-Norman, but in large part they must date back to that interesting time when the kingdom of Munster stood firm, splendid, and secure, through the genius and valour of a Cormac and of a Brian. There was one notable omission in Cormac's military achievements; he never seems to have come in contact with the Danes, and that for

---

became a king, he must have married as a bishop. (*Four Masters*, A.D. 909, O'Donovan's note.) O'Curry's efforts to clear Cormac's episcopal character of the stigma of matrimony are most amusing (see his *Lectt.*, vol. i.)

the simple reason that the earlier years of the tenth century were marked by a check to the Danish invasions both of England and of Ireland. Alfred and the Saxons in England had successfully routed them some years before; the Celts in Ireland, following their example, rose against them and simultaneously expelled them from all their strongholds, including the great central one of Dublin. A peace of forty years then ensued. They renewed their incursions, however, at its close in greater strength than before, and re-established the Danish kingdom of Dublin, which continued to make rapid progress all through the tenth century.

It is, indeed, from the year 919 that the greatness of Dublin and its dignity as a city, and the most important city of Ireland, must be dated. In 919 Sitric, who was of the family which in the previous century had ruled the Scandinavians settled on the Liffey, returned with his clansmen to their ancient haunts.[1] The Irish knew right well by bitter experience how necessary it was to attack them at once, before they had time to consolidate their power. The King of Ireland mustered therefore all his forces and, aided by the chieftains of Ulster, attacked the Danes at Kilmashogue Mountain, just above Rathfarnham, on Wednesday, September 15th, 919, but was utterly defeated, and slain by them, together with twelve of his allied princes. Of that battle we still find traces. One of the prettiest bits of scenery round Dublin is found in Glen Southwell, called otherwise the Little Dargle, next St. Columba's College. A river which rises in Ticknock valley at the back of the Three Rock Mountain, pursues a rapid course bounded by precipitous banks till it falls

---

[1] See Haliday, p. 54.

into the Dodder near Rathfarnham. This river flows through Glen Southwell, and there you will still find the remains of a massive cromlech, marking in all probability the spot where were buried the remains of the brave chieftains who vainly strove to resist the tide of Danish invasion. The Scandinavians now firmly established themselves in Dublin. It was a splendid point of vantage for them. Members of the same clan held the Lordships of Man, of Northumbria, and of York, with which the sea offered an easy and speedy means of communication, so that when danger threatened any one of them, the others could at once send supplies and assistance. It is no wonder then that Dublin should have rapidly grown under the Danish rule.

The Danes added, too, some elements which Celtic life sadly needed. Thus they excelled in domestic architecture, as I showed in my last lecture. They were wise and courageous rulers and traders too, and rapidly established a vigorous commerce. The Danes had their war ships, but they also had their trading vessels, with which they sought the produce of other lands. They were honourable, too, in their commercial transactions. The Dublin Danish merchants paid their debts and offered peace and security to foreign settlers. The Bristol merchants supplied them with cloth and iron and other commodities, and established a connection with Dublin, which has never since been broken. A curious instance occurs to me illustrating the trading activity of Dublin in those Danish times People sometimes think that Brian Boru expelled the Danes in the beginning of the eleventh century. He defeated them most certainly, as I shall hereafter show, but he did not expel or extirpate them. The Danish kingdom of Dublin stood firm in its strength till Strongbow landed, and Henry II. annexed the Lordship of Ireland to his kingdom of England. The Danish community continued to be a power in Dublin and in Ireland at large even for a century later than Strongbow. The *Chronicle of Man* tells us how in the thirteenth century, one hundred years, that is, after the conquest of Ireland, the Danish inhabitants of Dublin sent a deputation to Earl Haco, a Scandinavian chief then ravaging Scotland, entreating him to come and deliver them from the power of the English invader.

And now for my story illustrating the commercial activity of Dublin, which will show how West of England cloth was imported by the Danes before Strongbow's conquest. The very year before the English invasion, another Earl Haco from Orkney swooped down with his followers upon the Scottish and Irish coasts. They harried the southern isles, spring and summer, year after year. They were nominal Christians indeed, but their Christianity had as little moral power over them as that of the Kerry gentry had in the last century in Mr. Froude's celebrated pictures of the *English in Ireland*, or as that of a Connaught or Italian bandit of our own time, who says his prayers most devoutly before he shoots his victim. The northern Saga tells us, "The folk was so scared at him in the southern isles, that men hid all their goods and chattels in the earth or in holes of rocks. He sailed so far south as Man, and thence to Ireland. But when they came south under Dublin, they met two vessels coming from England, laden with English cloth and great store of foods. They offered them battle, which the merchantmen prudently declined, suffering themselves rather to be quietly plundered; and Haco and his allies returned north, using broadcloth as his sails, whence his cruise came to be known as the broadcloth cruise."[1] They were not only active in mercantile matters, they showed themselves open to new ideas as well. The tenth century beheld the Dublin Danes abandoning their old paganism and embracing Christianity. They founded the see of Dublin, they built Christ Church Cathedral, and established across the Liffey the Abbey of St. Mary, in the neighbourhood of the present Capel and Abbey Streets. We can even still recover the boundaries of their kingdom of Dublin as it existed before the conquest. The dioceses of Ireland, and of England too, as Mr. Green has shown us in his *Making of England*, are almost always conterminous with tribal limits.[2] The dioceses of England were established in the seventh and eighth centuries. The dioceses of Ireland were not established till the twelfth, shortly before the invasion of the Anglo-Normans. The other dioceses of Ireland were conterminous with Celtic tribes, but it is a most curious fact that the diocese of Dublin is to this day conterminous, not with any Celtic tribe, but with the ancient Danish kingdom of Dublin. The very topography of the diocese proves this. It extends from Holmpatrick and Skerries on the north, and these names are Danish. It extends to Arklow and Wicklow on the south, and both Arklow and Wicklow are Danish or Scandinavian names. The diocese of Dublin extends west but a few miles, to Leixlip, seven or eight miles from Dublin, and Leixlip is a Danish name, Leix or Laxlip,

---

[1] Dasent's *Burnt Njal*, ii., p. 371.
[2] See Dr. Reeves' *Memoir* on the Dioceses of Dublin and Glendalough, for the same view about Irish dioceses.

salmon-leap, a name which still survives in its original shape in an old Danish weir on the Shannon, a few miles above Limerick, which to this day is called the Lax weir. And round the whole diocese it is just the same; the nomenclature is all Danish; headlands, islands, towns, territories—Howth, Bray, Dalkey, Fingal, Wicklow, Harold's Cross, Gormanstown, Grangegorman, Oxmantown, Harold's Grange,—all remind us that the Danish sway extended over this district, and did not extend beyond it.[1] And here let me mention another most interesting point, which illustrates one of the most elementary, and at the same time important, truths with which an historian, whether civil or ecclesiastical, must reckon. History is all continuous. Just as the skilful geologist or palæontologist can reconstruct from an inspection of the strata of a quarry the animal and vegetable life of past ages, so can the historian reconstruct out of modern forms, rights, and ceremonies, often now but very shadowy and unreal, the essential and vigorous life of society as it existed ten centuries ago. History, I repeat, is continuous. The life of societies, of nations, and of Churches is continuous, so that the life of the present, if rightly handled, must reveal to us much of the life of the past. Now for an illustration of this. We are not altogether surprised to find an illustration of the kingdom of Dublin in the diocese thereof. We all know that the Church has been at all times essentially conservative; conservative of old creeds, old rights, and old customs. But what think you when we can turn to the Dublin Corporation, and find there an evidence of the existence and of the boundaries of this Danish kingdom? Yet so it is. The Lord Mayor of Dublin

---

[1] See Haliday, pp. 138-142.

used to be, among his other high and lofty functions, Admiral of the Port of Dublin, in virtue of which office his jurisdiction extended, in all its plenitude, from Holmpatrick and Skerries on the north, to Arklow on the south, which again are the extreme limits of the united diocese of Dublin and Glendalough.[1] The Danes of Dublin were a naval people. The Danish kingdom of Dublin was essentially a naval power. It extended its domain inland but a few miles, to Leixlip; but on the coast line far away to the north, and again to the distant south, did it claim and exercise jurisdiction. That jurisdiction was found by Strongbow in active existence, was continued by him, and then was transferred by the English to the corporation which they instituted, by whom it was maintained and preserved through various vicissitudes, of which Mr. Haliday tells the tale, till fifty years ago.

But how, you may say to me, did the boundaries of the diocese come to be conterminous with those of the Danish kingdom of Dublin? A full answer to this query would lead me to anticipate much which I must touch upon in a subsequent lecture. Let it now suffice to say, that the Danes formed one principal channel through which the Papal See renewed and accomplished its designs upon the independence of the Irish Church in the course of the eleventh and twelfth centuries. The Danish Christian bishops scorned the native Celtic ones, and claimed alliance with Canterbury and Rome, not with Armagh. As a natural consequence, when the Papal legates were parcelling out Ireland into dioceses, they selected the district ruled by the Danes as the site of an archbishopric, and determined its boundaries accordingly. This is a subject which

---

[1] See Haliday, pp. 139, 246.

naturally has, or ought to have, a great interest for ourselves, as inhabitants of the very spot where a thousand years ago the Danish kingdom flourished. In order to bring this more practically home, let me point out to you what other traces still remain of this ancient kingdom, and what was the social state of its citizens. Abundant materials, trustworthy, historical materials, remain, enabling us to reconstruct the state of society amid which some of our ancestors acted their part, for numerous families still exist about Dublin whose descent is to be traced from this Danish colony, as the Seavers, the Seagraves, the Coppingers, the Macdougals, and the Harolds. Some may be inclined to attribute my estimate of the dignity and importance of the Danish kingdom of Dublin to the *perfervidum ingenium* of an Irishman. Such, however, will not be their estimate if they only take the trouble to consult Sir George Dasent's book, to which I have so often referred, or any other of the Chronicles or sagas of the north, or if they will turn to such an accessible work as the *Chronicle of Man*, translated in the last century into English by Mr. Johnstone. But I can even further say, *Si vis monumentum, circumspice*. Walk out of our own front entrance, and passing the iron gate which leadeth into the city, you find yourselves at once under the jurisdiction of the city police, because you are no longer in college, but are now on College Green. Now this word Green brings you back to the days of the Danish kingdom. How comes it that College Green is now called by that name when not even a microscope could discover a solitary blade of grass there? It owes this name Green to the Danes. Every Scandinavian settlement had attached to it a Green or place of assembly, surrounding a Thingmote or hill, on which the leaders and chiefs took their seats, and from whence the laws and determinations of the assembled freemen were proclaimed. This Scandinavian institution flourishes to this day in the Isle of Man, where laws passed in the House of Keys have no binding force till proclaimed from the Tynwald. The Thingmote continued, under the name of the Althing, in Iceland till the year 1800, meeting about midsummer on the very same spot where it assembled in the year A.D. 1000.[1] The Althing or Hill of Laws in Iceland gives us the best idea of what these Scandinavian assemblies were like. There is a precipitous hill, with a church at its base, representing the old pagan temple, which, in the earliest ages of Scandinavian colonisation, was always placed next the Thingmount or Thingmote. Booths were placed all round the hill which formed the centre of the national life. At that spot regular meetings of the Icelanders were held, at which every freeman was required to be present. Trials took place there, bargains and compacts were concluded, quarrels adjusted; while, like true Teutons, they crowned the whole series of transactions by abundant eating and drinking. The annual meeting at the Althing was the great event in Icelandic life eight hundred years ago. They gave the young men and the young women the one annual chance they had of meeting their old acquaintances and making new ones. The farms were widely scattered; the settlements distant one from another. To the Althing came, therefore, the whole population, and tarried there during the space of fourteen days, not only making laws, but also utilising the sole opportunity which the young people possessed of marrying and being given in marriage. Now Hogges Green, or College Green,

---

[1] See Dasent's description of it in his Preface, pp. cxxiii.-clxx.

served to the Danish kingdom of Dublin the very same purpose.

Remember the fact which I have just mentioned—College Green was called Hogges Green. Now this name had no connection with the useful though unmusical animal which is now so customary an adjunct to Irish cabins. Neither had it anything to say to the Irish word Ogh, a virgin, as some historians of our city have imagined, deriving as they did the title Hogges Green from a nunnery which formerly existed where Suffolk and Wicklow Streets now stand. But it is called Hogges Green from the Scandinavian word Hogue or Hoga, a hill or tumulus, for such a hill used to rise upon the very site of the present St. Andrew's Church. Now exercise your imaginations. Remove every house from College Green. Sweep away this college and all its buildings. Remove the Bank of Ireland and leave an open space down to the shelving banks of the Liffey, even then of a dark rich brown colour. Place upon the site of St. Andrew's Church a steep hill rising fifty feet above the present street level, or as high as the highest summit of the roof of the church. Carve that hill out into terraces and call it the Thingmote, and then you have Hogges Green, or the assembly ground of the Danes of Dublin, as it existed 900 years ago. They had their pagan temple too. It stood near the present new market. St. Andrew's Church succeeded it when the Danes became Christian, and was built on the site of the pagan temple—according to the well-known plan of the Mediæval Church, which designedly availed itself of pagan sacred sites, to conciliate the affections and utilise the customary practices of the new converts—and it was only on the removal of the ancient Thingmote, less than two centuries ago, that St. Andrew's

Church was removed and built on the vacant site.[1] St. Andrew's Church and churchyard now represent this ancient Danish Monument. Nor was a temple the only institution connected with these Thingmotes. Places of public execution as well as of public worship were naturally associated with them. The very spot where we are now assembled, the fields and stretch of strand now occupied by our own park and college, were then called the Stayne, from the long stone cromlech where the capital sentences decreed by the assembly were at once carried out. This long stone escaped all the vicissitudes of time, the invasions of the Danes, the wars of Celts and Saxons, the struggles of Royalists and Republicans. It occupied its time-honoured position where the Crampton Memorial now stands, till the close of the seventeenth century. Then we find the last notices of it. The city of Dublin, in 1679, made a grant of a piece of land to William Christian, at Lazar's Hill, near the long stone of the Stein; while Lord Anglesea, about the same date, made another of "a parcel of the strand at the Long Stone of the Stein over against the College." But time would fail me to tell of all the monuments of Danish times the observant eye can still trace in the institutions of Church and State; let it suffice to refer the inquiring student to Mr. Haliday's book on the Scandinavian Kingdom of Dublin, where his curiosity will find ample satisfaction. The Danish kingdom, the social life and constitution of which I have thus endeavoured to depict, continued to flourish

---

[1] The soil of the Thingmote now forms Nassau Street, accounting for its height above the College Park. See Haliday, pp. 164-166, where a picture of it is shown with terraces, or exactly as it was in pagan days. The Thingmote was seized and used as a fortress by some soldiers who mutinied in 1647.

throughout the tenth century. It had its Sitrics and Amlaffes as sovereigns, all most probably descendants of Turgesius, the first great Danish conqueror. They fought with the kings of Meath, Ulster, and Munster. Sometimes they were victorious, at other times they were defeated. But now there arose Brian, a really great king, worthy of their steel. The achievements of the great Irish hero will, however, demand a lecture devoted simply to himself. Let me say one word in conclusion. Looking back now over the way I have led you, can we not read one useful lesson? Preaching and prayers, visiting and schools, are most important parts of a clergyman's work. Nothing can supersede them. But when they have been duly performed, how much time often hangs heavy upon some clerical hands. Yet it ought not to be so. Old customs, old tales, old manuscripts even, folk-lore in its thousand varying and important shapes, still linger in the remote districts of our land. If this lecture have taught you, in however slight degree, of what vast importance to the historian these things ofttimes are, a lecture upon the Scandinavian Kingdom of Dublin will not unprofitably or unfitly have found its place in a series devoted to the Ecclesiastical History of our native land.

# LECTURE XV.

## *BRIAN BORU, AND THE TRIUMPH OF CHRISTIANITY.*

BRIAN BORU is one of Ireland's national heroes. Some of these heroes are mythical characters. Some of them had little claim when in the flesh to the title of heroes. But as for Brian Boru, he is a truly historical personage, and his heroic character is as firmly grounded as that of Alfred the Great, whom he resembles in many respects. We shall take his career after the manner of old-fashioned sermons, under three great heads or divisions. (1) His youth; (2) His conquest of Ireland; (3) His final struggle with the Danes of Dublin. You may, indeed, naturally ask the oft-repeated query, What documents have we throwing any historical light on these topics? My reply would simply be this. I should point you to the Master of the Rolls' great series of English and Irish texts illustrating the early history of these kingdoms. There you  will find Dr. Todd's work on the wars of Brian, Mr Hennessy's editions of the *Chronicles of Lough Cé* and of the *Chronicon Scotorum.* Compare them then with the independent Icelandic Sagas, and you will have abundant contemporaneous evidence illustrating the career of the great Brian. Let us then apply ourselves to our task of tracing the history of one who finally destroyed paganism as a power in Ireland.

Brian was descended from one of the royal families of southern Ireland, possessing a hereditary claim to the throne of Cashel or of Munster. I do not think, indeed, it would enlighten you much were I to give you his full genealogy as the Irish historians trace it, through twenty-two generations back to Cormac Cas and Olid Olum, who divided Ireland in the second or third century with Conn of the hundred battles.[1] Brian was the son of a chief named Kennedy, who had also an elder son named Mahon. These children were born about the time when the Danes established the kingdom of Dublin, that is, somewhere about the year 930. Their earliest memories were of Danish rapine and plunder. Their position naturally marked them out as objects of attack by the Danes of Limerick, for it was with the Danish colonies which occupied the southern ports of Waterford, Wexford, Cork and Limerick the O'Briens first came into conflict. Limerick was essentially a Scandinavian town. Scandinavian names still linger round it, just as a Scandinavian castle, called Reginald's tower, still exists in Waterford, while again the very names Water-fiord and Wex-fiord testify to the Norwegian origin of the first settlers.[2] The kingdom of Limerick was specially powerful, and carried on perpetual and deadly conflict with Brian's family and kindred. Let me quote you a brief passage from the historian whom Dr. Todd translated, picturing the scenes of Brian's youth. " Now when Brian and Mahon

---

[1] This mythical genealogy is duly set forth in Keating's *History*, p. 563. Cormac Cas is regarded as the common ancestor of the clans O'Brien.
[2] There are five Fiords in Ireland—Ulfreksfiord (Larne Lough), Strangfiord, Carlingfiord, Wexfiord, and Waterfiord—all exhibiting physical features similar to the Scandinavian fiords. Haliday, p. lxvii.; Reeves' *Antiqq.*, p. 265.

saw the bondage and the oppression and the misrule that was inflicted on Munster, and on the men of Erin in general, they would not submit to it. They therefore carried off their people and all their chattels over the Shannon westwards, and they dispersed themselves among the forests and woods of the three tribes that were there. They began to plunder and kill the foreigners immediately after that. Neither had they any termon or protection from the foreigners. But it was woe to either party to meet the other or come together, owing to the plunders, and conflicts, and battles, and skirmishes, and trespasses, and combats that were interchanged between them during a long period." Let us now translate the historian's poetical expressions into the language of sober fact. Mahon and Brian, when they set their hearts upon freeing their country, recognised, like Alfred the Great under similar circumstances, their own weakness and inability to cope with the armour-clad and stalwart foreigners. They saw that guerilla warfare was their true game, a wearing out of the enemy by hanging on his flanks, cutting off his supplies, destroying him in detail. They had made their first attempts in the district covering the counties of Tipperary and Limerick. Then they crossed the Shannon to their native territory of Thomond, and buried themselves in the woods and forests which at that time covered the present County of Clare. Mahon soon grew weary of this rough and dangerous life; but Brian displayed the true spirit of a national leader and deliverer. He never despaired of the cause, no matter how desperate its state—and it was desperate at times. The Danes recognised the absolute necessity, for their own safety, of crushing this determined antagonist. They crossed the river in pursuit of him, and proved their engineering skill by raising the fortress of Bunratty, whence they might overawe the whole neighbourhood. I say they proved their engineering skill by doing so, because when the Normans, under Thomas de Clare, came to conquer this district, they selected the very same spot, where they erected a castle which stood many a vigorous siege down to the wars of the seventeenth century. Brian, however, was nothing daunted either by the defection of his brother or the nearer presence of his enemies. He acted like David when he fled from the face of Saul, and maintained a similar kind of warfare. David dwelt in the caves of Engedi and of Adullam, and the woods of Gilead, and in the hill of Hachilah which is before Jeshimon. Brian hid himself in the caves of the O'Bloods in the north-east of Clare, and in the Boughta mountains, near Gort in the County Galway, and there maintained himself till he was well-nigh reduced to the condition of Alfred when he became a goatherd, for Brian's army was at last reduced to the scanty number of fifteen men.

His brother now reappears on the scene. Mahon sought an interview with Brian, who reproached him for deserting the national cause. A poetical dialogue in one manuscript tells us of the interview. Mahon asks Brian where he had left his followers, as he had arrived almost alone and unattended. Brian answers that he had left them on the field of battle, cut down by the foreigners; that they had followed him in hardships over every plain, "not" (he adds) "like thy people, who remained inactive at home." He then recounted their achievements, and reminded his brother that neither their father Kennedy, nor their grandfather Lorcan or Laurence, would have sanctioned his cowardly truce with the Danes. Brian's reproaches took effect on his brother. He summoned his tribe, submitted to them the question of peace or war, which they naturally decided in favour of war, and then at once raised an insurrection against the dominant Danes. Mahon, as the elder brother, now becomes the prominent personage, though of course Brian remained the guiding and the moving spirit behind the scene. The Danes had conquered Kerry. Mahon flung himself upon them and routed them with the assistance of the inhabitants. Munster was now divided into two great sections. The curse of Ireland and of Irish action followed it on this as on every occasion. Jealousy and envy begat disunion and treachery. The chieftains took opposite sides. Ivar, Danish Prince of Limerick, summoned his allies. To him resorted every one who worshipped success and desired personal ease as opposed to national honour and freedom. The O'Mahony and the O'Donovan, two of the most powerful Munster chieftains, joined their forces to Ivar's; while Mahon and Brian rallied to their side the national spirit of southern Ireland. They drew their forces to a head in the neighbourhood of Cashel and Tipperary. The Danes attacked them at a place called Sulcoit, about two and a half miles north-west of Tipperary. Sulcoit means a sallow or willow wood; a name, by the way, still preserved in the designations Solloghod-beg and Solloghodmore, by which the neighbouring parishes are still known. The Scandinavians made one great mistake. They allowed Mahon to choose his ground, and under Brian's guidance he chose it so as to afford his light-armed troops every advantage. The whole neighbourhood was covered with dense woods of willows, whence its name. To this day the upper reaches of the Suir, which flows through these parts, is marked by plantations of willows, offering materials for a local industry. The Danes were unable to cope with the Irish in such a position. Their superiority in heavy armour hindered rather than assisted them, and as the result they were utterly routed, pursued to Limerick, and massacred there without mercy, a small remnant only, headed by Ivar their king, making good their retreat to Scattery island in the Shannon estuary, whence they sought shelter among their kindred in Dublin and in England. Mahon was now triumphant, and universally recognised as King of Cashel and of Munster. The fatal curse of division and of jealousy soon, however, displayed itself among the victors. The Molloys and the O'Donovans had allied themselves with the Danes, as I have already stated. Mahon seems to have forgiven their treachery, but they themselves could not forget it. They plotted against him, invited him to a conference, and then in the pass of Bearna Dhearg (red or bloody gap) through which the road from Kilmallock to Cork now passes, these treacherous chieftains assassinated the deliverer of their country. They murdered Mahon indeed, but they removed him only to make way for the stern avenger of his brother's death and a more vigorous champion of his country's cause. The fall of Mahon made Brian King of Munster, and placed him in the front rank against the Danes, who once again were raising up their heads. Let me give you a date or two. The battle of Sulcoit, which for the time annihilated the Danish kingdom of Limerick, happened in 968. Mahon reigned for eight years. He was murdered in 976, leaving the throne to his brother, who was then about forty-five years of age. The second period of Brian's life now opens upon us, when we have to trace his career of conquest till he stood as a victor, Emperor of Ireland, as he calls himself, before the high altar of Armagh, and indited by the hand of his chaplain the words you can still see in the *Book of Armagh*, in our own library.[1]

Brian's first duty was the punishment of his brother's foul assassination. This led him at once into fresh conflict with the Danes. The Irish historian from whom I have so often quoted, grimly notes that the murderers gained nothing by their crime. "For Brian who succeeded Mahon was not a stone in place of an egg, nor a wisp of hay in place of a club, but he was a hero in place of a hero, and he was valour after valour. He then made an invading, defying, rapid, subjugating, ruthless, untiring war, in which he fully avenged his brother."

Let me briefly sketch the steps by which Brian steadily raised himself to supreme power. He did not attain his end at once. He ascended the throne of Munster in 976. In 1002 he was recognised as supreme King of Ireland, a space of twenty-six years. Brian, as I have said, first applied himself to punish

---

[1] O'Curry, *MS. Materials of Ancient Irish History*, vol. i., p 654, gives these words incorrectly. The Latin of the correct text is certainly not classical; the spelling is very rude: "Sanctus Patri[ci]us iens ad cœlum mandauit totum fructum laboris sui tam babtismi tam causarum quam elemoisinarum deferendum esse apostolicæ urbi que Scotice nominatur Ardd Macha. Sic reperi in bebliothicis Scotorum. Ego scripsi, id est Calvus Perennis, in conspectu Briain, imperatoris Scotorum, et quod scripsi finiuit pro omnibus regibus Maceriæ." Which O'Curry thus translates: "Saint Patrick going up to heaven, commanded that all the fruit of his labour, as well of baptisms as of causes, and of alms, should be carried to the Apostolic city, which is called Scoticé Ardd Macha. So I have found it in the book collections of the Scots. I have written this, I Calvus Perennis, in the sight of Brian, Emperor of the Scots, and what I have written, he determined for all the kings of Maceria."

his brother's murderers. O'Donovan and his tribe summoned Harold, King of the southern Danes, to his assistance. Brian attacked the combined forces in O'Donovan's fortress and defeated them, slaying O'Donovan and his ally Harold. A more dangerous enemy remained behind. Molloy,[1] the other murderer, was himself a rival claimant to the throne of Munster, and had assumed its title. Brian formally declared war against him, defeated and slew him at a battle fought on the borders of Cork and Limerick. Within two years of Mahon's death, Brian had punished both his murderers. After the year 978 Brian advanced by rapid steps. He conquered the Waterford Danes. He defeated the chief of Ossory, Gillpatrick by name, an ally of the Dublin Danes,[2] and in 984 received the submission of the King of Leinster at his residence near Leighlin Bridge, in the County Carlow. Connaught and the North of Ireland as yet remained free from his attacks. He was a wise general. He took his foes in detail. He established himself at his favourite residence, Kincora near Killaloe. This gave him a commanding position. He could thence watch Limerick and the Danes. He could also attack the King of Connaught from the great Lakes of the Shannon, Ree and Derg, while Lough Ree again would help him to assail the rear of the kingdom of Meath. Brian's plans completely succeeded. Between 984 and 998, Connaught was conquered, while Malachy himself, who claimed to be supreme King of Meath, of Ulster, and of all Ireland, was compelled to make a treaty on the

---

[1] Maelmuaidh is the Celtic form of this name given by Keating, p. 544, ed. O'Mahony.
[2] Ancestor of the Fitzpatricks, Barons Castletown of Upper Ossory.

shores of Lough Ree, by which he yielded the supreme rule over the southern half of Ireland to Brian, retaining, however, his own authority over the northern half of the country.[1] But this treaty did not stand for long. Brian was determined to be supreme king. It was easy, therefore, to frame a pretext for a quarrel; a powerful and aggressive foe never has wanted one since the time the wolf of the fable sought an excuse for devouring the lamb. Malachy was accused of plundering Leinster, and challenged to war. He sought assistance in vain on every side. His own kinsmen, the O'Neills of Ulster, declined to help. The Celtic character recognised in Brian one made to rule and one determined to rule, and bowed before him as the corn bows before the wind. Malachy paid the southern conqueror the tribute demanded, and the year 1002 beheld the aged Brian universally acknowledged as King of Ireland. I shall close this section of his life by just noting that Brian proved his right to power by his exploits, not merely in the region of war, but also in that of peace, some of which remain and are even still in use. He erected or restored the cathedral of Killaloe, the churches of Inis-Caltra in Lough Derg, the round tower of Tomgraney in county Clare. He built bridges over the Shannon at Athlone and Lanesborough, he constructed roads, he strengthened the forts and island fortresses or Crannoges (the Swiss Pfahlbauten) of Munster.[2]

[1] Malachy has been rendered famous by Moore's Melody, "When Malachy wore the Collar of Gold which he won from the proud invader," referring to a battle gained by him over the Danes at Tara, A.D. 979. His character has been the subject of dispute. He is accused by Keating of meditating treachery at the battle of Clontarf. Dr. Todd vindicated him in a paper read before the Royal Irish Academy, *Proceedings*, vii., 500, 501.

[2] The Crannoges of Ireland and Switzerland have attracted

He dispensed a royal hospitality, he administered rigid and impartial justice and established peace and order through all the country, so that, as the historian puts it, " a woman might walk in safety through the length of Ireland, from Tory Island in Donegal to Glandore Harbour in Cork, carrying a ring of gold on a horse-rod," a state of affairs so seldom realised in those troublous ages, that it is no wonder it has been immortalised in the famous though probably over-drawn stanzas which sing :—

> " Rich and rare were the gems she wore,
> And a bright gold ring on her wand she bore;
> But oh! her beauty was far beyond
> Her sparkling gems, or snow-white wand.
>
> " On she went, and her maiden smile
> In safety lighted her round the green isle,
> And blest for ever is she who relied
> Upon Erin's honour and Erin's pride."

We have now arrived at the third great period into which Brian's life and work may be divided. He had conquered the Danes of Limerick in youth. He had conquered Ireland in the prime of life. But the toughest conflict remained behind. He conquered the

---

much attention, and been the subject of many communications to the Royal Irish Academy, to which the reader will find ample and accurate references in the Index attached to the *Proceedings* of that body, t. vii. I would specially call attention to the papers of Sir W. Wilde, vii., 147, and of Dr. Reeves, pp. 153 and 212, where the subject is exhaustively treated. The Crannoges are stockaded islands which, according to Wilde, p. 148, were occupied so lately as the reign of Charles II. In Switzerland they have been treated as pre-historic. In Ireland we have thus had pre-historic customs and habits surviving till almost living memory. See Dr. F. Keller's work, *Die Keltischen Pfahlbauten in den Schweitzer Seen*, and a memoir on the same subject in the (Zurich) *Mittheilungen der Antiquarischen Gesellschaft*, Bd. xii., Hft. 3. See Wilde's *Catalogue of the Museum of the Royal Irish Academy.*

Danish kingdom of Dublin in extreme old age. I have several times noted the genius of a true general and conqueror displayed by Brian. He used his opportunities with skill and judgment and prudence. He defeated his enemies in detail, and then, by kindly treatment, won them over to his side. He avoided above all things provoking his opponents into one grand united effort. Leinster, Connaught, Meath, Ulster, were all conquered in succession. But hitherto he had avoided conflict with the Scandinavians of Dublin, certain as they were of support from their allies in Man, Scotland, Northumbria, and York. His conquest of Meath in 998 brought him into contact with them, as his boundaries now marched side by side with those of the Danes, from the sea near Drogheda to the Curragh of Kildare and the waters of the Liffey. The Danes recognised their danger and boldly faced it. They sought allies among the Irish, and, as usual, sought them not in vain. Treachery was once again the deadly enemy of Ireland. The Leinster men rebelled against Brian, and, headed by their king and allied with the Danes, marched against Brian. Brian's old age was rendered splendid by two great victories over the Danes. The battle of Clontarf marked his death scene. The battle of Glenmama marked the year 1000. Of this latter battle nothing is commonly known, and yet it was in its way just as important as the more celebrated struggle by the sands of Clontarf. The battle of Glenmama was a great struggle with the Danes organised by the same sovereign, Sitric of Dublin, who commanded at the battle of Clontarf. He is no mythical character. We have his likeness still remaining stamped on the coins minted by him at Dublin, which you can see depicted in Worsaæ, *Danes and Norwegians*, p. 339. There we behold the features of a determined man, covered with a helmet and clad round the shoulders with a royal robe. He was a nominal Christian too, for his coins bear the sign of the cross upon them, though like many a Christian his religion sat very lightly upon him, and as the struggle grew fiercer would seem to have been entirely discarded. And now let us give our whole attention to Brian's first great struggle against the Dublin Danes aided by their treacherous Leinster allies. Brian, as soon as he learned their designs, collected his forces and marched towards Dublin. The allies on their side boldly advanced to meet him, and the hostile armies joined battle at Glenmama, the Glen of the Gap, near the ancient but rather backward town of Dunlavin, where the Wicklow mountains begin to sink into the rich plains of Kildare. Fortune as usual favoured Brian, and the Danes were defeated with the loss of King Sitric's eldest son and four thousand of his mail-clad warriors.

This battle was a crushing defeat for the allies. The Leinster men were dispersed in every direction. Accustomed to the bogs, they escaped more easily than the Danes; but their chiefs were so hard pressed that one prince was fain to take refuge in the branches of the ancient and majestic yews which to this day enclose the Church of St. Kevin at Holywood.[1] There he was captured by Morrogh, Brian's eldest son, an incident of which we shall soon hear more. I may just remark, that no ancient Irish battle-field has been more completely identified and followed in all its details than this one. In Dr. Todd's book, preface, p. cxliv.,

---

[1] A mountain parish of the diocese of Glendalough, situated between Dunlavin and Blessington, on the road to Dublin.

you will find the site of the battle and the various lines of flight accurately determined by the investigations and local knowledge of the late Rev. J. F. Shearman, formerly Roman Catholic curate of the parish, affording, indeed, an interesting instance how the clergy may profitably utilise rural leisure and life in the most backward localities, for the purposes of historical research.[1] Mr. Shearman traced most carefully the various routes by which the Danes sought safety, and was successful in gathering up relics of this most momentous struggle, which was indeed a complete victory for the Irish king. Brian was a thoroughly modern general in spirit. He did not commit the mistake of the English and French after the Alma. He left his defeated enemy no time to organise fresh resistance. Aged as he was, he pursued them across rivers, bogs, and mountains, till he entered with the fugitives the gates of Dublin, and made himself master of the fortifications. Brian used his triumph as victors have ever used them. He plundered the city, he destroyed the fortress, he enslaved so many of the Danes that, as the historian (cap. lxix.) tells us exultingly, "No son of a soldier deigned to put his hand to a flail or any other labour on earth; nor did a woman deign to put her hands to the grinding of a quern, or to knead a cake, or to wash her clothes, but had a foreign man or a foreign woman to work for them."

Here again, however, Brian pursued his usual policy. He did not push his victory too far. He weakened his foes, but did not destroy them. He even formed a

---

[1] Mr. Shearman was a devoted archæologist. His enthusiasm at times led him into mistakes and visionary identifications. He did real work, however, and has left some interesting papers behind him; see Todd's *Wars*, p. 145, note.

league with the Danes, and strove to secure the allegiance of the Leinster men by dethroning the king who had organised the revolt, and substituting for him Maelmordha, the prince whom Brian's son had dragged down from his hiding-place amid the branches of the yew trees of Holywood.

Now we come to the crowning victory of Brian's chequered and lengthened career, the battle of Clontarf; but before I proceed to describe it, I must trace the events which led up to it. Fourteen years separated the battle of Glenmama from that of Clontarf. These fourteen years were a period of comparative repose for Brian. Yet the Danes had only been waiting an opportunity to renew the struggle for their lost sovereignty. A chance circumstance gave them the desired occasion. A woman, as so often has been the case, was the cause of quarrel. The Irish kings and the Danish princes were perpetually intermarrying, notwithstanding their frequent and vigorous warfare. The dark-eyed Irish women captivated the Northmen. The King of Leinster had a beautiful daughter, named Gormflaith. Her face was very fair, but her temper and character were very different. She was a handsome virago. She first of all married Olaf or Anlaffe, King of Dublin, by whom she had a son Sitric, the hero of Clontarf. Olaf, however, could not put up with Gormflaith, and so he divorced her. Then she married Malachy, King of Ireland. He, too, after a little time dissolved the marriage bond, which seems to have hung very lightly upon these ancient Irish kings. Then, thirdly, she married Brian Boru himself, when he was now an old man. But neither could Brian endure her, and so a third time she was repudiated. She was, however, a woman who could not be insulted with impunity, and she had her revenge. Brian was living at peace in the year 1013, at his favourite palace of Kincora, near Killaloe. It is a beautiful and well-known spot. To the north lie the wide-spreading and island-studded waters of Lough Derg, in another direction rise the mountains of Clare and Galway, while in another Keeper Mountain, and the Slieve Bloom and Devil's Bit range bound the horizon. Though Brian had dissolved his marriage with Gormflaith, yet, by some curious arrangement, he permitted the rejected wife to reside in the palace which once had owned her as mistress; a bad device surely to secure his own peace and comfort. To this palace of Kincora, the King of Leinster, Gormflaith's brother, now arrived bringing a tribute imposed upon him by Brian. That tribute consisted of three large pine-trees suited as masts for shipping, cut in the great forests of Leinster, which existed till three centuries ago in the neighbourhood of Portarlington and Tullamore.

This tribute was the spark which caused the explosion. As the Leinster men were approaching Killaloe, they had to cross a boggy mountain, where the waggon carrying the trees stuck fast. Oliver Cromwell when crossing the same range to attack Limerick met with the same fate. His artillery stuck fast in the bog, and I have heard, on good authority, that some landholders in that district can show the title-deeds to their estates, graven in copper plates, granted for help rendered on that occasion.[1] The King of Leinster was an energetic man. He acted like the younger Cyrus in his famous expedition, described by Xenophon. When his baggage carts stuck fast, the historian tells us how

---

[1] So I was informed twenty years ago by the late Mr. J. F. Rolleston, D.L., of Ffranckfort Castle, Roscrea.

Cyrus jumped into the mud, clad in his royal vestments, and stirred his men to exertion by his vigorous efforts. So did Gormflaith's brother. He leaped from his horse, clad in a silk tunic embroidered with gold thread and decorated with silver buttons, the gift of Brian himself, and applying his shoulder to the work soon extricated the waggon. In doing so he knocked off one of the silver buttons. When he arrived at Killaloe he applied to his sister to sew it on. She took the tunic and flung it, silk, silver buttons and all, into the fire, bitterly reproaching her brother for accepting such a present, and accusing him of cowardice in submitting to the foolish old man who now ruled Ireland. She had a vicious, a vigorous, and a dangerous tongue. She reminded him of the deeds of his forefathers, and her words sank deep into the mind and heart of the Leinster prince. Still he was not prepared to revolt. He had once felt Brian's heavy hand, and did not care to incur the danger a second time. A trivial incident decided him. Brian's eldest son Morrogh was playing a game of chess with one of his cousins. Maelmordha, the Leinster king, was looking on. He suggested a move to Morrogh which lost him the game.[1] Angered at this, Morrogh said to his adviser, "That was like the advice you gave to the Danes, which lost them Glenmama." The king, moody and bitter as he was, sharply replied, "I will give them advice now, and they shall not be again defeated." "Then," said Morrogh, tauntingly touching his uncle on his sorest point, "then you had better remind them

---

[1] Chess was a favourite game with the ancient Irish. See the Introduction to O'Donovan's *Book of Rights*. The whole of this story will be found in Dr. Todd's book, and in Keating's *History of Ireland*, O'Mahony's edition, p. 569.

to prepare a yew tree for your own reception." The King of Leinster would have been no true Irishman had he endured this. He took horse at once, swearing to be terribly avenged. Brian, weary of war and strife, strove to stop the quarrel. He despatched messengers, entreating his brother-in-law to return and listen to an explanation. The messenger overtook him at the bridge of Killaloe, as he was mounting his horse. But his blood was up and he would listen to nothing. He became violent even. He struck Brian's messenger a blow on the skull, "and broke all the bones of his head," and then fled three days' journey to his own tribe. They at once revolted, and uniting themselves with the O'Neills, and the Danes of Dublin, they attacked Malachy, King of Meath, as Brian's representative and chief ally. Malachy at first was victorious, and ravaged the territory of his opponents as far as Ben Edair or Howth. But the tide soon turned. The Scandinavian mail-clad warriors of Baldoyle and Dublin hurled Malachy back, and pursued him as far as the celebrated sanctuary of St. Fechin at Fore, in the county of Westmeath.

It is now that Brian appears for the last time on the scene. Malachy despatched messengers imploring aid in the quarrel, which was really Brian's own. The aged king at once responded, and proceeded to act with his usual vigour and skill. He divided his army into two parts. Morrogh, his eldest son, commanded one division which took the enemy in the rear, advancing from Ossory along the line of the Barrow, and, penetrating by the vale of Imail, plundered the whole country as far as St. Kevin's monastery at Glendalough. Brian himself advanced by the great southern road, leading the forces of Munster and of Connaught, till he united with his son at the green of Kilmainham. There they formed an encampment, and proceeded to blockade the city from the feast of St. Kieran in harvest, September 9th, to Christmas, when, their provisions being exhausted, Brian was obliged to retire to Munster to recruit his exhausted stores.

Things remained quiet during the winter, but in spring war was resumed. About the festival of St. Patrick, March 17th, Brian organised another expedition and advanced against Dublin. The Danes on their side had not been inactive during the winter. Gormflaith, who escaped from Killaloe as soon as mischief was afoot, had been the moving spirit. Nothing could tame or satisfy her vengeful soul. She compelled her son Sitric, the Danish King of Dublin, to send emissaries in every direction, soliciting aid from his Norwegian and Danish kinsmen. She sent to the Kings of York and Northumbria, and they sent help in the shape of two thousand soldiers, who are described as all pagans, hard-hearted, ferocious mercenaries, having no veneration, respect, or mercy for God or man, for church or sanctuary; and, says the Irish historian, whose language waxes stronger as he remembers their appearance and their deeds, "there was not one villain of that two thousand who had not polished strong triple-plated armour of refined iron, or of cool uncorroding brass, encasing their sides and bodies from head to foot."

She sought assistance in more distant regions still. She sent an embassy to the Orkneys,[1] where she induced Sigurd, Earl of Orkney, to join the Scandinavian league. He promised to send troops and to be present himself, on condition, however, that Gormflaith should

---

[1] Dasent's *Burnt Njal*, ii., 327; Todd's *Wars of the Gaedhil*, p. 153.

become his wife, and the crown of Ireland be his portion in case of victory. Gormflaith, whose vanity and vengeance were alike flattered, readily consented. She had not, however, as yet exhausted her resources. She received intelligence that two pagan Vikings were then lying at the Isle of Man, Brodar and Ospak by name. She sent Sitric to them, bidding him engage their assistance at any cost. They received her offer with diverse feelings. They were brothers, indeed, but brothers who had followed very opposite courses. Brodar had been baptized and taken deacon's orders, but had relapsed to paganism; while Ospak was inclined heartily to accept Christianity. Brodar, delighted at the prospect of striking a blow at his old faith, agreed to Sitric's proposals, stipulating, however, that, if victory fell to his side, he should be King of Ireland and Gormflaith should be his wife.

To this again Gormflaith consented, notwithstanding her prior engagement, requesting merely that the treaty and its conditions should be kept secret, and, above all, that Sigurd of Orkney should know nothing of it. Ospak, however, Brodar's brother, refused Sitric's advances, escaped by stratagem from Man, and, sailing for Limerick, joined Brian's forces, accepted Christianity, and fought on Brian's side at Clontarf. Gormflaith's efforts were indefatigable, and were so far crowned with success that a formidable array of allies, including a body of Icelanders, promised to assemble at Dublin by the following Palm Sunday. The confederacy now assumed a distinctly pagan aspect. The little Christianity ever possessed by the Danes was flung to the winds. A pagan standard, a black raven, worked by the hand of Earl Sigurd's mother, " with mickle hand cunning, and famous skill," led the troops to battle, which was joined on Good Friday, April 23rd, 1014. We have many details of that fierce struggle left on record by eye-witnesses or actors therein. Let us strive to gather them together, and thus gain a definite idea of the last struggle on Irish soil between paganism and triumphant Christianity. The battle was fought all over the ground now occupied by the north side of Dublin, from the wood of Clontarf to the site of the present Four Courts, where stood the only bridge then spanning the river Liffey. It began early in the morning, at sunrise, soon after five o'clock. A strong north-east wind was blowing, as the inhabitants of Dublin still so often experience in April to their bitter cost. The Danish inhabitants of Dublin crowded the walls of the town, which clustered thick round the hill now crowned by Christ Church Cathedral, whence a splendid view of the fight presented itself. The immediate occasion of battle seems to have been an attempt on the part of Brian's forces to prevent the landing of some Danish reinforcements, or else to crush them just when landed. Brian was a pious prince according to his lights, and as such did not wish to select the most solemn day of the Christian year for a deadly struggle.[1] This attempt, however, brought on a general engagement, which lasted the whole day, from sunrise till close on sunset. The opposing armies fought in three divisions, drawn up in line four deep. Morrogh, eldest son of Brian, commanded the Irish, while Sigurd, Earl of Orkney, and Brodar, the apostate deacon, headed the pagan forces. The Irish historian whom Dr. Todd has

---

[1] The Icelandic story is that Brodar, who was a magician, found by his sorceries that, if the fight were "on Good Friday King Brian would fall, but win the day. If they fought before, they would all fall who were against him" (Dasent, ii., 333).

translated bestows thirty chapters on his account of the battle array and the varied incidents of the fight. A full narrative of it would be wearisome. I shall just mention its leading features. It was a thoroughly Celtic fight, without any skill or plan or manœuvres, consisting merely of a series of individual encounters, which are told in a very Homeric style. The battle opened with a fight between two rival champions, who had challenged one another the night before as they were drinking together; for the hostile armies seem to have been on very free-and-easy terms. The battle then became general. The O'Tooles of the Dublin mountains, who were allied with the Danes on the one side, and the O'Rourkes and O'Bryans from Leitrim and Westmeath on the other, separated from the main body of their supporters, and joined battle on their own account; which they waged so fiercely that they well-nigh exterminated one another.

The historian delights in recounting the achievements of Morrogh O'Brian, the commander, and of Torlogh, his son, which seem to have been met by equally brave deeds on the part of Earl Sigurd and Brodar among the Danes. The Raven Standard ever fluttered in front of Sigurd, who carried destruction with him wherever he went. Again and again the standard bearer was slain, till no one at last was found willing to carry a banner which, while it secured victory to the Danes, brought certain death to the bearer. So Sigurd seized it, wrapped round his body his mother's fatal gift, and then sought out Morrogh O'Brian. The historian cannot find Celtic epithets, plentiful as they are, sufficient to express the noble qualities of Morrogh, who seems indeed to have been a courageous and vigorous prince, and one whose career, had he survived the battle, might have changed the course of Irish history. He is compared to Hector, Samson, Hercules. "He was the gate of battle, the hurdle of conflict, the sheltering tree and the impregnable tower against the enemies of his fatherland and of his race during his time and his career" (ch. cvii.) Fortune, however, did not favour him. Morrogh and Sigurd met in single combat, and Sigurd went down before Morrogh, his head severed from his body. Another Dane, named Eric, then closed with Morrogh, determined to avenge his leader's death. Morrogh's sword being shivered to pieces upon Eric's armour, he seized the Dane with his hands, flung him beneath his feet, wrested his sword out of his grasp, and passed it thrice through his body. Eric, however, had his revenge; he summoned all his failing strength, drew his long skene or knife, plunged it into Morrogh's bowels, and laid them bare. Morrogh had sufficient strength to cut off Eric's head, and then fainted. He lived till next day, when he died, after receiving the Holy Communion and making his will. The rout then became general. A portion of the Danes sought their ships. The Irish pursued them into the sea, where vast numbers perished. Torlogh, grandson of Brian, distinguished himself in the pursuit, though only fifteen years of age, and met his death in doing so. He followed the beaten foe down to the strand of Clontarf, upon which the sea waves, raised high by the double influence of an easterly wind and a flowing tide, were now dashing themselves in those great foam-crested rollers which every Dublin man knows so well. One of those billows struck Torlogh, and drowned him at the weir of Clontarf, where he was found grasping the hair of two Danes with whom he had been fighting.

The flight of the pagans was marked by another and a crowning disaster for the Irish.  Brodar, seeing that safety could not be gained seawards, fled towards the woods, which then crowned all the heights which bound Dublin on the north and north-west, the last remnants of which are now to be seen in the Phœnix Park.[1] Brian had taken his station on one of these hills to engage in prayer, like Moses, attended only by a few servants.  The king was seated on a fur rug, where he prolonged his petitions from early morning till the afternoon, receiving occasional reports concerning the progress of the battle, from Latean, his attendant.  As the sun began to descend toward the west, the apostate deacon Brodar and two other warriors approached the king's station, seeking refuge in the woods.  One of the three had been in Brian's service, and he called Brodar's attention to Brian.  "The king, the king," said he. "No, no, a priest, a priest," replied Brodar.  "By no means," said the soldier; "that is the great King Brian."  Brodar then turned round with a battle-axe in his hand.  The aged king gathered his remaining strength, aimed a blow at Brodar, which wounded his legs, while Brodar cleft Brian's head in twain.  He then continued his flight to the woods, but was shortly afterwards taken and slain.  Malachy, King of Meath, who had remained in reserve, now advanced upon the field and completed the work, routing the enemy on every side, thus terminating the domination, though not the presence, of the Danes in Ireland.[2]

---

[1] The oaks which roofed Westminster Hall were said to have grown in these woods.
[2] The battle of Clontarf has been the subject of much investigation.  The best works dealing with it are those of Dr. Todd, *Wars of the Gaedhil*, of Dasent, and of Haliday already quoted. The student should also consult John O'Donoghue's *Historical*

*Memoir of the O'Brians;* Torfœus, *History of the Orkneys,* chap. x; J. Johnstone's *Antiqq. Celto-Scandicæ,* pp. 110-127, where the Icelandic narrative is given; Munch, *Norske Folks Historie,* vol. ii., 644—648, where the Icelandic and Northern authorities about the battle of Clontarf are investigated with great care. The Rev. Dr. Haughton has thrown the light of science on the subject in a paper, *Proc.* Roy. Irish Acad., vii., 495, where he shows that the time of high water in Dublin Bay, on April 23rd, 1014, exactly coincided with that reported in the *Annals,* viz., 5.30 A.M., and 5.55 P.M.; see Dr. Todd's Paper on the Battle of Clontarf, *l. c.,* vii., 498; and *Wars of the Gaedhil,* Introd., p. xxvi. It is not often that science so strikingly confirms the statements of history.

# LECTURE XVI.

## *THE SEE OF DUBLIN AND UNION WITH ENGLAND.*

THE work of the historian demands a very wise and discriminating eye. It is very easy to make history. We are all more or less making history. The family historian will find in the lives of the most obscure materials on which he can work. But to write national history requires an eye which can seize the main lines of national life; which can trace the working of great principles, and which, neglecting minor details, no matter how exciting or dramatic, can grasp the great turning-points of history, and show how they have determined the fortunes, and shaped the development, of the entire community. Any other kind of historical writing seems to me simply to stand on the level of annals, requiring merely mechanical perseverance, not mental capacity. It is for this reason that I do not attempt to deal with the fortunes of the various kingdoms into which Ireland was divided. I might occupy lecture after lecture with detailing the endless wars between the O'Connors of Connaught, the O'Briens of Munster, the O'Rourkes, the O'Flahertys, and the O'Tooles of our own mountains, and you would be nothing the wiser as to the great lines upon which Irish history marched till this island fell under the dominion of England. The great turning-points of Irish history are those with which I deal, and to one of them do I now request your attention,—the See of Dublin, its foundation, its development, and its influence in leading to final union with England. The See of Dublin dates from the eleventh century. Romancers in ecclesiastical history will undertake to trace back the line of bishops of this city to the time of St. Patrick, but without any solid historical grounds for their imaginations. Monastic bishops are often mentioned as living in the adjacent monasteries, and exercising there the offices of abbat or bishop. They were found at Tallaght, Kilmainham, Clondalkin, and Glasnevin; but they were bishops without a fixed see or territorial jurisdiction, and offer no analogy to that regular episcopal succession which has existed since the See of Dublin was established by the Danes. The Danes established the See of Dublin. They established it in opposition to the See of Armagh, they connected it with Canterbury and the Normans, and thus made it one of the great channels through which English and Norman influences flowed into Ireland. Let me show you how this took place.

The Danes of Ireland were largely converted to Christianity during the tenth century. Their Christianity was, however, only very superficial, and a large pagan party long continued to exist among them. Sitric, the king who gathered the Danes to Clontarf, was a Christian. His coins are marked by the cross;[1] and yet his most vigorous and determined allies at Clontarf

---

[1] A considerable number of his coins were found at Rome in 1884, mingled with those of Alfred and Athelstan. See an account of this find in Lanciani's *L'Atrio di Vesta*, with an appendix on the Coins by De Rossi (Rome: 1884); the *Contemporary Review*, December 1884, p. 912; and a further notice below.

were pagans, and, as I have shown, followed a pagan standard. Their Christianity seems to have come from England, and to have resulted from the labours of English and continental missionaries. It was imperfect, too, in its organisation. They possessed priests, but depended either upon the bishops of the native Irish Church for ordination, or else imported their clergy from England, where a large and increasing body of Danish clergy existed in the beginning of the eleventh century. We have an interesting document still existing, showing us how long the Danish communities continued without any local bishops. The See of Dublin was founded about 1040. Yet fifty-six years later, we find the Danes of Waterford without a bishop, and we have in Ussher's *Sylloge*,[1]—a collection of documents about Ireland in those early times, which I have often quoted, —a letter signed by the King of Ireland, a number of bishops, and the leading men of Waterford, asking Anselm, Archbishop of Canterbury, to consecrate Malchus, a monk of Winchester, to the episcopal office for that city. The letter is an interesting one. It shows how conscious the Danes of Waterford were of their own imperfections. The letters of Anselm in this *Sylloge* are all both curious and important, because they prove how constant and vigorous was the intercourse between Canterbury and the various Danish communities in Ireland during the latter half of the eleventh and the first half of the twelfth centuries. The petition from Waterford begins thus: It is addressed to Anselm, Archbishop of the Angles, and to all the bishops of his

---

[1] Epist. xxxiv., Works, ed. Elrington, t. iv., p. 518. See Eadmeri *Historia*, in the Rolls Series, pp. 76, 77 (London: 1884), where the same story is told. Malchus, first Bishop of Waterford, was consecrated by Anselm, assisted by the Bishops of Chichester and Rochester, December 28th, 1096.

province, from the clergy and people of Waterford. It then proceeds, "Holy Father, the blindness of our ignorance has long compelled us to suffer the danger of our salvation, because we have, like slaves, chosen to withdraw ourselves from the Divine yoke, rather than freely to yield ourselves to pastoral obedience. But now we have become conscious how profitable is the care of duly appointed pastors, when we reflect that neither can an army without due government engage in war, nor a ship encounter the perils of the deep. How, therefore, can our frail bark contend against its enemies, devoid of pastoral care?" Now, I have quoted these words, not because I purpose to enter upon the history of the Church of Waterford,—this would be a complete violation of my principle that we should confine ourselves to the great lines of national life,—but rather to show you how very long the Danish communities continued partly pagan, partly Christian, ravaging and plundering still as of yore the Celtic monasteries, and devoid of that complete episcopal government which might have done somewhat to restrain their erratic courses.

The See of Dublin was founded about A.D. 1040. The occasion of its foundation was a very natural one. The Danish princes of Dublin became Christians, and with Christianity they became travellers as well. Sitric, of Clontarf renown, and then an Anlaffe, and then again a Sitric, sought England and the Continent, and travelled as far as Rome itself. Wherever they went they beheld the majestic fabric of episcopal rule, consolidated by the master mind of Hildebrand, who then directed the Roman court, and established that system of papal domination which ruled Europe during the mediæval period. About the middle of the eleventh century, Sitric, King of Dublin, returned from a pilgrimage to Rome a devoted servant of the Roman See. The last year or so has seen a most interesting proof of his devotion coming to light. The late Pope Pius IX., whatever were his faults, was a magnificent patron of art and learning. The extensive excavations which have laid bare the face of ancient Rome were almost entirely due to his support and patronage. His chief agent in the work has been that archæologist of world-wide fame, De Rossi. The latest achievement due to his learning and labour has been the excavation of the Atrium Vestæ, where the sacred pledges of the Roman Empire were religiously preserved till the close of the fourth century, when Roman paganism made its last struggle for existence.

In the course of his excavations De Rossi came across a most interesting find in the shape of a vast collection of Anglo-Saxon and Danish coins of the tenth and eleventh centuries, which had been sent to Rome as the firstfruits of the earliest collection of Peter's Pence. Among these coins appear specimens of those of Alfred, Athelstan, and, though last not least for our purpose, of Sitric, the Danish King of Dublin. Sitric, however, not only paid Peter's Pence; he determined to found a see in strict communion with Rome, and not, like the ordinary Celtic ones, in opposition to, or at least in utter disregard of, the claims of the successors of St. Peter. He established therefore the See of Dublin about the year 1040, and appointed thereto a certain Dunan, or Donatus as his name was latinised, who was the first real bishop of this city. This Dunan was in all probability an Irishman or Celt, not a Dane. The very name Doonan is not yet extinct in the neighbourhood of Dublin. He was, I say, most probably an Irishman, because the Danes were too warlike or too commercial to become clergymen. It was just the same upon the invasion of the Roman Empire by the barbarians. The clergy were all Romans, used the Roman language, and dressed in the Roman dress. I remember an amusing instance of this. Gregory the Great was a thoroughgoing Roman of the ancient style. He prided himself, indeed, on his descent from one of those old Roman houses which had come down from the time of the republic. The barbarians came to Italy, however, with their new ideas and their new fashions, which the young blood of Italy soon began to ape. It became the fashion with the Roman young gentlemen to wear breeches in imitation of their northern conquerors. The clergy, too, followed suit. They began to imitate lay and barbarian dress; but Gregory would stand none of that, so he issued an edict that the clergy were to clothe themselves in the ancient Roman style, that they were to avoid all barbarian fashions, and specially were to avoid the wearing of breeches. The clergy, therefore, continued Romans and Latins, and thus by degrees re-established that dominion over their barbarian foes of which the fortune of war for a time deprived them. It was just the same with the Danes. As men of war holding their possessions by the sword, they despised the clerical profession. The Celts sustained that necessary office, however; and thus we find that all, or nearly all, the early bishops of Dublin were, as far as we can ascertain, of pure Celtic descent.

Donatus left his mark upon the city of Dublin. The Dublin of that date remained largely unchanged till the seventeenth century. To a great extent it can still be reconstructed by the imagination of a skilled archæologist. Dublin clustered then round the Castle or Dun of Dublin and St. Michael's Hill, which rose steep and threatening above the bridge which served to connect the north and south sides of the Liffey. Sitric and Donatus wished to have a noble church. Formerly the pagan Danes had offered their human hecatombs on the Great Stone at the Thingmount on College Green. Now Christianity demanded purer offerings and a more worthy and more expensive temple. The churches of the Irish, too, were often but of earth and wood, their stone buildings were small and poor, as you can still see so near at hand as Dalkey, Killiney, and Howth. Sitric and Dunan determined to build a church, modelled after the magnificent structures which they had seen on the Continent and in England; and as the result they produced the Cathedral of the Holy Trinity, commonly called Christ Church, which, after many additions and changes, Mr. Roe's magnificent restoration has reduced to somewhat the same proportions as Sitric and Dunan gave it.[1]

It is very curious to note how persistent and abiding

---

[1] I have received the following note from Mr. Drew, the learned architect of Christ Church Cathedral, concerning the only trace of the Danish origin of Christ Church Cathedral which has escaped the wreck of time. The "lately recovered plan" there referred to is due to his own architectural instinct, which predicted the existence of the cloisters hidden beneath the accumulation of ages—a prediction which was singularly verified during the excavations made in the precincts during last spring. These excavations revealed the ruins of the Chapter House, which escaped even Mr. Street's eye.

"An entry in the Leasehold Map of Christ Church Cathedral, dated 1761, gives the names of four holdings in the precinct described as 'part of Coolfabius.' The lately recovered plan of the cloistral buildings indicates that 'Coolfabius' so-called lay outside the cloisters, to the eastward of the 'Fratry.' A terrier of the leaseholds as existing shortly after the dissolution of the are first characteristics. Dublin Castle, when Sitric resided there, was connected with Christ Church Cathedral, and ever since that time the connection has continued. Within Christ Church Cathedral the viceroys were formerly sworn in, and Christ Church has been ever since regarded as the Parish Church of the Castle. But Dunan did more than erect Christ Church. He built St. Michael's chapel, which lasted till our own day, on the site now occupied by the Synod Hall, and erected, close by, an episcopal palace, afterwards turned into the Courts of Law, and used for that purpose till the close of the last century. Dunan held the See of Dublin for nearly forty years, till his death in 1075. A great change had meanwhile come over the fortunes and views of the Danes. The Normans had conquered England, and, in pursuance of a consistent policy, had placed their own countrymen in every important post of Church as well as State. The Danes and Normans regarded themselves as fellow-countrymen. The Danes despised the Celts of Ireland as thoroughly and profoundly as the Normans did the Saxons of England or the Celts of Wales. They refused, therefore, to have mere Irish bishops, and determined to import prelates having an English stamp, and rejoicing in an English consecration.

Now bear this in mind : from the year 1070 onwards

---

monastery which is preserved in the cathedral throws some light on the original etymology of this strange word. It is there written by the scribe as 'Colsabus,' subsequently as 'Colfabus.' It would appear that the original form *Colsabus*, as transcribed from some older document, was the correct form of the word. It seems to be a topographical word in Scandinavian form, meaning 'Col's Farm.' The name which has thus survived brings us back to the Danish occupation of Dublin, when cattle fed up to the walls of the cathedral." Streatfeild's *Lincolnshire and the Danes*, p. 178, would seem to suggest a different derivation.

the three great Danish communities—Dublin, Waterford, and Limerick—were in communion with Canterbury, not with Armagh. It will perhaps interest you at this precise conjuncture of events to know the names of the bishops who ruled the See of Dublin during the first century of its existence.[1] Here they are in order. Donatus from 1038 to 1074; Patrick or Gillpatrick from 1074 to 1084; Donatus O'Haingly from 1085 to 1095; Samuel O'Haingly, his nephew, from 1095 to 1121; Gregory, the first prelate designated as Archbishop, from 1121 to 1161; and the famous Laurence O'Toole, who presided over the see during the period 1162 to 1180, which introduced the Normans, subjugated Ireland beneath English rule, and brought the Irish Church under the undisputed sway of Rome and the pope.

Let us now take three of these bishops as representative men, and study their history, for their lives were turning-points. I select Patrick, Gregory, and Laurence O'Toole. Patrick, who ruled the diocese from 1074 to 1084, comes first. The Kingdom of Dublin was just then under the dominion of Gothric, the Danish King of Man, who had gained possession of it in 1066, the very year of the Norman conquest of Ireland. But the family of Brian Boru still retained its ancient glory.[2] Torlogh O'Brian, the grandson of

---

[1] When this lecture was delivered, the See of Dublin was vacant through the resignation of Archbishop Trench.

[2] The political and social life of Ireland during the eleventh century was one perpetual scene of war and bloodshed. The moral state of the country seems then to have touched its lowest point. The descendants of the great Brian quarrelled among themselves. Donogh, one of his sons, murdered his elder brother Teige. The murderer retired to Rome, while his nephew Torlogh seized the supreme power. Torlogh O'Brian, whose name occurs below, was the most vigorous sovereign of the eleventh century. He ruled the whole of Ireland about the year 1080. He was succeeded by his son Mortogh, whose reign also was vigorous and

the great Brian, was an old man, yet he showed that he possessed something of Brian's genius for war and statesmanship, and so Gothric was very soon compelled to submit himself to Torlogh as supreme king. I have noticed this point, because both Gothric and Torlogh play a considerable part in the history of Bishop Patrick. Now, we have concerning all those individuals documents, whose historic value and truthfulness the most sceptical cannot doubt. Notices in the *Annals* of Dublin, of Canterbury, and of Man, letters from Lanfranc, Primate of Canterbury, from the Pope Gregory VII.—all these remain, and can be inspected by any of you who will take the trouble of turning to Ussher's *Sylloge* in the fourth volume of his works (Epp. xxv., xxvi., and xxvii.) Donatus died, as I have said, in 1074. The Danes of Dublin at once met, chose a bishop, most probably out of the clergy attached to the Cathedral of Christ Church (Ussh., *Syll.*, ep. xxvi.), and directed a letter to Canterbury, whither they sent him for consecration. Its address is from "The clergy and people of Dublin to the Venerable Lanfranc, Metropolitan of the Church of Canterbury;" so that the people of Dublin then claimed and exercised a vote in the election of their chief pastor.[1] They then

---

flourishing. He was the last of his family who ruled the whole country. After Mortogh O'Brian the O'Conors of Connaught gained the supremacy. Upon Mortogh's death in 1119, the dissensions between the members of Brian's family became still more bitter; they murdered, mutilated, and blinded one another. In 1137 they entered into alliance with Dermot MacMurrough, by whom Strongbow was introduced into Ireland. See O'Donoghue's *Hist. Mem. of the O'Brians*, chap. v.

[1] The following is the notice of Bishop Dunan's burial in Christ Church and Bishop Patrick's election, taken out of the *Dublin Annals*, A.D. 1074:—"Dunanus, Episcopus Dubliniensis civitatis, in Christo quievit, et in ecclesia S. Trinitatis, juxta magnum altare, ad dextram ipsius, est sepultus. Eodem anno

proceed to inform Lanfranc of their choice of Patrick to fill the vacant see, he being a presbyter of honourable birth and character, well instructed in apostolic and ecclesiastical discipline, Catholic in faith, and well taught in doctrine. Finally, they entreat Lanfranc to proceed to his consecration with all possible speed. The primate of Canterbury was nothing loath. The Norman had a very poor opinion of the Irish Church, and Canterbury was naturally anxious to extend its primatial jurisdiction, which its prelates were at that very time endeavouring to assert over the provinces of York and Scotland as well as over Ireland.[1] So Lanfranc consecrated Patrick and sent him back with letters commendatory, one addressed to Gothric of Dublin, and the other to Torlogh O'Brian, King of Southern Ireland, which shed much light upon the social condition of the country at that period.

---

ad regimen Dubliniensis Ecclesiæ, populo et Clero consentientibus et eligentibus, in ecclesia S. Pauli Londoniæ Patricium sacravit antistitem." In the case of Patrick the people and clergy consent and elect, but fifty years later the lay element appears even more decided and distinct in the election of Archbishop Gregory. The address of the epistle to Ralph, Archbishop of Canterbury, is from "Omnes Burgenses Dublinæ Civitatis, cunctusque clericorum conventus;" the burgesses of Dublin seem to have claimed precedence over the clergy in the election (Ussher, *Sylloge*, ep. xl.)

[1] See Wilkins, *Concilia*, i., 327, where Lanfranc in 1072, writing to Pope Alexander II., claims that his predecessors have been primates over York, the whole island of Britain, and also over Ireland. Anselm, more than thirty years later, in 1108, put forward the same claim in a dispute with King Henry I. "Archiepiscopus Cantuariensis primas est totius Angliæ, Scotiæ, et Hiberniæ, et adjacentium insularum" (Eadmeri *Hist.*, p. 189, Rolls Series, 1884). Eadmer, indeed, often refers to Ireland as subject to the dominion of Canterbury. In his account (*Hist.*, lib. ii.) of the consecration of Malchus, first Bishop of Waterford, he describes his see as lying "in one of the provinces" subject to Canterbury. Ussher discusses this point in t. iv., p. 567, Works, ed. Elrington.

Lanfranc makes the same complaint in both. The Irish were very loose in matrimonial matters. It was the same under Torlogh's sway as under Gothric's. Men left their wives without any canonical cause, married others, although near in blood to themselves or to the deserted wives. They even took wives who had been deserted by their husbands.[1] In Gothric's kingdom the Danes seem to have gone a step further, and were in the habit of exchanging wives. The letter to Torlogh is well worth consulting for another reason. It quite disposes of the notion that the Irish Church succumbed to Roman supremacy and Roman discipline when it consented, three hundred years earlier, to receive the Easter cycle of the Western Church. Lanfranc in his letter to the Irish king complains most bitterly of the Celtic irregularities. (1) They did not recognise the prohibitions of the Roman Canon law concerning the degrees of consanguinity and affinity; (2) Bishops were consecrated in the Celtic Church by one bishop; (3) Infants were baptized without consecrated chrism;[2] (4) Holy Orders were given by the Celtic bishops for money. Now, you will observe that it is in his letter to Torlogh Lanfranc complains of these things simply because he ruled over the Celts, while in his letter to Gothric he makes no complaint

---

[1] Lanfranc's letters to Gothric. Ussher, *Sylloge*, ep. xxvi. "In regno vestro perhibentur homines, seu de propria, seu de mortuarum uxorum parentela conjuges ducere; alii legitime sibi copulatas pro arbitrio et voluntate relinquere; nonnulli suas aliis dare et aliorum nefanda coummutatione recipere."

[2] The Gallican and Irish Churches of the fifth and sixth centuries used only one unction *either* at baptism *or* at confirmation. The Roman Church used unctions on both occasions (see Hefele's *Councils*, iii., 160, Clark's ed.). The use of one unction only was a point of complaint against the Celtic Church, at the period of Augustine's mission. Lanfranc's letter is sufficient to prove the independence of the Irish Church in the eleventh century.

of ecclesiastical irregularities, because the Danes of Dublin had long since conformed themselves to Roman discipline.

I have styled the consecration of Patrick a turning-point in Irish history, and with great justice. His profession of obedience to the See of Canterbury was a wholesale betrayal of the liberties of this Church. It was of a very complete character, and ran thus:[1]— "Whoever presides over others ought not to scorn to be subject to others, but rather make it his study to humbly render, in God's name, to his superiors the obedience which he expects from those placed under him. On this account I, Patrick, elected prelate to govern Dublin, the metropolis of Ireland, do, Reverend Father Lanfranc, Primate of the Britains and Archbishop of the Holy Church of Canterbury, offer to thee this charter of my profession; and I promise to obey thee and thy successors in all things appertaining to the Christian religion."

Time will not allow me to discuss this act of submission; and there is less need to do so, as it has been already very fully and very fairly examined by the eminent Roman Catholic historian of Ireland, Dr. Lanigan, in his twenty-fourth chapter. I shall only say that it opened the way for Norman influences, which now poured into Dublin, making it a thoroughly Norman and Roman colony, so far as ecclesiastical matters were concerned. Patrick was not content with his submission to Lanfranc. He travelled to Rome apparently, and sought the papal presence. He told Pope Hildebrand of his hopes for the conversion of Ireland, and induced him to write a short but flattering letter to King Torlogh about the year 1084.[2] It was

---
[1] See Ussher, iv., 564. [2] *Ib., Sylloge*, ep. xxix., Works, iv., 498.

a judicious act on the part both of the pope and of the bishop to do so. Armagh was their great opponent. As in the Easter controversy Ulster stood out longest against the Roman party, so was it now. The primate of Armagh was the centre of opposition to Dublin, Canterbury, and Rome. But Torlogh O'Brian could now be utilised. He was, in the earlier portion of his life, king merely of Southern Ireland. In 1080 to 1082, however, he conquered Ulster,[1] and so now, in 1084, the pope and the bishop of Dublin combine to utilise him for their own purposes in opposition to hostile Armagh. The work of Anglicising and Romanising the Church of Dublin now went on apace. The three next bishops, Donat O'Haingly, Samuel O'Haingly, and Gregory, were all consecrated at Canterbury by Lanfranc, or by his successor Anselm, and all promised canonical obedience to that see. The primates of Canterbury, too, exercised an active supervision over the affairs of Dublin. Thus Lanfranc had a particular love for Donatus O'Haingly, and bestowed upon him a number of rich vestments and important books for the use of Christ Church Cathedral. His nephew, Samuel O'Haingly, made away with these gifts, and appropriated them to his own use, pleading that they were the private property of his uncle, the previous bishop. Anselm was watching him, however. Complaints of his conduct were made to the primate of Canterbury, who sent the Dublin prelate a letter, which we still possess in Ussher's *Sylloge*, ep. xxxix., telling him that the monks of Canterbury could prove that these gifts had been given, not to Donatus personally, but to him in his episcopal capacity, and ordering him to restore them, or cause them to be restored, if

---

[1] See O'Donoghue's *Hist. Memoir of the O'Brians*, p. 50.

he had alienated them to any stranger. The complaints which had been forwarded to Anselm had evidently proceeded from the Chapter, towards whom Bishop Samuel had been acting with a high hand. He had even turned some of the monks out of the monastery attached to the Cathedral of Christ Church. These Anselm commanded him to restore. Samuel had begun to exalt his office, too. Dublin was daily rising in importance, and Samuel did not see why Dublin, the seat of a king, should not hold its head as high as a provincial town like Canterbury. He therefore caused his cross to be carried aloft before him as he marched across St. Michael's Hill to his cathedral door, after the manner of archbishops. This was too much for the Primate of Canterbury. "I have also heard," he says, "that you make the cross to be carried before you on the way, which, if it be true, I command you not to do so again. For this privilege does not belong except to an archbishop who has been confirmed with the pall by the Roman pontiff; nor is it fit that by any unusual presumption you should appear remarkable and reprehensible to men." But now the time was come when Dublin should gain by canon law what Samuel desired. Samuel passed away in 1121, after an episcopate of twenty-six years. He was succeeded by Gregory, who held the see for forty years, and saw it installed in the high position it has ever since occupied. Gregory's election was remarkable in one respect. He was, like St. Ambrose of Milan and many other early bishops, a simple layman when elected to the archiepiscopal office. And there may have been good reason for this choice. The archbishop of Armagh, upon the death of Samuel O'Haingly, seized the Cathedral and See of Dublin. He had been legally recognised three or four years before at the Synod of Usnagh as Primate of All Ireland, Dublin alone excepted, which the synod reserved to the jurisdiction of Canterbury.[1] But the primate would not tolerate English intrusion into Ireland, so he attempted, after the manner of his predecessors, to assert his spiritual supremacy by physical force. The burgesses of Dublin, and the worthy merchants and shopkeepers of that day, were English—or I should say perhaps, Norman—to the backbone.

They rose against the Irish primate and his clergy, turned them out of the city, and in union with the Dublin clergy elected Gregory, one of their own number, who doubtless signalised himself by the vigour of his resistance to the intruding primate. They at once despatched Gregory to Canterbury for consecration. Their letter on that occasion is an interesting one. It shows that the Dublin laymen at that time claimed and exercised equal rights with the clergy in episcopal elections, and also betrays their bitter dislike of Armagh and the purely Irish or Celtic Church. The letter is thus addressed : " To the Most Reverend Ralph, Archbishop of Canterbury, all the burgesses and all the clergy of Dublin send greeting." It then proceeds to tell him that they send to him Gregory, their elect, for that (to quote their very words) " we were always willingly subject to the direction of your predecessors,

---

[1] The hill of Usnagh (Usneach) is a remarkable elevation in the barony of Rathconrath, county Westmeath, about six miles southwest from Mullingar. It was anciently considered the centre of Ireland, and was, after Tara, one of the principal places of national assembly. See Keating's *History of Ireland*, p. 300, O'Mahony's edition. The Synod of 1112 was held there. It has been identified with the Synod of Rath-Bresail. An account of its decrees will be found in Keating, p. 596; Wilkins, *Concilia*, p. 392; Waræus, *De Præs. Hib.*, 12; *Four Masters*, A.D. 1111.

from whom we remember that our people received the ecclesiastical dignity. Know, then, that the bishops of Ireland entertain a very great jealousy against us, and most of all the one who resides at Armagh, because we are unwilling to submit to their ordination. Therefore, we supplicantly request that you will promote Gregory to the holy order of episcopacy, if you wish to retain any longer this diocese which we have preserved for you during a considerable time." Here we meet with a notable coincidence. The Dublin burgesses were so thoroughly Anglicised that they chose Gregory, a layman, their bishop, so that even his lower orders, those of deacon and priest, might be Norman as well as that of bishop; yet, it was during Gregory's episcopate that Armagh finally achieved its supremacy over Dublin, and Dublin, by attaining the archiepiscopal rank, shook off the yoke of Canterbury. Let me show you, as briefly as I can, how this came about. In the earlier years of the twelfth century, say about the years 1110 to 1120, the Roman and Canterbury party had placed quite a ring of its own adherents round Ireland. Waterford was held by Bishop Malchus, a monk of Winchester; Gilbert, Bishop of the Danes of Limerick, was legate for the pope; while the Bishop of Dublin was, of course, a chief support thereof. Gilbert of Limerick was the most vigorous, influential, and aggressive of them all. He had travelled far and wide, and had lived long at Rouen with Anselm before his consecration. He was an enthusiastic admirer of the order and liturgical system of the Church of Rome. He conceived, therefore, the project of reducing Ireland to the same condition by introducing the accurately graduated, the closely articulated hierarchical system which prevailed in England and the Continent, instead of the ecclesiastical chaos then existing in the Celtic Church. His mind, too, was of that type which Rome has ever loved. It was intensely systematic, but very narrow; loving uniformity with a passionate love, and hating that lack of it which is always associated, and must be always associated, with individual freedom and personal activity. Bishop Gilbert was much displeased, therefore, not only with the disorderly character of the Church government prevalent in Ireland, bishops abounding in every direction without any fixed sees, or any competent incomes; he equally disliked the vast variety of liturgical uses which found place therein. We still possess (Ussh., *Sylloge*, xxx.) a letter from him to the bishops of Ireland, where he declares the variety of liturgies used in Ireland schismatical, and the Roman liturgy the only Catholic one. Appended to this letter we have a treatise, to which I would call your special attention. It is styled *De Statu Ecclesiæ*. It was originally accompanied by a diagram illustrating the text. The object of this treatise was to expound the very elaborate and intricate system of Church government which the genius of Rome had built up in the West. It explains the monastic system, but devotes special attention to the hierarchy, which it traces from the ostiarius and the lector up through the seven orders to the priesthood. Then it minutely sets forth the relation of the priest to the bishop, of bishop to archbishop, archbishop to primate, and finally of the primate to the pope, laying down in passing the duty of paying tithes, which had not hitherto been enforced in Ireland.[1] The system which Gilbert thus expounded,

---

[1] On the division and application of ecclesiastical property in Ireland see a learned note in Bishop Reeves' *Colton's Visitation*, pp. 112-119. He there points out that the Irish Church retained

he endeavoured to enforce. About 1120 he held a synod of the bishops and clergy of Ireland at Rathbreasail, sometimes identified with the synod of Usnagh already mentioned, where he divided Ireland into twenty-four dioceses, subjecting them all, except Dublin, to the supreme direction of Armagh.[1] Such an ecclesiastical reform and redistribution bill was wanting in completeness. It satisfied no one, and only led to frequent disputes, till in 1157 the pope sent a special legate to bring the Irish Church into conformity with the rest of Western Christendom so far as diocesan arrangement was concerned. I shall have more to say when treating of Armagh about the influences which brought about this result. Let it now suffice to note that Cardinal Paparo held the Synod of Kells on March 9th, 1152, in which Ireland was divided into four provinces, Armagh being constituted the primatial see, while Dublin, Cashel, and Tuam were raised to the rank of archbishoprics, and endowed, in conjunction with Armagh, with archiepiscopal palls.[2] Archbishop Gregory was, therefore, the first archbishop of the See of Dublin, which had been founded one hundred and twelve years before.

And now we come to the last archbishop or bishop of

---

till 1833 the fourfold division of Church funds mentioned by Pope Gelasius in the year 494. The quarter Episcopals were only abolished in the dioceses of Clonfert and Kilmacduagh in that year. This is an interesting evidence of the conservative tendency of Ireland, upon which I have so often insisted in these lectures. [1] See Reeves' *Antiqq.*, p. 139.

[2] See Wilkins' *Concilia*, i., 425. The four ecclesiastical provinces corresponded to the four kingdoms, while as for Meath, being usually held in conjunction with Ulster, it was included in the province of Armagh. At this time, too, there was no bishopric of Meath as such. The Kingdom of Meath was divided into the dioceses of Clonard, Duleek, Kells, Clonmacnois, etc., and so continued till the reign of King John. The rural deaneries of Meath now correspond to the ancient bishoprics of that kingdom.

Dublin who falls within our period. I have fixed as a limit for myself the Norman invasion, and that limit I do not intend to pass on this occasion. Some other time, if Providence permit, I hope to trace the history of the Church of Ireland from the Norman invasion to the Reformation. Now I shall only say a few words concerning the origin, training, and the life of the last bishop of independent Dublin,—the celebrated St. Laurence O'Toole. The previous bishops of Dublin had been Danish or Norman by sympathy and education. Dublin had now gained Home Rule in ecclesiastical matters. It had broken its thraldom to Canterbury, and the firstfruit of its independence was this. It elected as its second archbishop a genuine Irishman, Irish by birth, by education, and by consecration. Archbishop Gregory died October 8th, 1161, and was succeeded by Laurence O'Toole, whose name proclaims his origin. He was the son of an O'Toole prince of Imail, in the county of Wicklow, a beautiful and romantic vale, which lies beneath the shadow of the stupendous cliffs of Lugnaquila. By his mother's side, too, he was of local origin, for she was a Byrne or O'Byrne, and anyone that knows the counties of Dublin and Wicklow is aware of this, that the O'Tooles and the Byrnes are to this day the most numerous families in the whole district. Laurence O'Toole was from earliest youth dedicated to the ecclesiastical state. He was seized as a hostage when ten years old by Dermot MacMurrogh, who afterwards betrayed Ireland to Henry II. At his hands he seems to have suffered very severe treatment, which laid the foundation of a hostility which continued throughout life, and had important consequences for the country at large.

Laurence was trained at Glendalough, which was then a famous seat of learning. There he made such rapid progress that he was chosen abbat of the monastery, when only twenty-five years of age, and ruled with such diligence, learning, piety, and charity, that the people and clergy of Dublin fixed their eyes upon him, and unanimously elected him archbishop upon the death of Gregory. But the learned abbat prized the retirement and the studious shades of Glendalough too highly. He distinctly said, *Nolo episcopari*. The electors, however, wisely recognised that the fittest bishop is not the man who thrusts himself forward, but that rather the very modesty, self-distrust, and humility which lead him to decline, point him out as the fittest to rule the Church of God. So they pressed Laurence. They refused to elect any one else, and Laurence, at last recognising in their importunity the finger of God pointing him to still higher and more onerous work, accepted the position thus offered. The election of Laurence O'Toole cannot have been very pleasing to Dermot MacMurrogh. He was then king of Leinster, and as such seems to have exercised a kind of suzerainty over Dublin and its Danes. We have ourselves, as members of Dublin University, an interest in Dermot. He was a dissolute and abandoned character. In 1153 he seduced the wife of O'Rourke, Prince of Breffny, an action which finally brought about his ruin, for O'Rourke persecuted him with undying hostility, till he drove him from his kingdom to seek shelter at the Court of Henry II. Still, like many another licentious villain, he thought to atone for his wicked actions by his charitable donations. He founded, in 1146, a nunnery, called St. Mary de Hogge, where now is Suffolk Street, and erected the Priory of All Saints, in 1166, on the very spot where we now stand, endowing it with estates, some of which still belong to Trinity College, and others of which constitute the Baldoyle estate of the Corporation of Dublin. Time, however, would fail me to tell the full story of Laurence's life and work. Let it suffice to say he was a diligent administrator of his diocese, he was a stern reprover of vice, he energetically opposed the treacherous designs of Dermot, and vigorously denounced his wicked life. He courageously opposed the invading English, so long as he saw a chance of success, and then, when fortune declared against him, he used all the influence of his name, his position, and his character, to gain the best terms he could for his vanquished flock. Laurence O'Toole lives embalmed in the memory of the See of Dublin, and justly so; for he was an honour to it, and possessed all the qualities which conspire to make a distinguished bishop. He was pious, learned, and devout. He was distinguished for his generosity, his mercy, and his courage; he was devoted to the work and cause of God's Church, as he knew and understood it; and he died as he lived, doing that work. The Normans were then the conquerors. England and the English peasantry had felt their heavy hands one hundred years earlier. The stately castles which, all in ruins as they now are, mark the course of the Boyne tell how the De Lacys and the Dexters laid the same heavy hand on the Irish people in the earlier years which followed the conquest. Laurence O'Toole was so troubled at the miseries which he saw all around, that he determined to go and plead with Henry II. for his miserable flock. He crossed, therefore, to England, but Henry was gone to Normandy. Thither the archbishop followed him, though almost worn out with disease. He was not destined, however, to reach the king. He travelled as far as the Abbey of Eu, where death overtook him. Seeing the tower of the abbey in the distance, he said, "This is my rest" ("Hæc est requies mea"). He was gladly received by the brethren of the abbey, who perceived, however, that the end was near. He was exhorted, therefore, to make his will. "God knows," he replied, "out of all my revenues I have not a single coin to bequeath." He then received the Eucharist, and breathed out his soul to God in those words of the Psalmist which have so often in that same supreme moment of existence supported the spirits of God's elect ones, "Be merciful unto me, O God, be merciful unto me; for my soul trusteth in Thee, and under the shadow of Thy wings shall be my refuge until this tyranny be overpast." And thus falling back upon the great foundation truth of humble trust in God's mercy, in which all Christians can agree, he ended his mortal warfare on the 14th day of November, 1180.[1]

---

[1] He was canonised by Pope Honorius III., in 1225. Alexander III., in the third Lateran Council, A.D. 1179, appointed him papal legate in Ireland. See Ceillier, *H. E.*, xiv., 1143.

# LECTURE XVII.

## *ST. MALACHY AND THE SEE OF ARMAGH.*

THE See of Armagh differs from the See of Dublin in many respects. The See of Dublin claims the primacy of Ireland. The See of Armagh claims the primacy of All Ireland, the little word "all" making the whole difference. The See of Dublin has often contested the chief place with the See of Armagh. The quarrel began, as I showed you in my last lecture, during the time of Danish supremacy. The quarrel continued fierce and bitter all through the time of papal supremacy. Again and again did the archbishops of the two sees appeal to the king and to the pope on this point. Edward VI. made the Dublin prelate the superior. Queen Mary reversed the process, and awarded the primacy to Armagh. Ussher maintained before Strafford the metropolitan and primatial rights of Armagh; and the difference which began in Danish times was not settled till the last century, when the Roman Catholic Primate Macmahon wrote a very exhaustive and conclusive work on the question, since which time Dublin has quietly submitted to the claim of Armagh.[1] Armagh, indeed, has one evident point of

---

[1] A learned paper by Ussher on this question will be found in Elrington's edition of his Works, vol. i., Appendix, p. cxxix—cxliii. Exactly the same question was raised in England in the eleventh and twelfth centuries between Canterbury and York; see Wilkins, *Concilia*, Index, *s.v.* "Eborum."

superiority above Dublin. The origin of the Northern See is lost in antiquity. The origin of the Dublin bishopric can be fixed to a year, and that a comparatively modern year.

Let me now trace for you the history of the primatial See so far as we can ascertain it prior to the twelfth century, and then I shall strive to show how it attained its present modern position. The See of Armagh claims to have been founded by St. Patrick, and it may have been so. If you take up Ware's *Bishops*, you will find the whole list of bishops duly traced in orderly succession from St. Patrick down to the seventeenth century,—a list which Cotton's *Fasti* continues to the present time. But then, if asked for historical proof of this succession, we should be unable to produce it, as our authority for the names and order of the primates from St. Patrick, to the year 900, is the *Psalter of Cashel*, which is generally attributed to Cormac MacCullinan, King and Bishop of that city, about the year 908.[1] Now, suppose that Cormac was the author of earlier portions of the list contained in the *Psalter of Cashel*, and that I am bound to tell you is a matter of controversy; but yet supposing him to have been the author of that list, we may well ask what is the value of it. Cormac lived in Munster, he was king of a division of Ireland, practically as far and as divided from Armagh as Dublin is from Canterbury; he was writing four hundred and fifty years after St. Patrick's time, and he gives us a list of bishops and the number of years in which they presided over the See. All we can say is this, he may or he may not have had abundant and sufficient

---

[1] This list is given in King's *Primacy of Armagh*, p. 67, and in Colgan's *Trias Thaumat.*, p. 292.

materials for his task, but we have no evidence assuring us of its trustworthy character. On the contrary, we find that this list is brought down to the eleventh century more than a hundred years later than Cormac. It seems much more likely, therefore, that it was composed and inserted in the *Psalter of Cashel* after Roman ideas and views became current in Ireland, and testifies merely to the tradition of that time. Now, let us ask another, and a distinct question, Have we any early evidence that there existed a See in Armagh from St. Patrick's time, and that it enjoyed any peculiar precedence among the bishoprics of Ireland? The answer to this must be in the affirmative. The *Book of Armagh* proclaims upon its face that it dates from the eighth century. It was for ages counted one of the sacred relics, the possession of which proved its owner to be the true primate. In that book we find a very ancient canon, which has given rise to much controversy. It runs as follows: "Whensoever any cause that is very difficult and unknown to all the judges of the Scottish nation shall arise, it is rightly to be referred to the See of the Archbishop of the Irish, to wit, Patrick, and to the examination of the prelate thereof. But if, by him and his wise men, a cause of this nature cannot easily be determined, we have decreed that it shall be sent to the See Apostolic, that is to say, to the Chair of the Apostle Peter, which hath the authority of the City of Rome." This canon, found in one of the most ancient MSS. belonging to the Church of Ireland, has given rise to much controversy.[1] Bishop Moran, late of

---

[1] The existence of an entry in a volume like the *Book of Armagh* does not prove such entry coeval with the earliest portion of the Book. It might be centuries later, as such a

Ossory, has seen in it a clear proof that the Ireland of the seventh and eighth centuries submitted completely to papal supremacy. Archbishop Ussher, on the other hand, is equally well satisfied with it, and is quite willing to pay equal obedience to it. "If I myself had lived in Patrick's days" (writes he in his *Religion of the Ancient Irish*, cap. viii.), " for the resolution of a doubtful question I should as willingly have listened to the judgment of the Church of Rome, as to the determination of any Church in the whole world; so reverend an estimation have I of the integrity of that Church as it stood in those good days."

But quite apart from the controversial aspect of this canon, it seems to me conclusive on the point of the precedence, authority, and dignity of the See of Armagh at the date of its insertion in the ancient codex which we still possess. Armagh was, then, in the eighth century the chief See and the final court of appeal for the churches of the Scottish nation.[1] And the course of history as I have expounded it confirms this view. Danish and Celtic enemies, all alike, made Armagh the central point towards which their attacks were directed. Turgesius, the celebrated Danish conqueror of the year 840, seized the city, and established himself as pagan priest as well as pagan king, in place of the Christian primate whom he expelled. His action clearly proves that Armagh possessed a religious

---

volume was used as a book of record. The Queen's name is written on the fly-sheet of the *Book of Kells*. This will scarcely justify a historical student in the year 2886 maintaining that Queen Victoria was a contemporary of Turgesius, the Danish invader of Ireland A.D. 800.

[1] Cumınian, as I have already pointed out, seems to recognise a supremacy in Armagh in the seventh century, by calling Patrick "Papa noster," "Our Pope" (see p. 160).

significance, for Ulster at least, enjoyed by no other see. The primate fled to the south, bearing with him, according to the ancient Irish historian of the Danish wars, the sacred relics which connected Armagh with St. Patrick. But yet, notwithstanding an abundance of notices of Armagh, it must be confessed that the history of the See prior to the twelfth century is exceedingly puzzling. The histories of the Abbey of Armagh and of the See of Armagh are inextricably mixed up together, so that it is almost impossible to say whether any individual mentioned in our *Annals* as the Coarb[1] of St. Patrick was Abbat of Armagh or Bishop of Armagh. This much, however, is quite clear. The Church of England did not look upon the Irish Church or upon the See of Armagh as occupying a very regular or a very canonical position. At the close of the eighth century and the opening of the ninth, the English Church was still in the first burst of papal zeal. Through the labours of a very able and very devoted series of prelates it had been brought into complete conformity with Roman canon law, and had completely cast off all traces of that Irish connection to which it owed its earlier Christianity. The English were now inclined to look down upon and to pity the barbarous and schismatical Irish. So they passed a canon in the Council of Celclyth in the year 816, prohibiting " Irish clerics from officiating in England, because no position of dignity or honour of any kind is assigned to metropolitans " (Wilkins, *Concilia*, i., 170); whence it is clear that whatever tradi-

---

[1] See about this word and the office expressed by it, Ussher, *Treatise on Corbes, Herenachs, and Termon Lands*, Works, vol. xi., p. 419, ed. Elrington; Robert King's *Primacy of Armagh*, pp. 17-32. It was applied to the Pope as the successor of St. Peter (Reeves' *Colton's Visitation*, p. 11).

tional reverence was then paid to Armagh, it did not occupy any such canonical position or primacy as Canterbury held towards the English Church of that age.[1] The eleventh century first brings the See of Armagh into the clear light of day. At the very beginning of the century, in 1002, Brian Boru stood before the high altar of Armagh, and laid twenty ounces of gold thereupon in acknowledgment of the superiority of Armagh over Munster as well as over Ulster. In fact it is to Brian Boru I should feel inclined to ascribe that prominent position of Armagh over the whole of Ireland, and not over Ulster merely, which it has since enjoyed. Brian had a great reverence for the primatial See. By his will he left two hundred and forty cows to the successor of Patrick, the Abbat of Armagh. To the Church of Armagh he left his body, prescribing the very route which the funeral should follow, first to Swords, then to Duleek in Meath, then to Louth, where the bishop and clergy of Armagh were to meet it, and thence to the northern cathedral, where he was to be buried. From the time of Brian the history of the Armagh primacy is pretty clear. In Brian's day the bishop of Armagh was one Maelmury or Marianus. He was a married man, and belonged to a family who for two hundred years at least held possession of the See. They transferred it at times from father to son, but in any case always kept it for their own relations, till

---

[1] This canon of Celclyth is quite sufficient evidence that Roman discipline had no currency in Ireland in the early part of the ninth century. It seems to throw some light, too, on the nature of the Celtic liturgy. It must have been similar to the Roman, or else the Irish clergy would not have known how to use it, and there would have been no need of prohibiting them from celebrating mass, as this canon expressly does.

such a gross abuse was terminated by St. Malachy and the Roman party in the twelfth century. Those who endeavour to show that the Irish Church was always organised in strict conformity with Roman discipline are greatly puzzled by this hereditary succession to the See of Armagh. They have discovered a device, however, to account for it, and it is this. The married primates of the eleventh century were not bishops at all. They were only laymen who seized the temporalities of the See, and called themselves Coarbs of St. Patrick, while they employed a true bishop to act as their deputy and perform all ecclesiastical offices, and they have found a happy modern example which they think exactly illustrates the circumstance, in the case of the Duke of York, son of George III., who was not only commander-in-chief of the British army, but was also appointed Bishop of Osnaburgh in Germany when an infant of a few months old, in order that he might enjoy the episcopal revenues, though he never received any kind of ordination whatsoever.[1] Several circumstances, however, conspire to prove that these hereditary bishops acted as true bishops. (1) The bishop of Brian's day was succeeded in his office by no less than two sons. Yet at his death he was revered by the whole of Ireland, and is described by the *Annals of the Four Masters* as " the head of the clergy of the West of Europe ; the principal of all the holy order of the West, and a most wise and learned doctor ; " than which no stronger words can well be invented to describe a bishop invested with full ecclesiastical functions. (2) His son

---

[1] Supposing this contention true, it would be but a poor support for the Roman view ; for surely the Pope would never have tolerated such a gross abuse in a Church subject to his authority.

Amalgaid, who presided over the See from 1021—
1050, acted as a real primate over all Ireland, and
was the first bishop of Armagh who exercised such
power by making in the first year of his episcopate,
1021, the first primatial visitation of all Munster;
and lastly his great grandson, Maurice or Murtogh,
successfully held the See for five years in opposition
to St. Malachy, elected thereto by the votes of the
Roman party, who were desirous of reducing Armagh
to a more Christian and canonical condition.

But, doubtless, you are well tired of the eleventh
century and its confused ecclesiastical state. Let us
pass on to the twelfth century, when a greater regularity began to prevail, and those forms of ecclesiastical
discipline and law were put into operation which had
been already established all over Western Europe.
Gilbert, Bishop of Limerick, was, as I have told you,
the moving spirit in this revolution. He was papal
legate, was thoroughly endued with the Latin and
Roman spirit, and found a willing assistant in the
person of Celsus, consecrated Bishop of Armagh September 23rd, A.D. 1106. Celsus belonged to the family
which had held the See for two hundred years; he was
grandson of a previous primate, and is said by some
to have been himself a married man; yet he became
the instrument in the skilful hands of Gilbert and
St. Malachy of overthrowing the hereditary succession
to the primatial see.

The life of Celsus having been so very influential
for the Irish Church, let me give you a brief account
of it. Celsus was chosen bishop in 1106, when he
was only twenty-seven years of age; he ruled till
1129, when he died in his fiftieth year. He led a
very active life. He presided at several national

synods, as, for instance, at the Synods of Usnach and of Rathbresail already referred to, when Ireland was divided into twenty-six dioceses, and the first formal attempt made to get rid of that anarchical state of Church government which had hitherto prevailed. I fix, indeed, upon the archiepiscopate of Celsus as a turning-point in the history of Armagh and of the Irish Church, on account of the decrees of this Synod of Rathbresail. Episcopacy had been the rule of the Irish Church prior to that synod, but dioceses and diocesan episcopacy had had no existence at all. St. Bernard of Clairvaux has left us a most valuable document concerning the Church of Ireland in his life of St. Malachy. He was an independent witness, and at the same time a most competent one, because he was the intimate friend and associate of St. Malachy of Armagh, and heard from his own mouth those particulars about the state of Armagh, and of Ireland at large, which we find in that work. But Malachy was not his only source of information. He had a number of Irish clerics left by Malachy at Clairvaux, or sent thither by him, in order that they might be duly initiated into the Cistercian discipline and order. From Malachy, and from these Irish monks, St. Bernard had direct evidence about Ireland and its customs. Then again, he sent his own French monks over to found the celebrated abbey of Mellifont, near Drogheda, where the beautiful ruins still testify to the grandeur, dignity, and wealth of the Cistercian order. From all these sources Bernard gathered his information about the Church of Ireland as it existed prior to the Synod of Rathbresail; and he tells us expressly that no dioceses existed in the Ireland of the eleventh century, but that bishops were multiplied and changed without order or regularity, according to the mere pleasure of the Armagh metropolitan, so that almost every church had a bishop of its own (*Vit. S. Mal.*, cap. 7). Primate Celsus was a good man, but a timorous one. He was wanting in one of the first qualities desirable in an archbishop, —he was wanting in backbone; and he felt that a stronger hand than his was required to deal with the nepotism which reigned supreme at Armagh. So he looked around him, and selected for that purpose Malachy of Connor, to whom, when he found death approaching, he sent his pastoral staff as a formal act of appointment. St. Malachy was the person who finally reduced Ireland beneath the supremacy of Rome, and introduced complete Roman discipline. That subjection was, indeed, formally ratified and confirmed by the Norman invader and his creatures at the Synod of Cashel in 1172, but the real work was done by St. Malachy. To his career let me, therefore, call your special attention.

Malachy was born about the year 1095, his father was called O'Morgair or O'Mungair, a name afterwards changed to O'Dogherty. His father was senior lecturer of the University or school of Armagh, where Malachy himself was educated under the direction of a celebrated anchorite of the day, named Imar, who lived in a cell near the cathedral, devoted to study and to religious exercises of that severe ascetic type which had a special charm for an enthusiastic ecclesiastical mind. At Armagh, Malachy was ordained priest and deacon about the year 1119, after which he went to study theology at Lismore, the great school of Southern Ireland. Here his admiration for the Latin system was abundantly confirmed. Already the influence of Gilbert of Limerick and of his writings had told upon him. He, therefore, desired to avail himself of the instruction which could be obtained in the schools of Lismore, then presided over by a Bishop Malchus, who had been trained for years at the great Norman monastery of Winchester.[1] Lismore had been for centuries in active communication with France and England, and was by this time in thorough sympathy with the Latin Church. The schools of Lismore completed the work which Gilbert and his writings had begun in St. Malachy, and he returned to Ulster a devoted adherent of Roman ideas. Malachy now rose rapidly through the various grades of the Latin hierarchy. He was made abbat of the famous monastery of Bangor, on Belfast Lough, and, in 1125, Bishop of Connor, embracing within its limits the present county of Antrim. As a bishop Malachy devoted himself to his work. His activity was ceaseless and his self-denial extreme. St. Bernard describes him in one place as perpetually traversing towns and villages on foot, preaching the Gospel, attended only by some chosen disciples. In another place he thus sets forth the simplicity of his life and the fervour of his piety: "He had neither servants, nor estates, nor revenues. His episcopal table possessed no money for its support. He had not even a house of his own. He was incessantly visiting his parishes, serving the Gospel and living by the Gospel, as the Lord hath appointed, saying, 'The workman is worthy of his hire.'" Poverty

---

[1] Malchus was the first bishop of Waterford (see p. 309). He is mentioned in Bernard's *Life of Malachy* in very high terms: "Hic erat senex plenus dierum et virtutum, et sapientia Dei erat in illo. Natione quidem Hibernus, sed in Anglia conversatus fuerat in habitu et proposito monachali in Vintoniensi monasterio; de quo assumptus est in episcopum in Lismor civitate Mumoniæ, et ipsa nobiliore inter cæteras regni illius."

seems, indeed, to have been Malachy's voluntary choice, though some Irish bishops were compelled to accept it *nolentes, volentes*. In the sixteenth century the ancient See of Annaghdown, in Galway, was returned to the crown as worth only twenty pounds per annum. At the third Lateran Council, Alexander III. discovered an Irish bishop whose income consisted of the milk of three cows. When they went dry, his people supplied him with three others. But Malachy had ample diocesan property, as we learn from the simple fact that some thirty years after his time his successor could largely endow two religious houses with very considerable estates.[1] Malachy's earnest, vigorous labours among the mountains and glens of Antrim must have constituted an epoch in the history of the diocese, and shed a halo of piety and devotion round his efforts for the reformation of the Celtic Church.[2]

But higher promotion still awaited him. Primate Celsus had fixed upon Malachy as the only one fitted to destroy the power and influence of the clique which for two centuries had controlled the See of Armagh. He chose him, therefore, as his successor, and sent him his pastoral staff in token of his choice. But Malachy was prudent as well as zealous. He

---

[1] See Reeves' *Antiqq.*, pp. 99, 162. King's *Primacy of Armagh*, pp. 87-101, gives a long account of St. Malachy gathered out of St. Bernard's *Life*, and the *Irish Annals*. The reader will there find an elaborate discussion of the tangled chronology of Malachy's life.

[2] Malachy's efforts constituted a real reformation of the Celtic Church. The Celtic Christian organisation had utterly broken down. The bishops had become the mere creatures of the princes, and nothing but the strong central organisation of the Roman Church could have ruled and tamed in any degree the wild Celt.

knew the difficulties of the task and the danger to be incurred at the hands of the dominant faction ; for the Irish of that day would have thought as little of murdering an unpopular primate as a Kerry Moonlighter of to-day thinks of shooting an unpopular landlord.  He declined, therefore, to accept the primacy till formally elected at a national synod convoked about 1134 by Gilbert of Limerick, the papal legate, and attended by the chief princes of the whole island.  Armed now with full power of Church and State, he proceeded to execute his mission, in which he was eminently successful.  He expelled his opponents, and recovered from them the emblems of the See, the sacred pledges of primatial authority, which alone guaranteed in the minds of the populace the character of a true primate, viz., the Book of the Gospels, said to have been written by St. Patrick himself, which is our present *Book of Armagh*, and the Staff of Jesus, said to have been given by our Lord Himself to the Apostle of the Irish people.  St. Malachy, however, was not ambitious of place, power, or riches.  He made a bargain with Gilbert and the synod which elected him primate that, when he had effected their purposes and reformed the Church of Armagh, he should be permitted to retire again to his beloved obscurity.  Malachy understood the secret of a quiet and of a happy life, which does not consist in the blaze of publicity or the glare of high station, and can only be found in the valley of humiliation and amid the shadows of obscurity.  Malachy, therefore, when he had fulfilled his task, retired to the See of Down in the year 1137, and was succeeded in Armagh by Archbishop Gelasius, who held the primacy for thirty-seven years, till two years after the Norman invasion of 1172.  Malachy resigned the See of Armagh, indeed, in 1137, but he continued, though in a subordinate position, to occupy the foremost place in the Church of Ireland. His position in the Irish Church was somewhat like that of the late Bishop Wilberforce in the English Church of twenty years ago. No matter who was primate of Canterbury, the Bishop of Oxford or of Winchester was the foremost bishop of the English bench ; and so no matter who was primate of Armagh in those changeful and fateful years which preceded the Norman conquest, Malachy, the Bishop of Down, was the leader of the Irish Church. And now came an epoch in Malachy's life, and not in his life merely, but in the history of the Irish Church and of Ireland itself. I showed you in my last lecture how the Danes introduced English and Norman fashions in religion, and thus paved the way enabling the Church of Rome to overthrow our ancient national customs and independence. Malachy completed the work which the Danes began. The Danes and Danish bishops were bitterly hostile to Armagh and the Irish bishops. It was left to Malachy to reconcile Celts and Danes by rendering them both the subjects of the pope. Let me show you how this came about. About the year 1140 Malachy proceeded to pay a long-meditated visit to Rome. He took York, and then Clairvaux on his way as being the seat of St. Bernard, the most learned doctor, the most profound and devout spiritual physician then existing.

The biography of our saint by Saint Bernard contains some interesting illustrations of the social life of these remote times. Malachy evidently crossed the Channel by the shortest possible route. The pagan Dane was still abroad and paying but little attention to episcopal or primatial dignity. He sailed probably from Strangford or Donaghadee to the opposite coast of Scotland, whence he made his way to York. His retinue was not an extensive one. It consisted of five priests, with a few servants. Yet they were able to muster but three horses to carry the whole party. During their stay at York their deep piety commended them to a certain prior, named Wallenus, who offered the bishop a kicking and restive horse, which he evidently did not value very highly. Malachy, acting on the principle of not looking a gift-horse in the mouth, willingly accepted the beast, any little addition to his travelling resources being most acceptable. The worthy prior expressed sorrow that a better animal could not be placed at his service. The bishop, however, thanked him warmly for his gift, and intimated his intention to retain the animal for his own special use. And we may well suppose that it was as the result of his new owner's sanctity that the animal gave up his kicking and restive and ill-bred habits, and became a respectable, well-conducted beast, fit for the use of a middle-aged gentleman of episcopal dignity. Malachy next visited Clairvaux, where he formed a lifelong friendship with St. Bernard, which has resulted in the most authentic biography of an ancient Irish bishop which we possess. He then passed on to Rome, where he was graciously received by the reigning Pope Innocent II., and named by him papal legate for Ireland in succession to the aged Gilbert of Limerick, who had succeeded as well as man ever did in carrying out a most difficult task. Forty years previously Gilbert had begun his work; all Ireland, headed by Armagh, was then hostile to Rome, save the three Danish cities of Dublin, Waterford, and Limerick. Gilbert worked, wrote, and, above all, chose his instruments with the one object of reforming the Irish Church from what St. Bernard called Celtic "barbarism" to papal order. And now, as life was passing away, he saw his task completed when a former primate of Armagh was named papal legate, and knelt a suppliant seeking the gift of the pall, the outward and visible mark of a magnificent slavery, bestowed by Rome upon her obedient children. The pall, indeed, was the great object of Malachy's visit to Rome. He had carefully studied and thoroughly assimilated the Roman system of hierarchical government, as expounded in Gilbert's work *De Statu Ecclesiastico*, which I have already analysed. He lamented the defective state of the Irish Church. It had no real primate, no metropolitans, no archbishops ornamented with the pall and entitled to take their seats side by side with the great dignitaries of England and the Continent. Malachy, therefore, besought the pope to raise Cashel in the south and Armagh in the north to archiepiscopal rank, and to confer the pall upon the occupants of these sees. The pope consented at once to raise them to the rank of archbishoprics; but the question of the pall required more deliberation. He told Malachy that the pall must be requested by a national synod of the Church of Ireland, and would then be granted. Malachy spent some time at Rome sight-seeing and visiting the holy places connected with the memory of martyrs and apostles, and then took leave of Pope Innocent, who treated him with the greatest respect, presenting him with the mitre and stole used by himself in the celebration of mass. Malachy returned to Ireland by Clairvaux, where he arranged with St. Bernard for the instruction of his followers in the Cistercian discipline, and for the immediate introduction of that order into Ireland instead of the ancient Irish monastic rule which had prevailed since the fifth century.

Malachy returned to Ireland by the same route as he pursued when setting out. He passed north to Scotland, and sailing from Portpatrick to Donaghadee, devoted himself with all his heart to his three great objects—(1) The evangelisation of his diocese, comprising the eastern portion of the county Down; (2) His work as papal legate; (3) The introduction of the Cistercian order. In these two latter he completely succeeded. The Cistercian order was at once established. To this day you can behold in our own neighbourhood the handiwork of Bernard's monks, for the very first monastery erected by them was the celebrated one of Mellifont, near the banks of the Boyne, four miles from Drogheda. There, in a retired glen, near the site of the famous battle-field, stands St. Bernard's Chapel, one of the most perfect specimens of the early Gothic, of the twelfth and thirteenth centuries. In his other object St. Malachy succeeded too, though, like many another man, he lived not to see his complete success. He called a synod at Holmpatrick, in the north of the county Dublin, in the year 1148, where a petition for the palls was agreed to, and Malachy was commissioned to present it in person to the pope, who was then visiting France. He departed at once to Clairvaux, but found the pope had left. Malachy's work, however, was done. He was seized with a fever in that monastery, and there where he most desired to rest he expired, on All Saints' Day, November 1st, 1148. In body indeed he departed from the Irish Church, but in Spirit he remained present with it. He resigned his primacy at Armagh eleven years before to Gelasius, when he had thoroughly broken the old clan or tribal idea connected with that See. Gelasius, his successor, was elected in the canonical manner by the votes of clergy and laity, and continued faithfully to second all Malachy's efforts towards reducing the Irish Church to Roman conformity. Malachy's death ensured the fulfilment of his long-cherished wishes. The pope yielded to the petition of the synod of Holmpatrick, and despatched Cardinal Paparo as supreme legate to Ireland, where he established, at the synod of Kells, March 1152, that diocesan system which has ever since continued without material alteration. That assembly made Cashel, Tuam, and Dublin archbishoprics, constituted Armagh the seat of the primacy, and (as the Annals of St. Mary's Abbey put it) made Gelasius himself "the first archbishop of Armagh, that is, the first who used the pall, although others before him were called archbishops and primates out of reverence to St. Patrick, the apostle of Ireland, whose See was from the beginning held in the greatest honour, not only by bishops and priests, but by kings and princes" (Ware's *Bishops*, ed. Harris, p. 59). The remainder of Gelasius' history is of the same type. He continued to the end a faithful servant of the Roman See. Armagh had hitherto been the centre of opposition to Rome. Henceforth, and for four hundred years, Armagh remained devoted to Rome. Opposition to Roman claims continued, indeed, in the schools of Ireland. The old Irish traditions and the old Celtic spirit of independence lingered still in places like Clonard. Gelasius determined to reduce the colleges to order and uniformity, as he had already reduced the greater part of the clergy. So he held a synod in the year 1162, at the ancient Irish Abbey of Clane, whose site can still be traced on the banks of the Liffey, in a beautiful spot some twenty miles from Dublin, where it was decreed that no one should be admitted a reader or professor of Divinity who had not studied at Armagh, or been admitted to an *ad eundem* degree in that college.

By this decree Gelasius gave a monopoly of teaching, or at least of examination, to Armagh, and hoped thereby to extinguish all opposition to papal claims. Opposition, however, did not at once die out. Two proofs of this remain. Dermot MacMurrogh's Charter for the foundation of All Saints' Priory, the predecessor of our own College, required papal confirmation. Innocent V. issued a bull for this purpose in 1276, enacting that it shall be subject to the diocesans being Catholics, and in communion with the Roman See, which evidently proves that some bishops still continued to assert an independent position,[1] while the papal grant to Henry II. states plainly that the pope made over Ireland to England, that it might be brought into complete conformity with Catholic usages. Notwithstanding, however, a sporadic resistance offered here and there, the days of the Celtic Church and its independence were for ever past and gone. Irish national independence and Irish ecclesiastical independence, in fact, terminated practically together, and their fate was finally sealed when the first archbishop of Armagh, Gelasius, visited Dublin in 1172, and made his formal submission to King Henry II.

I have now completed the task which I undertook. I have traced for you the history of the Church of Ireland during its period of Celtic independence. We

---

[1] See *Registrum Prioratus Omnium Sanctorum*, ed. Butler, p. 7 (Dublin: 1845).

have followed its fortunes from Patrick to Columba; from Columba to the Danes; from the Danes to Rome, and the Normans, and England. I trust that, if you have learned nothing else, you have at all events learned this, that Irish history is not the utterly tangled and fabulous maze of which we have sometimes heard; but that it is a story full of interest, full of romance, and capable of receiving illustration and fresh light from the daily advance of archæology, philology, and history. You can all do something to help on that work. Ignorant barbarism has been a great enemy of the antiquities of Ireland. The most valuable monuments have been destroyed to mend roads or build a wall. Cultivate the study of Irish antiquities in your own parishes and neighbourhoods; prove yourselves guardians of everything really ancient. Farmers have not alone been the culprits. The rector of Drumcliffe, in the county of Sligo, lately informed me that during last summer he found an English tourist hammering away with a geologist's hammer at the ancient and beautifully carved stone cross which stands in his parish. He was attacking it to get geological specimens, and received my friend's expostulations very indignantly. You will find every parish in Ireland rich in memorials of the past, some of them sadly needing guardianship. Nothing, too, will tell so well with your people as a lecture on their own local history. Gather up and transcribe and publish every notice of antiquity which you can find, and thus, no matter how backward the place of your ministry, you will find life richer, fuller of interest for yourselves, and will earn, too, the gratitude of those who strive to reconstruct the past story and to paint the past chequered fortunes of our common fatherland.

# INDEX.

AARON, 11.
Abbott, T. K., Prof., 227.
Abraham, St., 3, 173.
Adamnan, *De Locis Sanctis*, 99, 187.
—— *Vita S. Columbæ*, 97, 98, 99.
Adelfius, bishop, 10.
Agape in Egypt, 225, 226.
Agricola (Roman general), 13, 14, 15.
—— (heretic), 50.
Aidan, St., 161.
—— king, 125.
Aidus, St. (of Sleaty), 30.
Aileran, St. (of Clonard), 220, 229.
Alban, St., 11.
Alcuin, 209.
All Saints' Priory, 327, 348.
Altus, centurion, 18.
Amalgaid, primate, 337.
Ammianus Marcellinus, 17.
*Analecta Bollandiana*, 24, 26, 28, 29, 30, 48, 84, 88, 92.
Ancyra, 62.
Anicetus, pope, 157.
Annaghdown, see of, 341.
Annegray, 138.
Anselm, St., 320.
Antonines, age of, 9, 15, 16.
Archæological Society (Somerset), 10.
—— *Journal*, 248.
Archæology, Ulster *Journal* of, vii, 16.
Arculf, bishop, 99.
Ariminum, council of, 11.
Aristobulus, 6.
Arles, council of, 10.
*Armagh, Book of*, 26, 84, 86, 89, 92, 218.

Armagh, foundation of, 91.
—— see of, Lect. xvii.
Arthur, king, 5.
Assemani, S.E., *AA. MM.*, 173.
Athlone, 83, 84.
Atkinson, G. M., *On Iniskilly Amulet*, 124.
Atkinson, Prof. R., 170.
Attacots, 17, 18.
Augustine (of Ireland), 221.
—— St. (of England), 4, 154.
—— St. (of Hippo), 12, 172.
Augustus, emperor, 14.
Aurelius, Marcus, 3.

BAITHENE, 107, 129, 221.
Ballymoon, battle of, 269.
Ballyligpatrick, 59.
Banduri, 176.
*Bangor, Antiphonary* of, vii.
Baring-Gould (*Curious myths*), 5.
Baur, 168.
Bayet, Ch., *L'Art Byzantin*, 242.
Bede, 5, 12, 51, 90, 120, 134, 154, 229.
Bernard, St., 338-346.
Biblical Archæology, Society of, 8.
Bingham, *Antiqq.*, 75, 151, 152.
Bith, 13.
Bobbio, 142, 146.
Böcking's *Notitia*, 17.
Boeckh's *Corp. Ins. Græc.*, 43, 62.
Bollandus, J., life of, 144.
Boniface IV., pope, 147.
*Book of Armagh.* See "Armagh."
—— *of Durrow.* See "Durrow."
—— *of Kells.* See "Kells."

Book satchels, Irish, 188.
Braid, river, 58.
Brawny, barony of, 196.
Brehon law, 203-205.
Brendan, St., 101.
Brian Boru, 197, 267, 283-306.
Brigid, St. (of Kildare) vi, 200.
Britain, conversion of, 74-78.
Brodar, the apostate, 301, 303, 305.
Broichan, 123.
Broughshane, 74.
Brude, king, 113, 120.
Brugh-na-Boinne, 71.
Brunehault, queen, 139.
Bunratty, castle of, 286.
Burke, Sir B., 193.
Butler's *Coptic Churches*, 188.
Butler's (Dean) *Hist. of Trim*, 219.
—— *Regist. Prior. Onm. SS.*, 348.

CALVUS PERENNIS, 289.
Canice, St. (Kenneth, Cainnech), 120.
Caractacus, king, 6.
Carbri, 79.
Cashel, rock of, 271.
Cashels (Caiseal), 117, 184-188.
Cassianus, Joannes, 169, 177.
Cassir, 13.
Cathach of St. Columba, 108.
Cedd, St., 162.
Ceillier, *Hist. Aut. Eccles.*, 11, *pass.*
Celclyth, council of, 334.
Celsus, primate, 337-341.
Cethiacus, bishop, 82.
Chess in ancient Ireland, 298.
Chrism in baptism, 155, 318.
Cistercian order in Ireland, 346.
Clairvaux, abbey of, 338, 344-346.
Clane, synod of, 348.
Claudian (poet), 17, 18.
Clermont-Ganneau, 8.
Clonmacnois, 84.
—— description of, 260.
Clontarf, battle of, 296-306.
—— authorities on, 305.
*Codex Kossanensis*, 207.
Cœlestine, pope, 47.
Cœlestius, 21.
Cogitosus, 29.
Coins, foreign, in Ireland, 16.
Colcu (of Clonmacnois), 209, 230.
Coleraine, 16.

Colgan, *Trias Thaumat.*, 13, 30, 33, 123.
—— *AA. SS. Hib.*, 101, 126, 180, 201, 214, 249.
College Green, 278.
Colman, bishop, 163, 229.
Columba, St., Lectt. v., vi.
—— family of, 100, 114.
—— birth of, 100.
—— education of, 100.
—— in Iona, 114.
—— death of, 128.
Columbanus, Lect. vii.
—— birth, 132.
—— works, 133.
—— education, 134.
Combefis, *Lecti Triumphi*, 236.
Comes Britanniarum, 17.
Comgall, St., 120, 134.
Conall (of Donaghpatrick), 79.
Connall (son of Endeus), 82.
Connaught, St. Patrick in, 81.
Constantine, the Great, emperor, 7.
Conway, copper block at, 10.
Coote's *Romans in Britain*, 7. 50.
Cormac MacArt, king, 17, 66, 72.
Cormac MacCullinan, 219, 268, 270.
—— writings of, 270.
Coroticus, 26, 28.
Corprius, bishop, 201.
*Corpus Ins. Lat.*, 10.
Cotelerius, *Monumenta*, 177.
Crannoges, 291, 292.
Crimthann, 17.
Croghan (Cruachan), 86.
Cualanni, 52.
Cummian, 25, 29, 159.
Curses, monastery of, 65.
Curzon's, *Monast. of Levant*, 169.
Cusack's *St. Patrick*, 48, 95.
Cuthbert, St., 185.
Cyprian, St., 41, 88.

DAGAN, bishop, 156.
Dagobert II., king, 209.
Daire, 92.
Dalaradia, 53.
Dallan Forgaill, 126.
Dalmatius, 176.
Dalriada, 55, 113.
Danish Invasion, Lect. xiii.
—— date of, 255.

# INDEX. 353

Dasent's *Burnt Njal*, 205, 265, 300.
Davies, F. R., 78.
Decurion, 37.
De Rossi (J. B.), 6, 308, 311.
Derry, 106, 115.
Desert (Disert, Dysert), 178, 179.
De Vogüe, 176, 237, 239-242.
Diarmait, king, 108.
Dichu, 53, 61.
*Dictionary of Christ. Biog.*, 6, 11, passim.
—— *Antiqq.*, 75, 226.
Dicuil, 214.
Diodorus Siculus, 14.
Diuma, St., 162.
Dobda, 219.
Domitian, 7.
Domnach (Donagh), meaning of, 83.
Domnon, 82.
Donaghmore (Mayo), 83.
Donaghpatrick, 79.
Donatus (Dunan), first bishop of Dublin, 311.
Doulough (Duilech), St., 177, 178, 180, 181.
Downpatrick, 16.
Dowth, 71.
Drew, Mr., on Christchurch, 313.
Drumceatt, 109, 125.
Drumcliffe, 110, 349.
Dublin, castle of, 262.
—— corporation of, 276.
—— diocese of, 275.
—— see of, Lect. xvi.
Duchesne, 190.
Dumbarton, 36, 37.
Dunraven, Ld., *Irish Architecture*, 117, 185.
*Durrow, Book of*, 107.

EADMER'S *Hist.*, 309, 317.
Eanfled, queen, 162.
Easter cycle, 151, 155.
—— fire, 74.
Eborius, bishop, 10.
Egbert, St., 165.
Eginhard, 248.
Endeus, 82.
Ephemeris Epigraphica, 8.
Erc, St., 76, 81.
Erigena, Joannes Scotus, 218, 227, 228.

Etchen, bishop, 105.
Ethne, 86.
Eulalia, SS., 11.
Eusebius, 3, 11.
Eutighern, bishop, 201.
Evagrius, 180.
Exuperius, St., 40, 171.

FEIDELN, 86.
Feidhlimidh.  See Phelim.
Ferguson, Sir S., 19, 67, 73, 196, 205.
Fergus, the great, 55.
Fiacc, St., hymn of, 32.
Fidelis, 216.
Finan, St., 162, 229.
Finnian, St. (Clonard), 100.
—— (Moville), 107.
Finn, MacCumhaill, 67.
Fintan, St., of Taghmon, 158.
Fiords in Ireland, 284.
Fleming's *Collect. Sacra*, 148, 220.
Fochart, battle of, 200.
Fochlut, 46, 81.
Fontaines, 139.
Forannan, primate, 259.
Fore, abbey of, 182.
Forget's *De Vita Aphraatis*, 184.
*Four Masters, Annals of*, 13, 17, 38.
Frazer, Dr., on sacred crystals, 125
Fredegund, queen, 139.
Freeman's *Hist. Essays*, 244.

GALATIA, 2, 62.
Gall, St., 131, 144, 247.
Gartan, 100.
Gebhardt u. Harnack, *Texte u. Untersuch.*, 155.
Gelasius, primate, 342, 347.
Gemman, 230.
Georgia, 19.
Georgii *Mirac. S. Colluthi*, 226.
Germanus, St., 50.
Giant's Causeway, 16.
Gilbert, J. T. (*Facsimiles*), 107, 108, 207.
Gilbert of Limerick, 323-325, 339, 345.
Gilpatrick of Ossory, 290.
Gladys, 6.
Glasnevin, abbey of, 183.
Glenmama, battle of, 293.

23

Glastonbury, 5.
Gontran, king, 137, 138.
Gormflaith, queen, 296-301.
Gormlaith, queen, 270.
Gothric, king of Dublin, 315, 318.
Gottschalk, 228.
Gozpertus, abbat, 248.
Graham, H. D., *Iona*, 116.
Grail, Holy, 5.
Granard, monastery of (Larro), 83, 84.
Graves, bishop, 207.
—— on *Book of Armagh*, 218.
Green, J. R. (*Making of England*), 4.
Gregory, first archbishop of Dublin, 315, 322.
Gregory, St. (Tours), 27, 238.
Gregory the Great, pope, 4, 148.
Guasacht, 61, 84.
Guest, 13.

HACO, earl, 274.
Haddan and Stubbs, *Councils*, 10, 11.
Hadrian, 16.
Haliday's *Kingdom of Dublin*, 258, 261.
Hallelujah victory, 51.
Handbells, Irish, 188.
Handcock's *Hist. of Tallaght*, 104.
Harold (Fairhair), 256, 264.
Harris' *Ware's Works*, 183.
Hartley, Prof., 207.
Haughton, Rev. Dr., on battle of Clontarf, 306.
Hefele, bishop, *Councils*, 11, 151, 153.
Hennessy, W. M., viii, 78, 123, 181, 193, 230, 250.
Henry II., king, 348.
Herbert, Hon. Aub., 89.
Hermes, 8.
Hieronymus. See "Jerome."
Hilda, St., 163.
Hippolytus, 151.
Hogan, Rev. E., viii, 29. See *Analecta Bolland*.
Hoggesgreen, 279, 280.
Holmpatrick, 53.
—— synod of, 346, 347.
Honorius, 16.
Hort, Dr., on *Book of Adam*, 216.
Hübner (*Corp. Ins. Lat.*), 10, 16.

ICELAND, 217, 264.

Iconoclasts, 246.
Ierne, 14.
Iona, 114.
Inis Ainghin (Hare Island), 201.
Inisclcraun (Inisclothran), 187, 237, 238.
Inisfallen, *Annals of*, 24.
Inisghoill, 85.
Inismurray, 110, 184.
Inispatrick, 53.
Innocent, pope, 40, 348.
Irenæus, 3.
Isdegerdes, king, 173.

JEROME, St. (Hieronymus), 4, 12, 18, 40, 171.
Jerusalem, 19.
Jewish controversy, 155.
Jonas, abbat (*Vita Columbani*), 133, 138.
Joseph of Arimathea, legend of, 5, 6.
*Journal, Hell. Stud.*, 7.
—— Kilkenny Arch., 57.
—— Ulster Arch., vii, 16.
Joyce, Prof., *Irish Names*, 117, 179.
Julius, St., 11.
Justinian, emperor, 243.
Justin Martyr, 55.

KEATING'S *Hist. of Ireland*, 13, 17, 79.
*Kells, Book of*, 104, 206, 207.
Kieran, St., 101, 200, 201.
Killala, 83.
Kilmashogue, battle of, 272.
King, Rev. Robert, *Primacy*, 331, 341.
Kingsley, C., 183.
Knowth, 71.

LANCIANI, *L'Atrio di Vesta*, 308.
Lanfranc, archbishop, 316, 320.
Lanigan, *Hist. of Ireland*, 319.
Laoghaire (Leary), king, 74.
Laserian, St., of Old Leighlin, 158.
Latean, Brian's horse-boy, 305.
Laurence O'Toole, St., 315, 325, 329.
Laurentius, archbishop, 155.
Lazarus, legend of, 5.
Labarte's *Hist. of Indust. Arts*, 247.

# INDEX. 355

Le Bas and Waddington, 7, 8.
Le Blant, E., *Ins. Chrét. de la Gaule,* 3, 174.
Legio ii. Augusta, 10.
Lentheric, M., 4.
Letronne, 214.
Lightfoot, bishop, 2, 55.
Limenach, 85.
Lochru, 76.
Loigles, well of, 81.
Lottner, C. F., 3.
Lucian, *Pseudomantis,* 216.
Lucius, king, 6.
Lugnademon, 90.
Lugnædon, 85.
Lupait, 32.
Luxeuil, 139.
Lyons, 3.

MABILLON, *AA. SS. Bened.,* 4, 177, 225.
MacCarthy, Rev. Dr., on *Stowe Missal,* vi, vii.
MacFirbis, 110.
MacFirbis (annalist), 193, 230.
Macmahon, primate (R.C.), 330.
Macmurrogh, Dermot, king, 326, 327, 348.
Maelmury (Marianus) primate, 335.
*Magazine, British,* 89.
—— *Macmillan's,* 63.
—— *Meath Parochial,* 84.
Mahoun (Mahon), 197, 284-288.
Mai, Cardinal, 142, 147, 225.
Maine, Sir H., *Hist of Instit.,* 107, 203, 204, 205.
—— *Ancient Law,* 203.
Malachi, king, 290, 299, 305.
Malachy, St., or Malachi O'Morgair, St., Lect. xvii., 339-347.
Malalas, John, 215.
Malan's *Book of Adam and Eve,* 188, 216.
Malchus, bishop of Waterford, 309.
Manchan, St., 221.
Man, *Chronicle* of, 278.
Mansi's *Councils,* 11.
Marianus Scotus, 131, 180.
Marinus, St., 12.
Marius Mercator, 12, 22.
Martial, 6.
Mayo, monastery of, 164.

Mel, St., 84.
Menæa, 6.
Methodism, 9.
Milchu, 44, 57.
Military system, Roman, 8.
Minerals and mines in Britain, 9.
*Mittheilungen Instit. Athen,* 7.
—— *der Antiq. Gesellschaft,* 131.
Molassius, St. (Molaise), 110, 184.
Molyneux, Dr. T., 58.
Mommsen, 8.
Monasticism, 167.
Montalembert's *Life of St. Columba,* 97, 127, 147.
Montfauçon's *Palæographia,* 225.
Moore's *Cybele Hibernica,* 78.
Moran, archbishop, viii, 332.
Morgan (Pelagius), 12.
Morrin's *Patents,* 91.
Mosul, monastery of, 184.
Muirchu Maccumactheni, 29.
Muratori, vii, 147, 204.
Muratorian fragment, 142.
Murtogh (Maurice), primate, 337.

NARBONNE, council of, 173.
Nero, 16.
Nestorius, 22.
New Grange, 71.
Niall, of the Nine Hostages, 17, 38, 125.
Nice, council of, 11.
Nicodemus (*Evangelium*), 6.
Nilus, S. (*Epp.*), 105.
Nina, St., 19.
Nitria, 168, 229.
Noris, Card., *Hist. Pelag.,* 22.
*Notes and Queries,* 78.
*Notitia Dignitatum,* 17.

O'BRIAN, Morrogh, 294, 303, 304.
O'Curry's *Lectt.*, 65, 123, 249, 289.
O'Donoghue, *Hist. Mem. of the O'Brians,* 305, 316.
O'Donovan, Dr. (*Book of Rights*), 68, 193, 196.
—— (*Hy-Fiachrach*), 81.
Œnghus (Ængus), 179, 212, 249.
*Oesterreich. Monatsschr. für den Orient,* 237.
O'Haingly, Don., 315.
—— Samuel, 315.

O'Hanlon's *Irish Saints*, 137.
Olga, empress, 82.
Ollamh Fodhla, 68.
O'Neills, 199.
Onuphrius, 177.
Orosius, 12.
Ospak, viking, 301.
Oswy, king, 162.
Oysters, British, 9.

PALLADIUS, 23.
Pallu de Lessert, 63.
Palmyra, 8.
Pamphylia, 19.
Papiro or Paparo, Card., 347.
Patricius, 16.
Patrick, St., 4.
—— miracles of, 34.
—— mission of, 46, 61.
—— family of, 39.
—— captivity of, 43.
—— country of, 35, 36.
—— names of, 39.
—— sisters of, 32, 85.
—— at Croaghpatrick, 89.
—— staff of (*baculus Jesu*), 90, 342.
—— and the snake legend, 90.
—— visit to Rome, 93.
—— preaching in Dublin, 94.
—— death of, 94.
—— burial of, 95.
—— writings of, 26.
—— hymn of, 95.
Patrick, second bishop of Dublin, 315.
Pelagia, St., 180.
Pelagius, 12, 20.
Pellechet, M., 5.
Pertz, *Monumenta*, 225.
Petrie, Dr., 25, 65, 95, 117, 193.
Pfitzner, Dr. W., 8.
Phelim (Feidhlimidh), king, 199, 262.
Picts, 13, 121.
Piers, Sir H., 182.
Plautius, A., 5.
Poitiers, 3.
Polycarp, St., 151.
Pomponia Græcina, 5.
Porter, J. S., 16.
Potthast, *Bibliotheca*, 225.
*Proceedings* (Roy. Irish. Acad.), 3, 12, 13, 16, 26, 29, 75, 85, 218, 220, 224.

*Proceedings* (Somerset Arch. Soc.), 10.
Prosper, 12, 23.
*Psalter of Cashel*, 331.
Ptolemy, 15.
Pudens, 6.
Putland, Mr., of Bray, 15.
Pytheas, 15.

QUARTODECIMANS and the Irish Church, 151, 154, 155.

RADERIUS, 181.
Rahan, church of, 84.
Rambaud's *History of Russia*, 82.
Randon, fortress of, 192.
Rath-Bresail, synod of, 322.
Rathfarnham, 16.
Reeves, bishop, 12, 13, 54, 90, 97; 188, 200.
—— on Augustine, 224.
—— *Ancient Ch. of Armagh*, 259.
—— Cotton's Visitation, 324.
—— Adamnan's *Columba*, 97, *pass.*
—— on Stephen White, 13.
—— *Antiquitt.*, 54, 105, *pass.*
Reichenau, 100, 144.
Restitutus, bishop, 10.
*Review, Contemporary*, 43, 144, 175, 249, 308.
*Revue Archéologique*, 7.
—— *Celtique*, 64.
—— *Critique*, 5, 8.
Richborough, 9.
Roman army in Britain, 8, 14.
—— coins, 16.
—— fleet, 15.
Round Towers, Lect. xii.
—— Dr. Petrie on, 234.
—— writers on, 234.
Ruan, St., 65.
Rufus, 6.
Ruinart's *Acta Sinc.*, 41.

SABAS, St., 236.
Sabatier, 224.
Salmon, Dr., 143, 151, 202.
*Saltair, Na Rann*, 188, 216.
Salvian, 4, 50.
Sardica, council of, 11.
Saul, church of, 54, 95
*Saxon Chronicle*, 256.
Scotia, 13.

# INDEX.

Scots, 13.
Scott's (*Ulfilas*), 143.
Sechnall, St. (Secundinus), 32, 95.
Sedulius, commentator, 224, 228.
—— poet, 226.
Seebass, Dr. Otto, 138.
Segienus, St., of Iona, 159.
Senan, St., 249.
Serapion, 181.
Severus, 7, 66.
Shamrock and St. Patrick, 78.
Shearman (Rev. J. F.), 24, 295.
Sidonius Apollinaris, 38, 50, 173.
Siegfried, R. T., 3.
Sigurd, earl, 300.
Simeon Stylites, 174.
Sitric, king, 272.
—— coins of, 308, 311.
Sixtus, St., 11.
Skene's *Celtic Scotland*, 13, 97, 183.
Slane, hill of, 74, 208.
Slemish, hill of, 44, 58.
Solinus, 91.
South Shields, 8.
Sozomen, 177.
Stevens, *Hist. of Methodism*, 9.
Stokes, Dr. Whitley, 85, 95, 123, 182, 188, 212, 216, 219, 249, 269, 270.
—— Miss, *Christ. Archit. in Ireland*, 234. 245.
—— *Irish Christ. Ins.*, 201.
—— *Kugler's Handbook*, 246.
Strabo, 14.
Stubbs and Haddan (*Councils*), 11.
—— bishop, 134.
Suibhneus (Sweeny), 214.
Sulcoit, battle of, 287.
Sviatoslaf, 82.
Sweetman's *Calendars*, 179.
Sysinnius, 172.

TACITUS (*Annals*), 5, 6.
—— (*Agricola*), 13, 14.
Tallaght, 80.
Tara, 16, 62, 96.
—— roads of, 80.
Teabhtha (Teffia), 83.
Tectosagæ, 63.
Telltown, 79.
Temple Douglas, church of, 100.
Tennyson, Lord, 5, 174.

Termon-Lands, 200.
Tertullian, 7, 88.
Theodore (Mopsuest), 22.
Theodosian code, 155.
Theodosius, 17.
Theodotus of Ancyra, 41.
Thingmote (Thingmount, Althing), 278-281.
Three Rock Mountain, 16.
Tigernach, 55.
Tirechan, 29, 75, 76, 79, 82, 84, 88.
Todd, Dr., 85, 95, 200.
Tolistobogii, 63.
Torques, 70.
Trajan, 16.
*Transactions* (R. I. A.), 69.
Tregelles, Dr. S. P., 143.
Trim, church of, 91.
Trocmi, 63.
Tuadhcar, bishop, 201.
Turgesius, 258.

ULSTER, *Annals of*, 214.
—— *Journal of Archæology*, vii, 16.
Ultan, St., 29.
Urbicus, Lol., 55.
Usener, H., 180.
Usnach, hill of, 222, 322.
Ussher, archbishop, *Antiqq.*, 5, 6, 12, 65, 259.
—— *Religion of Ancient Irish*, 224, 333.
—— *Sylloge*, 209, 230.

VESPASIAN, 16.
Victoria, queen, 125.
Victorius, abbat, 153.
Victor, pope, 157.
Victor (Victoricus), 46, 58.
Vienne, 3.
Vigilantius, 171.
Viollet le Duc, 243.
Virgilius, St., 50.
Virgil, the geometer, 219, 224.

WADDINGTON, Le Bas and, 7, 8.
Waggon-roofs, Irish, 188.
Wallenus, prior, 344.
Ware, Sir James, 230, 347.
Warren's *Celtic Liturgy*, vi, vii.
Wasserschleben, viii, 105, 138, 159.

Wesley, John, 9.
White, Stephen, 13.
Wilde, Sir William (*Beauties of Boyne, etc.*) 71, 220.
Wilfrid, 163.
Wilkins' *Concilia*, 40, 317.
Windele (*On Sacred Pebbles*), 124.
Windisch, *Irische Texte*, 95.
Worsaæ's *Danes and Norwegians*, 293.
Wright, Dr. W., 8.

Wright's *Cat. Syr. MSS.*, 184.
Wülcker, R. P., *Das Evangel. Nicodemi in Abendl. Literat.*, 6.

YATES, James, 10.
York, 8.

ZEUSS, viii, 117.
Zimmer's *Kelt. Stud.*, viii, 32.
Zosimus (pope), 22.
—— historian, 50.

www.ingramcontent.com/pod-product-compliance
Lightning Source LLC
Chambersburg PA
CBHW031421230426
43668CB00007B/384